INVADERS AND INFIDELS

INVADERS AND INFIDELS

BOOK 2: THE KHALJI DEVASTATION
OF INFIDEL DEVAGIRI

SANDEEP BALAKRISHNA

Title: Invaders and Infidels: The Khalji Devastation of
Infidel Devagiri–Book 2
Author: Sandeep Balakrishna

ISBN: 978-93-92209-49-9

First published in India 2023
This edition published 2023

Published by:
BluOne Ink LLP
A-76, 2nd Floor, Sector 136, Noida
Uttar Pradesh 201305.

Website: www.bluone.ink
Email: publisher@bluone.ink

Printed and bound in India by Thomson Press India Ltd.

This volume is dedicated to Sri Jadunath Sarkar....
A force of nature that chose history as its sacred calling.

Contents

Preface

*The benevolent face of the Turk was always and exclusively turned
towards his Muslim Ummah, and never towards the accursed
Hindus. Jalal-ud-din Khalji was second[1] to none among the Muslim
kings when it came to heaping atrocities on Hindus.*

When Qutub-ud-din Aibak died in a polo game in 1210, he
had left behind a rickety, fledgling Muslim kingdom
in Delhi. For the next eighty-odd years, its fortunes swayed
wildly, witnessing a record twelve short-lived sultans. Barring the
blood-soaked regimes of Iltutmish and Balban, it was a period
of incessant palace coups, fratricides and serial political murders.
Sita Ram Goel provides a pithy analysis of the tumultuous era in
his *The Story of Islamic Imperialism in India.*

> The popular notion that after the conquest of Muhammad Ghori,
> India formed a Muslim Empire under various dynasties, is hardly
> borne out by facts.... *Muslim power in India suffered a serious
> setback after Iltutmish.* Balban had to battle against a revival of
> Hindu power. The Katehar Rajputs of what came to be known
> as Rohilkhand in later history, had so far refused to submit to
> Islamic imperialism. Balban led an expedition across the Ganges
> in 1254. According to Badauni, in two days after leaving Delhi,
> he arrived in the midst of the territory of Katehar and *put to death
> every male, even those of eight years of age, and bound the women.*
> But in spite of such wanton cruelty, Muslim power continued to
> decline till the Khaljis revived it after 1290. [Emphases added]

Book 1 of *Invaders and Infidels* ends with Balban's wasted and
degenerate grandson Kaiqubad elevating a septuagenerian
governor named Jalal-ud-din Khalji to the post of war minister.
However, Balban's death had already extinguished the so-called
Muslim Slave dynasty and snuffed out the short-lived Turkic
Muslim rule in Delhi.

Book 2 traces the political ascent of the Afghanistan-based Khalji tribe. From the earliest times, the historical memory of Central Asia had classed the Khaljis as a 'low-born' tribe, a story that is narrated in some detail in this volume.

The most notable and the most notorious early Khalji who ravaged large parts of Eastern India was the semi-barbarian Bakhtiyar Khalji. Although he predates the Khalji Sultanate in Delhi, the complete story of his grisly career is told in this volume. He does find a brief mention in Book 1 of *Invaders and Infidels* but in the interests of providing a semi-comprehensive history of the Khalji tribe in India in one place, Book 2 reserves substantial space to him.

The unlikely rise of Jalal-ud-din Khalji, who became an ill-suited monarch and an unworthy successor to Balban, is one of those freak accidents of history that permanently altered the fortunes of Bharatavarsha for the worse. Purely in the realm of speculation, had Jalal-ud-din lost the battle for the throne of Delhi, southern India would perhaps have remained untouched by Islamic invasions for much longer. And, perhaps, there would be no occasion for the birth of the grand Vijayanagara Empire, which safeguarded and saved Hindus in the South from this clear and present Islamic danger. But history can be written only in hindsight, and therein lies the surest repository of wisdom.

Like the Muslim kingdoms that preceded it, the Khalji Empire was ephemeral. It too, imploded due to the same weaknesses intrinsic to every Islamic empire in India. That story will be fully narrated in Book 3.

At the time of Jalal-ud-din Khalji's coronation, Hindu political power in Northern India was in total disarray. There was no unifying Hindu leader who had the vision to combat and permanently expel the alien oppressor lodged in Delhi. Hindu political power was now concentrated mainly in the region of today's Rajasthan and Madhya Pradesh, but it was scattered power. Hindu kings had an abundance of grit, determination, strength and valour, but they were hopelessly disunited and scudded along the suicidal path of internecine wars. With predictable results. The other face of this coin was defaced with myopia: for the better part of these 80 years of internal warring among various Muslim dynasties, *no Hindu ruler had the vision to exploit the repeated juicy openings and vulnerabilities they provided.* The opposite is actually true. We have the shocking example of a powerful Hindu ruler of Ranastambhapura who falls for Iltutmish's guile and loses his life to foul murder at his hands.

Like Balban, even Jalal-ud-din Khalji's fleeting Sultanate was not entirely stable. His whole career was punctuated with recurrent bouts of doughty resistance from Hindus, and frequent plots against his own life by people in his inner circle and outside it. On more than one occasion, Jalal-ud-din proved unsuccessful and even cowardly in the face of Hindu resurgence. Peter Jackson, the scholar of medieval Muslim history of India, correctly observes[2] how, it is 'important…to recognize the limits of Muslim success. Victory did not necessarily entail the displacement of Hindu rulers'.

The surest proof for Jalal-ud-din Khalji as an inept and implausible monarch is the macabre manner of his murder. The book narrates how he walked into the web of vile treachery with open eyes.

—•┄•┄•—

Book 2 of *Invaders and Infidels* is woven around three major themes.

The first is a continuation of the historical narrative that began in Book 1—that is, the trajectory of alien Islamic invasions and subsequent Muslim regimes established in Delhi.

The second is to offer a fairly detailed picture of the Hindu facet of this story. This includes heart-rending accounts of widespread Hindu suffering, their heroic wars of resistance and their squandered chances for civilisational reclamation. Vivid details of the sacred geography of India—a primary actor in all these sagas—also provide the political and military context. The third is related to an epochal event. This is Ala-ud-din Khalji's maiden shattering of Devagiri, the gateway to the South. This singular episode instantly catapults him on to the throne of Delhi. Book 2 of *Invaders and Infidels* ends here.

Overall, Book 2 narrates a heady and often savage and depressing tale of a period rife with bloody intrigues, aggressive campaigns of Islamic expansionism and the avoidable destruction of several Hindu empires in a vast territory. It is also the preface to a much larger story of how the fortunes of Bharatavarsha would be irreversibly transformed with far-reaching consequences, the imprints of which, we still notice throughout this country and its neighbourhood.

Book 2 follows the same approach as its predecessor. The narrative is vigorous, the historical cast of characters and episodes are delineated, based entirely on primary sources. Timelines for different events are woven into the narrative in as continuous a sequence as possible. Given that multiple events occur simultaneously on the same timeline, it is impossible to maintain a strict chronology. However, enough care has been taken to ensure that the narrative is wholesome and unified and that the reader doesn't need to go back and forth. Whether I have succeeded in the attempt is for the reader to judge.

As always, my heartfelt thanks goes out to the wonderful folks at BlueOne Ink who have published this book in record time. Their patience, care and responsiveness in crafting various aspects of this book are exemplary.

Special thanks are due to Praveen Tiwari. For your unstinted support and graciousness.

Sandeep Balakrishna

PROLOGUE

'Sons of the Thief'

The Twenty-two Ghuzz Turks call them
Kal aç in the Turkic languages;
This means 'stay hungry and remain left behind'.

In 2006, the United States of America, under the banner of its USAID programme, built Zabul's first military airport, located two miles north-west of Qalat. In an oblique manner, this construction fused the US-dominated global order in the present with a strategic region of Bharatavarsha in the past. A region that was dangerously perched on the edge of losing its freedom forever.

At a freezing temperature of minus three degrees Celsius in January, Qalat[1] is a barren strip of land in southern Afghanistan, squeezed between Ghazni to its north and Kandahar to its south. Perhaps, the only extant structural proof of its antiquity is the Qalat city fort, a tattered remnant of countless annihilations. However, its other name[2] offers a clearer insight into its role as a blood-soaked amphitheatre of political history: *Qalati Khalji*.

For more than a millennium, the region around Qalat was known as Khalaj or Khalj, encompassing Zabul, Kandahar, Ghazni and Helmand. Qalat was the heartland of the Khalaj or Khalj tribe[3] whose descendants eventually birthed the Muslim Khalji dynasty in Bharatavarsha.

Fleeing Central Asia

A Turkic sheep-grazing nomadic tribe of untraceable antiquity, the Khaljis fled their original home in the steppes of Central Asia and were the earliest to cross the Amu Darya river. By the 9th century, they were so deeply settled in the Helmand region that they became almost indistinguishable from the local Pashtuns. Their intrinsic nomadic character allowed them to assimilate quickly, adapt to local conditions and learn new languages. Over time, this led to their integration into the Pashto-speaking Ghalzay (or Ghilzay) tribe of Afghans. Eventually, they too came to be regarded as Afghans.

In his raid of Zabul, the 9th century Turkish mercenary Yaqub bin Layth launched a targeted campaign against the Khaljis and subdued them.[4] In the 10th century, we see them described as 'a tribe of ancient immigrants to the region' who had retained their 'Turkish customs, clothing, external appearance and language'.[5] They were sheep-grazing pastoralists who maintained an enormous hoard of cattle and as professionals, habitually wandered through seasonal pastures.

For much of their history, the Khalji tribe was consigned to the lower dregs of the Muslim social hierarchy. The racist Turkic Muslim scholar, linguist and lexicographer al-Kashgari derived the meaning of word 'Khalaj' from *Kal aç: stay hungry*.[6] Even after the tribe was assimilated into the Afghan Pashtun fold and became the Ghalzay, it couldn't fully wash off the stain of low-origin taint. The word 'Ghalzay' or 'Ghal-ze' was also deciphered as 'sons of the thief'.[7]

Figure 1: A Khalji coin dated 8th century CE. The reverse shows Shiva standing holding his Trishul.[8]

The decisive twist in the fortunes of the Khaljis arrived with the Ghaznavids. After the Turkic Muslim governor Alptigin enthroned himself at Ghazni, he sent his slave and commander, Sabuktigin, in 963, to collect taxes and animals from the Khaljis and Turkmans.[9]

Sabuktigin led a 200 strong armed force. But to his surprise, he found that despite being nomads and not generally aligned with any army, the Khaljis coolly rebuffed him. Sabuktigin's surprise soon turned to alarm when he sensed their determination to resist. He decided not to fight, and his enraged troops obviously concluded that he was a weakling. These low-born immigrant nomads were surely no match for Sultan Alptigin's battle-hardened army, and here was Sabuktigin advising cowardice. But Sabuktigin was keen on discretion:

> Our master did not send us here for war but to collect money and animals. A small sum, overall. Not worth a war. But imagine if *they* beat us. Can you guarantee against such an outcome? As you said, a bunch of low-born nomads. If they beat us, imagine how low our master's prestige will fall. Also remember that our master didn't issue orders for war. I'm personally answerable to him, not you.[10]

This sounded reasonable. When Sabuktigin returned to Ghazni empty-handed, his master furiously repeated the same argument of the soliders. Unfazed, Sabuktigin skilfully rephrased the same response:

> Master, you had sent us there without an order to fight. And if we had fought on our own accord, we, your slaves, would have no longer remained slaves but would have become masters. And if we had been defeated, wouldn't we incur the wrath of you, our Master? But if you now wish us to return there and wage war and recover money or die in the attempt, our head is yours. Your command is all we seek.[10]

The Master, Alptigin promoted his protégé Sabuktigin and the matter was put to rest there for some years. Throughout, the Khalji tribe stubbornly refused to submit to the authority at Ghazni.

But that changed when Sabuktigin succeeded Alptigin in 977. In a binge of conquests, he wrested the whole of Afghanistan after his decisive victory over Jayapaladeva, the last great Hindu hero who had resolutely defended this vital frontier of Bharatavarsha.[11]

In 988, the Khaljis and the (native) Pashtuns in the entire zone surrendered to him and agreed to serve under him. This swelled Sabuktigin's army. He could now admit thousands of Khaljis and Pashtuns whenever he wished, and thereafter, they spent their lives in his service.

In 995, Sabuktigin, now lodged in Herat, sent summons to the rulers of Sistan, Guzganan[12] and the Khalji tribe. This time, it was obeyed. This pastoral nomadic tribe was gradually being transformed into a formidable military force.

However, it was under Sabuktigin's barbaric and fanatical son, Mahmud of Ghazni, that the Khaljis truly grew in power and prestige—the fuel of their ambition. He recruited them in swarms for his endless campaigns of military devastation, wanton pillage and plunder, and savage religious conversions in infidel Hindustan. The more the Khaljis participated, the wilder became their thirst for battle, booty, blood and bigotry.

In 1005-06, as Mahmud was busy ravaging Multan for a second time in order to punish the heretical Shia governor Dau'd, his arch enemy, Ilak Khan had already crossed the Amu Darya with a 50,000-strong army and began to menace Ghazni. Mahmud quickly decamped to Ghazni and summoned a hardened contingent of the 'Khalaj Turks, ever on their horses, manly sons of "swords"'. Ilak Khan was thoroughly crushed, but swore vengeance. He enlisted the support of another warlord, Qadir Khan at Tokaristan after which a 'sea of Turkish forces came like a torrent and occupied the utmost parts of Mahmud's kingdom'.[13] Undaunted, Mahmud 'rushed to Balkh with his Turkish, Indian, Khalaj, Afghan, and Ghazna troops'.[14] In the ferocious battle that ensued, Mahmud battered them so comprehensively that 'not a trace of them remained'.

When Hindu Women Sold Their Jewels to Expel Mahmud

Two years later, Mahmud, the 'Allah-ordained' sultan, decided that the time was ripe to punish that accursed infidel, Anandapala, who had shown such insolence during the punitive expedition against that Ismaili heretic, Dau'd. To Mahmud, this was a twofold insult: a loathsome idolater aligning with an impure heretic. But this time, Anandapala[15] had preempted Mahmud. When he heard of the latter's planned attack, he sent ambassadors throughout Hindustan and all Hindu kings responded positively. Their unity was now hinged on a determined objective: it was their Dharma, their sacred duty, to expel the unclean Mlecchas from Bharatavarsha forever. Forces from regions[16] as diverse and far-flung as Kalinjara,[17] Ujjaini, Gwalior, Kanauj, Ajmer and Delhi marched to assist Anandapala. This formidable martial confederacy sped towards Punjab. Led by Anandapala, they met Mahmud on the rugged plains of Peshawar. A stalemate ensued for 40 days. Neither side wanted to shoot the first arrow. But during this pregnant deadlock, the 'troops of the idolaters daily increased in number, and aid came to them from all sides. The infidel Gakkhars[18] also joined them in great strength, and made extraordinary exertions to resist the Musulmans'.[19] It was the first and the only time in the history of alien Islamic invasions into India that Hindu kings would sequester their hostilities in order to expel the despised Mleccha interloper. Their steely resolve evoked plaudits from Mahmud himself. His chronicler Utbi describes the scene:

> *The Hindu females, on this occasion, sold their jewels, and sent the proceeds from distant parts to their husbands,* so that they, being supplied with all necessaries…might be in earnest in the war. Those who were poor contributed from their earnings by spinning cotton, and other labour. *The Sultan perceived that on this occasion the idolaters behaved most devotedly….*[20] (Emphasis added)

It was an exceptionally bloody battle that claimed prolific casualties on both sides. The substantial contingent of the infidel Gakkhars gave Mahmud a taste of his own medicine— mass slaughter of his well-equipped army of Islam. But, as fate would have it, Anandapala's elephant went berserk, and confusion won the day for Mahmud. This would not be the last of that ubiquitous contributor to many a historic Hindu defeat—an over-reliance on elephants in war, as well as on a single person for leadership and direction. As the confused army of Anandapala began to flee, Mahmud's contingent comprising 6,000 Arab horses, 10,000 Turks, Afghans and Khaljis doggedly pursued it. In two days, the invaders slaughtered 8,000 infidels.

This epochal Battle of Chach ended with Anandapala's surrender. He ceded most of his territories and remained Mahmud's vassal for the rest of his life.

The Rise and Rise of the Khalji Tribe

By now, the Khaljis in Mahmud's engorged Islamic army had grown in stature, numbers and dependability. The Khalji unit had become an inevitable component of his numerous raids into mainland Hindustan. Ironically, Mahmud's son and successor Masud I, provides tangible evidence of the meteoric growth in power and ambition of the Khaljis. As Book I of *Invaders and Infidels* narrates, Masud was regarded as an ugly blot on his towering father's zealous legacy of expanding the dominions of Islam throughout infidel Hindustan.

The Khaljis were quick to recognize that Masud was a pathetic weakling and began openly defying him. On the Muharram of 1040, an enraged Masud dispatched an expedition from Ghazni to quell them. It was partially successful. Notwithstanding this defeat, the Khaljis had already risen as an unstoppable martial race, who were in great demand. But in the same year, a terrified Masud had to hastily abandon Ghazni when the savage Seljuk Turks sacked the city.

The cut-throat politics of Central Asia that lasted for over a century after the death of Mahmud of Ghazni witnessed astounding swings in the fortunes of the Khaljis. This took a definitive turn during the blood-soaked power struggle between the Khwarazim Shahs and the Ghurids and later, the Mongols. All these powers recruited Khalji fighters in droves. Eastern Afghanistan, Peshawar and Kabul were the major theatres of this mutually destructive and confounded fighting, which ended with the decimation of the Khwarazim Empire. In its aftermath, Khaljis and Turkmans from Khorasan flooded Peshawar.

By this time, the Khaljis had found a new leader. He was one of their own. The Khalji blood flowed in his veins. A military commander, Saif-ud-din Ighraq was showing enormous promise of establishing an independent Khalji power base in the Kabul River Valley. But he had to earn his spurs first. Ighraq stormed Ghazni, now being ruled by a petty chieftain named Radhi al-Mulk and easily overpowered him. But Ighraq had no time to savour this victory because Jalal-ud-din Khwarazim (or Jalal-ud-din Mangbarni) exploded onto the scene, unannounced. It was his desperate attempt to revive the shattered Khwarazim Empire. He issued a veiled threat to Ighraq, dressed as a request for an alliance to wage war against a Mongol contingent lodged at Parwan,[21] in Northeastern Afghanistan. Their combined armies expelled the Mongols. Almost immediately, squabbling began over the division of the spoils. The wretch Jalal-ud-din had revealed his true colours as a crafty backstabber. The outraged units of Khaljis, Turks and Ghurids in his army abandoned him and travelled southwards.

A few months later, the flames of Mongol vengeance swept across the country, in the form of Gengis Khan and his army. It scorched 30,000 Khaljis, Turks and Ghurids in Herat, Ghazni and Merv. When he turned towards Mangbarni, the latter bolted[22] to Hindustan in 1221.[23]

Sixty years earlier, one batch of the Khaljis had enlisted under Muhammad Ghori, who had emerged as a ferocious leader from the House of Ghor. Their service to Muhammad's serial Islamic incursions into infidel Hindustan would pay them royal dividends for generations to come, surpassing their wildest imaginations. It would produce generals, commanders, nobles, aristocrats, courtiers and two sultans. But from that bloodthirsty race of warriors came a freebooter, who rose from the fumes of humiliation, and eventually gave Bihar and Bengal its first awful taste of an all-out Islamic invasion, planting the green flag of Islam there.

His name was Ikhtiyar al-Din Muḥammad Bakhtiyar Khalji.

The Vandal of Nalanda and the Butcher of Bengal

Emerging from the incinerating deserts of Garamsir[24] on the eastern bank of the Helmand river, Bakhtiyar Khalji became one of the freak accidents, rather unique in the blood-soaked annals of Islamic invasions into India. Born to severe disadvantage, Bakhtiyar embodied the tribal elements of the treacherous region. Ugly, coarse, cruel, rough, reckless and desperately in search of military employment, he was among the thousands of such young adventurers seeking opportunities for a share in the Jihad-cum-plundering campaigns under the banner of a powerful sultan or raider of infidel Hindustan. But Bakhtiyar also brought to this vicious table a special garnish, characteristic of the season—the searing ambition to carve out an empire of his own.

In 1193, Bakhtiyar travelled to Ghazni and stood in 'the Audience Hall of Dominion of Sultan Mu'izz-ud-Din Muhammad-i-Sam offering to enlist as a soldier'.[25]

It was hate at first sight for Mu'izz-ud-Din or Muhammad Ghori.

Bakhtiyar was short, ugly and had grotesquely long arms reaching down to his shins. His countenance was 'ill-favoured'. He would bring bad luck. Worse still, Bakhtiyar had no money to buy himself a horse and a suit of armour—both were mandatory for military enlistment. However, because every man who volunteered for military service was an asset, Muhammad offered him a small stipend, which the impetuous Bakhtiyar rejected, and left the place.

Bakhtiyar arrived in Hindustan after a long journey to try his luck with Ghori's slave, Qutub-ud-din Aibak, now stationed in Delhi as the custodian of his master's territories in infidel Hindustan. Aibak didn't even give him an audience.

His Muster-Master (*diwan-i-arz*) took one look at Bakhtiyar and summarily dismissed him for the same reasons: short, ugly, awkward and unprepossessing. Bakhtiyar was furious at these successive rejections. He would later come to realize that the *diwan-i-arz* had actually done him a favour by inadvertently spurring him on to a more spectacular career.[26]

Unwilling to allow anything to thwart his raging ambition, Bakhtiyar travelled to Badayun and got an audience with a *Sipah-Salar* (Commander of Troops) named Malik Hizbar-ud-din.[27] He, too, displayed open distaste for this unsightly applicant. Nevertheless, he gave him the job on a cash salary but refused to give him a *Jagir*. A *Jagir* was highly coveted because it meant that an applicant—Bakhtiyar—could possess his own troops.

The next stop for the unrelenting Bakhtiyar was Awadh. In 1197, he got an audience with its governor, Malik Husamuddin. Unlike Ghori and Aibak, this shrewd warlord instantly recognized Bakhtiyar's potential and his overweening ambition. If used with tact and discretion, Bakhtiyar would prove to be a great asset to him. Husamuddin granted him a *Jagir* of two *Parganas* in the south-eastern corner of the modern Mirzapur district after making astute calculations. So far, these two *Parganas* had not been visited by any invading Muslim army. It was a good location to test Bakhtiyar Khalji's mettle.

A crooked line from Mirzapur, extending 30 kilometres southeast, connects it with the historic town of Chunar, the site of the ancient hill-fort of Chunar.[28] A further 20 kilometres eastwards leads to the launchpad of Bakhtiyar Khalji's ambition—his *Jagir* comprising the Bhuili and Bhagwat villages. Now unremembered and unremarkable, this modest tract became the springboard for Bakhtiyar's grotesque but successful career of sweeping military conquests.

Figure 2: North view of the Chunar Fort: British library, public domain, https://commons.wikimedia.org/w/index. php?curid=22598978

Bakhtiyar's *jagir* also came with the goodies he needed—a lumpen band of kindred predatory mercenaries, horses, arsenal and armour. With Bakhtiyar Khalji's brutal intrusion, the small region also witnessed its first-ever military presence of alien Muslims. It had been under the protection of some minor Hindu chiefs, hailing from different branches of the Gahadawala dynasty.[29] They were no match for Bakhtiyar's brand of ethics-deprived and honour-bereft Islamic warfare that included lightning raids, large-scale cruelty and unrestrained plunder of money, women and children. It didn't take him long to expel these infidel chiefs.

Now, he turned his attention eastward. The flat open plains, stretching endlessly along the serpentine frontier-river, Karmanasa, which merges with the Ganga at Chausa, Bihar, were the tailormade playground for his insatiable empire-building hunger.

Large parts of this region were no-man's lands, unprotected by any powerful Raja. In small and large instalments, Bakhtiyar began ravaging this huge stretch, meeting with zero opposition. He burned down hundreds of defenceless villages and small towns, pillaging them for booty, women and slaves. With each raid, his territory, weaponry and army grew exponentially. The first shimmering pearl in his string of successes was his capture of Muner[30] and some parts of southern Bihar.

Bakhtiyar Khalji possessed an original craftiness that made him unique amongst all alien Muslim invaders of infidel Hindustan. Unlike Mahmud Ghazni, Muhammad Ghori, Aibak or Balban, he had no siege-train for capturing strong Hindu forts. His formula for successful raids included these: speed, the element of surprise, recklessness, savagery and an uncanny sense of timing. All of these tactics were anchored to a focussed goal early in his career: securing maximum loot with minimum bloodshed on his side. His rapid triumphs earned him the title, *The Doughty Lord Marcher*,[31] which he remained till the end, and which was also the cause for his ultimate and spectacular failure. Unlike Mahmud, Aibak, Iltutmish or Balban, Bakhtiyar rarely, if ever, engaged in prolonged sieges or manoeuvres that lasted months. Fully consistent with his character, his campaigns were underscored by impatience, brashness and ungainly hurry with little thought or time to weigh consequences. In a way, these very qualities bizarrely contributed to the sweeping successes early in his career, and he therefore found no reason to change the formula.

Bakhtiyar's newfound title and fame, and the furious pace at which he was amassing plunder and territory attracted likeminded Islamic predators. They poured into Hindustan from all directions, eager to enlist. Thousands of Khaljis vied with one another to join his ever-bourgeoning army. They were all enlisted. Apart from the unlimited opportunities for plunder, these Khaljis were fiercely proud that one of their own brethren had risen to such heights, in this infidel land. Almost an equal number of Turkic Muslim mercenaries also enrolled under him. If this was not enough, Sultan Qutub-ud-din Aibak himself extolled Bakhtiyar as the 'rising star of Islam in East Hindustan',[32] and sent him a *Khillat* comprising a robe of distinction and a laudatory letter.

Buoyed by this great honour, Bakhtiyar now surveyed the situation in the east. North Bihar was prohibitive. The infidel kingdom of Mithila, ruled by the powerful descendants of the Karnataka dynasty,[33] was impenetrable. He refocused his attention on southern Bihar, now a sitting duck. Almost for a full year, Bakhtiyar devastated the surroundings of Munger and pushed further westwards till he sighted a magnificent fort in 1197.

This was *Hisar-i-Bihar,* the fortress of Bihar, known to the Hindu civilizational consciousness as Nalanda.[34]

The Eternal Teardrop of Nalanda

Among the numerous meanings of the Sanskrit word *Nalanda,* the one that truly epitomizes it is the derivation, *na alam dadaati:* 'that which does not give less'.[35] As the premier solar centre that radiated knowledge and the finest traditions of scholarship, this meaning, as its derivation suggests, was one of undisturbed expansion: when has knowledge or the thirst for it ever been any less?

As one of the most ancient centres of human civilization, Nalanda has a continuously recorded history, dating back to 1200 BCE. Every *Darshana* and *Sampradaya,*[36] that grew in the soil of Bharatavarsha, has left its mark here. Every great Hindu and Buddhist king has offered their obeisance through patronage, funding and endowments. By virtue of its earliest, sustained and intimate association with the Bauddha Dharma, from the time of Gautama Buddha, Nalanda has, to this day remained a globally renowned nerve center of the religion of Tathagatha.[37]

After the turbulence that followed in the wake of the disappearance of the Gupta patronage and protection, Nalanda regained its pre-eminence in the 9th century under the Pala rulers. For the next 400 years, the Palas put Nalanda at the centre of their abundant Dharma-building activity and established an extraordinary network[38] of education centres in eastern India. This was the pearlnecklace of knowledge,[39] studded with four other universities—Odantapura, Jaggadala, Vikramashila and Somapura. These five great centres were the heart of Bauddha-Dharma in pre-medieval Bharatavarsha. Every aspiring Buddhist scholar throughout eastern and southeast Asia had to prove his mettle by first subjecting himself to rigorous education in one or more of these centres, before his own country recognized him.

———•·•·•·•———

In Bakhtiyar Khalji's bigoted eyes, it was only a fort, which, like others earlier, offered one more tantalizing opportunity for plunder, another virgin field to plant the victorious flag of Islam in this infidel land. From afar, Bakhtiyar surveyed *Hisar-i-Bihar* with a troop strength of about 200 holy warriors of Islam. He ordered his two *Janbaaz*[40] warriors, Nizam-ud-din and Samsam-ud-din to storm the gateway of the fortress. The brother-duo launched the attack. But Bakhtiyar, true to his 'intrepidity, threw himself into the postern of the gateway of the place'.[41] This is what happened next:

> *The greater number of the inhabitants of that place were Brahmans, and the whole of those Brahmans had their heads shaven; and they were all slain.* There were a great number of books there; and, when all these books came under the observation of the Musalmans, they summoned a number of Hindus that they might give them information respecting the import of those books; *but the whole of the Hindus had been killed.* On becoming acquainted with the contents of those books, it was found that the whole of that fortress and city was a college, and in the Hindu tongue, they call a college, Bihar.[41] (Emphasis added)

Bihar is a corruption of the Sanskrit word, *Vihara*, which means 'college' or 'monastery'. The contemporary state of Bihar takes its name from this word.

Figure 3: The end of the Buddhist monks in Bihar.[42]

What astonished Bakhtiyar and his bloodthirsty horde was that none of these shaven-headed Brahmans put up a fight. In reality, they were not Brahmans but Buddhist monks who, as usual, were immersed in studies and meditation. Much to the delight of these holy warriors of Islam. The same ghastly Islamic precedent was let loose even here: a heartless genocide of these pious and defenceless Buddhist monks ensued in record time. As their bloodlust subsided, Bakhtiyar and his army discovered fabulous amounts of wealth in the 'fort', accompanied by an expansive library of books. After making some inquiries, he learned that these books were filled with the darkness of *kaffir* knowledge. So he promptly burned down this treasure-trove of knowledge, painstakingly preserved over the eons. The spiritual and philosophical wisdom of the ages, consigned to flames. The physical structure of the Nalanda University became fire-fodder, burning continuously over three or six months.

Nalanda, 'that which does not give less', no longer had anything to give. This situation remains unchanged till date.

The fanatical razing of Nalanda is perhaps the cruellest example of the lived Hindu historical experience that gives credence to K.M. Munshi's memorable phrase that the Islamic conquest of India was the conquest of culture by those who lacked it. Sita Ram Goel echoes Munshi in a tangential fashion, when he characterizes the substance of the Islamic invasions of India in these words: 'It was neither the first nor the last time that a [peaceful] society succumbed in the face of determined gangsterism.'[43] Measured by the sheer scale and duration of its decimation, the Nalanda tragedy exceeds the burning of the ancient library of Alexandria by Christian fanatics.

After Nalanda, Bakhtiyar demolished the remaining pearls of the Buddhist necklace of learning in the region: Odantapura and Vikramashila. Today, Odantapura languishes as an unrecognizable structure on a mound, a few miles away from Bihar Sharif, a savage irony of nomenclature. In every place that Bakhtiyar raided, the destruction was thorough and irreversible. B.R. Ambedkar narrates this horrific tragedy with intense feeling:

The Musalman invaders sacked the Buddhist Universities of Nalanda, Vikramasila, Jagaddala, Odantapuri to name only a few. *They razed to the ground Buddhist monasteries with which the country was studded.* The Monks fled away in thousands to Napal, Tibet and other places outside India. A very large number were killed outright by the Muslim commanders. *How the Buddhist priesthood perished by the sword of the Muslim invaders has been recorded by the Muslim historians themselves....* Such was the slaughter of the Buddhist priesthood perpetrated by the Islamic invaders. *The axe was struck at the very root...by killing the Buddhist priesthood Islam killed Buddhism. This was the greatest disaster that befell the religion of Buddha in India....* Nobody remained to keep the flame of Buddhism burning.[44] (Emphasis added)

However, the shameful tragedy of our own time is the sustained propaganda specifically aimed at concealing and denying Bakhtiyar Khalji's laudatory record of the destruction of not just Nalanda but *Bauddha-Dharma* itself.[45]

The Story from the Buddhist Tomb

Buddhist primary sources reveal a fairly comprehensive and vivid panorama of Bakhtiyar's barbaric annihilation of this ancient, sacred *Dhamma* from its own land of birth.

> An undertaking accomplished without analysis,
> Who would regard it as wise?
> After worms have eaten,
> Although a letter may appear, they are not skilled philosophers.

These words flowed from the gifted intellect of the Buddhist scholar, saint and monk, Sakya Sribhadra. Hailing from Kashmir, he still adorns a reverential place in the annals of *Bauddha-Dharma,* in Tibet. He is known by the honorific *Khache Panchen* ('the Maha-Pandita of Kashmir'). He was also the last Indian (Buddhist) Pandita to visit Tibet for an elementary and familiar reason: Bakhtiyar Khalji had annihilated *Bauddha-Dharma* before his very eyes, in a manner of speaking. The sight that this Maha-Pandita had witnessed when he visited Magadha in 1200,[46] made him weep copiously. It had also impaled fear, deep in his heart. His beloved Odantapura and Vikramashila monasteries were now piles of rubble and billows of smoke, completely under the control of the impure and wicked Mlecchas.[47] These were ancient, sacred sites of learning where he had once taught and preached Buddha's *Dhamma*. Scared and grieving, he fled to the safety of the other great Buddhist centre, Jaggadala in northern Bengal.

———◆·•·◆··◆·———

Thirty-four years later, another pious and renowned Buddhist scholar and monk, Dharmasvamin, found his way to India, from Tibet, after months of gruelling journey. He came here carrying a profound dream. Of visiting all the cities, towns and villages hallowed by the footsteps of Gautama Buddha. He longed to see the fabled Bodh Gaya, where the Buddha had attained *Nirvana*. Then he would visit all the Buddhist

Viharas at Nalanda, Odantapura, Vikramashila and Jaggadala and study Buddhist philosophy at the feet of the prestigious scholars whose venerated names he had read and heard about in the meditative quietude of the Himalayan heights. But when he finally arrived, he saw how his dream had been transformed into a live nightmare on the ground. Everywhere he travelled in eastern India, he saw its grotesque dance: the smoking ruins and shattered wreckage of once-pristine Buddhist seats of learning.

Dharmasvamin got the first glimpse of this at Uddandapura or Odantapura. The battered remains of that fabled university was now the residence of a Turushka military commander. Nothing remained of Vikramashila either, the other pearl in the necklace of Buddhist learning.

All the *80* Viharas at Nalanda, now a mass of desolate detritus, had long been abandoned. Only two were semi-functional, operating in fear, secrecy and a desperation born in the innermost recesses of the souls of the Buddhist monks who wanted to somehow preserve their cherished *Dhamma*.

Dharmasvamin's biography,[48] *Upasaka Chos-dar* is the most definitive first-hand account that narrates the fatal and irreversible consequences of Bakhtiyar Khalji's devastation of eastern India from the perspective of his prolific Buddhist and Hindu victims. The narrative is vivid and detailed, and makes for an agonizing reading.

Dharmasvamin quickly realized that the land sanctified by Gautama Buddha had been mauled beyond recognition by the Turushkas. In his extensive journeys, menacing bands of weirdly-dressed (Muslim) soldiers freely indulging in loot and extortion was a common sight. In fact, Dharmasvamin was a personal victim of this Muslim brigandage:

Two such [Muslim] soldiers were in the ferry boat, which was taking Dharmasvamin across the Ganga....They demanded gold from him. Being a simple person or a simpleton, Dharmasvamin threatened to report them to the king, forgetting that Hindu and Buddhist kings were at this time unable to protect themselves, much less their subjects. *This threat made the Muslim soldiers wild and they snatched away the begging bowl of Dharmasvamin.* Two Buddhist lay passengers tried to assuage the Muslim soldiers by offering them precious things, but the soldiers replied, 'We do not want your wealth; we want this Tibetan'. The matter was eventually compromised by Dharmasvamin offering a Pana [typically a gold coin]....*Had the fellow passengers not intervened, Dharmasvamin would have been carried away as a slave, and Indian history would have lost this important sourcebook.*[49] (Emphasis added)

The stark light that hundreds of such painful incidents shines upon the patented nature of the Islamic conquests of infidel Hindustan and their ensuing consequences for Hindustan's infidels is now widely familiar. In this specific context, it is clear that Bakhtiyar Khalji's savagery singlehandedly uprooted *Bauddha-Dharma* from India, forever, by decimating all the physical spaces that had fed and nurtured it by an exhaustive genocide[50] of the monks and scholars who had kept it alive. Bakhtiyar's genocide was primarily impelled by a core Islamic doctrinal reason, encapsulated in a single word: *But,* or *Vigraha* or *Murti* (translated incorrectly as 'idol').

The Muhammadan historian [was] indifferent to distinctions among idolaters.... *The multitude of images used in mediaeval Buddhist worship always inflamed the fanaticism of Muslim warriors to such fury that no quarter was given to the idolaters. The ashes of the Buddhist sanctuaries at Sarnath near Benares still bear witness to the rage of the image-breakers.* Many noble monuments of the ancient civilisation of India were irretrievably wrecked in the course of the early Muhammadan invasions. *Those invasions were fatal to the existence of Buddhism as a...religion in northern India,* where its strength resided chiefly in Bihar and certain adjoining territories. The monks who escaped massacre fled, and were scattered over Nepal, Tibet, and the south. After 1200, the traces of Buddhism in upper India are faint and obscure.[51] (Emphasis added)

———•·—•·—•———

In Delhi, Qutub-ud-din Aibak was overjoyed.

Bakhtiyar Khalji, the rising star of Islam in eastern Hindustan, continued to ascend. Unaided by any imperial power, this short and ugly, but ruthless freelance mercenary had brought extraordinary gains for Islam in a difficult and hostile territory. His total devastation of southern Bihar, which brought him such unprecedented prestige, had also awakened the wily politician inside him. Unwilling to become anybody's subordinate, he opted for cunning diplomacy in the form of flattery. Bakhtiyar sought an audience at the august court of Aibak by addressing him as 'Sultan', an honour Aibak was not yet entitled to. This was because his overlord, Muhammad Ghori was still alive and thriving.

As anticipated, Aibak gladly granted him the audience.

Accordingly, Bakhtiyar[52] Khalji, 'one of the chief supports of the Islamic State in infidel Hindustan, he, the splendour of Islam, celebrated throughout Hind for his religious wars, joined the auspicious stirrups and came to pay his respects from the direction of Behar'.[52] His entourage, comprising opulent treasures and booty, finally arrived in the presence of the 'beneficent' Qutub-ud-din Aibak. He received Bakhtiyar with great honour and distinction. Indeed, no honour was too great for this lone and intrepid pillar of Islam in this land of infidel darkness.

It was a grand courtly ceremony with Aibak's chief officers and nobles in full attendance. From his personal royal wardrobe, Aibak presented Bakhtiyar with an ornate robe, indicative of prestige. More *Khillats* followed: a tent, a *naubat* (clarionet), a drum, a flag, a horse and trappings, a waist belt, a sword and a vest—all befitting a distinguished holy warrior of Islam. Obscene amounts of money, jewels and precious stones came next. Bakhtiyar respectfully accepted it all, and then in an astute move, he generously redistributed the wealth among Aibak's courtiers. This further elevated his stature in 'Sultan' Qutub-ud-din Aibak's eyes. The impressed host conferred that ultimate distinction—his special Imperial robe of honour, upon Bakhtiyar.

The whole thing turned out exactly as he had calculated. Qutub-ud-din Aibak had now given him tacit permission to raid and ravage the whole of eastern India as he pleased. And Bakhtiyar had shrewdly guarded his independence by faking subservience to Aibak's authority. Thus, until Iltutmish usurped the throne, no Muslim ruler from Delhi set foot in that region.

The Turushka Devastates an Ancient *Tirthakshetra*

Bakhtiyar Khalji now turned his attention to Bengal. His prior devastations in Bihar had so terrified the 'unbelievers of that region' that 'fear of him operated exceedingly in their hearts'.[53] His first target was the ancient and sacred city of Navadvipa (Nadia) on the banks of the Ganga.

For centuries, Navadvipa was renowned as a sacred *tirthakshetra* (centre of pilgrimage) on the banks of the Ganga, attracting thousands of *Sadhus*, monks, mendicants, scholars and pilgrims from across India. It is said that Ganga, as Bhagirathi, once flowed down the west of Navadvipa. In many ways, it resembled Kashi. Sadhus built cottages and Ashrams and spent the rest of their lives in spiritual pursuits on its sanctified banks. Navadvipa grew in prestige under the Sena kings, who made it one of their capitals. Naturally, it soon developed into a thriving commercial city, populated by merchants, traders, builders, craftsmen, entertainers, professionals, bureaucrats and servants.

In the early years of the 13th century, Navadvipa was ruled by the pious and venerable, but negligent Lakshmanasena. He would pay an expensive price for ignoring the ominous message regularly emanating from Bakhtiyar Khalji's ravaging exploits in the region. To make matters worse, Lakshmanasena had not even posted any armed troops to guard his city.

In the summer of 1200-01, Bakhtiyar Khalji stood outside the gates of this ancient *tirthakshetra* and laid the macabre edifice of the first-ever Muslim rule in Bengal.

Bakhtiyar had thoroughly studied his complacent target. For decades, Navadvipa, the commercial city, was also where the caravans of Turkish Muslim horse-dealers frequented in order to peddle their wares, which included Tartar-bred warhorses, chinaware and expensive brocades. Lakshmanasena was blissfully ignorant of the fact that some of these Muslim merchants also moonlighted as reconnoitring agents for any sultan or Muslim adventurer who sought information. This pattern of Muslim merchants, traders and businessmen doubling as spies would recur much later in Devagiri, Gujarat and other places as well.

Armed with this intelligence, Bakhtiyar Khalji started out from Bihar Sharif. He crossed the River Son (Shona in Sanskrit), sped through Munger and pushed eastwards, till he arrived at the forbidding jungles of Jharkhand. He camped there for the night. He was less than thirty kilometres northwest of Navadvipa. Early next morning, he led the march with a meagre force of 18 troopers. He divided the rest of his force into small but nimble units, which would follow this advance party at an interval of fifteen minutes. This was to be his most daring assault yet. His band of 18 slowed down at Navadvipa's gates and sauntered into the ill-fated city with nonchalant confidence. To its inhabitants, Bakhtiyar and his crew were one of those familiar travelling horse-salesmen they had long been accustomed to. He paid the customs duty at the gate and after about half an hour, sighted Lakshmanasena's palace. Behind him, another unit of his larger force had already reached the city's gates.

Inside Lakshmansena's palace, it was time for lunch. Outisde, his citizens too, had retired to their homes for their mid-day meals. As was customary, a leisurely siesta would follow. Navadvipa was languid, its streets largely deserted. Even if he had prayed to Allah, Bakhityar couldn't have asked for a better fortune.

At lighting speed, he drew his sword, a signal to his troop of 18 to 'commence the onslaught of the unbelievers'.[54] It began with the brutal massacre of the semi-alert guards of the palace, who didn't stand much chance. Bakhtiyar next rushed to the Inner Quarters, chopping and slashing everyone he encountered. The ruckus of this sudden assault was the cue for Bakhtiyar's second contingent. This larger unit had already entered the city. As the clamour rose from the gate of the palace and the market streets, this second contingent unleashed pure terror. Navadvipa's unarmed citizens were mercilessly sliced into pieces. The market was thoroughly devastated. The manic loot of the hard-earned wealth of the generations was inaugurated by the Islamic holy-war cry of 'Allah-hu-Akbar', which resonated through the streets. Then the remaining units of Bakhtiyar's troops stormed into this drowsy city of infidels.

This was how the virgin Islamic invasion of Bengal had begun—on a sleepy, unguarded afternoon. Its Hindus would repeatedly lose their freedom for centuries to come.

Lakshmanasena couldn't have his lunch.

The 13th century Muslim chronicler Minhaj Siraj describes Lakshmanasena's sorry fate with frank glee[55]:

> The Rae [Raja] fled barefooted by the back part of his palace; and the whole of his treasures, his wives, and [other] females, his domestics and servants, his particular attendants, were captured, and the Musalmans captured a number of elephants, and such a vast amount of booty fell to their lot, as cannot be recorded.[55]

But Lakshmansena managed to escape alone on a boat and reached Samatata[56] with some difficulty. The tottering Sena Empire was on its last legs, but following Bakhtiyar's savage incursion, it shifted its base to this place and somehow retained its power for a few more years. Lakshmanasena's 'boundless treasures, the accumulations of eighty years, fell into the possession of the Musalmans; and a large portion of them, the greatest rarities, were transmitted to Malik Kutub-ud-Din [Aibak]'.[56]

As the undisputed overlord, Bakhtiyar Khalji did to Navadvipa what was scripturally sanctioned for every victorious Muslim invader. He plundered all that was worth plundering and thoroughly wrecked the rest, ridding the city of all traces of infidelity and left it in desolation. When he was finished with it, Navadvipa was but a skeleton of its previous prosperity.

Unlike Bakhtiyar's career-starting raids in Bihar, the devastation of Navadvipa spurred him on to even greater ambition: of capturing all of Bengal. Entirely consistent with his impatience for rapid serial conquests, he did not pursue Lakshmanasena. Nor did he station a military contingent in Navadvipa.

The Sorrow of Gaur

Bakhtiyar's next target was even more enterprising—Gaur[57] or Lakshmanavati. It was the historic nerve-centre of the *Gauda-Desha* (Bengal) from the ancient times. Lakshmanavati had prospered as the 'metropolis of Bengal under its Hindu kings'.[58] When the colonial British surveyed it in the second half of the 19th century, local tradition had retained its civilizational memory: it was known variously as (a) *Adisur*: named after Adishura, the ancient king of Bengal; (b) *Ballal Sen:* named after Ballalasena, father of the aforementioned Lakshmanasena; (c) *Lakshman*: named after Lakshmanasena, Bakhtiyar's first infidel victim from Bengal.

Figure 4: Painting of Adi-Varaha discovered at the ruins of Gaur. Available in The Ruins of Gour: Described and Represented in Eighteen Views with a Topographical Map. *Compiled from the manuscripts and drawings of the Late H. Creighton, Esq. Circa 1817.*

Whether the luminaries of Gaur[59] had brought such prestige to the place, or the place itself produced such generational luminaries is difficult to say. But the doubtless fact remains, that from undated antiquity, Gaudiya[60] Brahmanas have played a resplendent role in the spread and preservation of the best of Sanatana philosophical, spiritual and cultural traditions. In fact, the repeated mass migrations of Gaudiya Brahmanas merit an independent study in its own right. Their descendants today are scattered along the western coast in Goa, Maharashtra and Karnataka. Their generational memory survives in their general appellation: *Gauda Sarasvata Brahmanas*.

Gaur was also the historic site of the renowned Five *Kulin* Brahmanas[61] of Bengal. The aforementioned King Adisura had invited five distinguished Brahmanas from Kanyakubja (Kanauj) in order to perform a grand Yajna. The most distinguished of them was Bhatta Narayana, author of the renowned Sanskrit play, *Venisamhara*. Over time, they made Gaur their home. Like its Buddhist counterparts at Nalanda and Odantapura, Gaur was the exalted nucleus of Sanskrit learning and literature, and the only battles it had witnessed so far were debates that took place among its scholars, where the ultimate victor was knowledge.

Gaur met with the same fate as Nalanda. Here too, Bakhtiyar implemented the same dastardly template that had worked so spectacularly early in his blood-drenched career. The renowned historian, Jadunath Sarkar describes it '…. like the warriors of the steppe and the desert in every age operating in a civilized country, the army of Bakhtiyar also first ravaged the open country without making [a direct] attempt on Gaur….'[62]

This open country roughly corresponds to a vast tract, a rich alluvial expanse of the earth lying between the main channels of Ganga and Brahmaputra. Bakhtiyar's devastation of Gaur was worse than that of Navadvipa. He began by wasting and capturing this tract and then moved directly into the metropolis. It didn't stand a chance. Bakhtiyar's holy Islamic warriors slaughtered all the infidels they could find and destroyed the 'idol temples of the infidels and erected masjids and other buildings'.[63] The obliteration was so exhaustive that Gaur was *physically* erased from existence. Nothing remained to indicate the traces of its flourishing Sanatana past.

The devastation of Gaur was the pinnacle of Bakhtiyar Khalji's genocidal career. It had finally enabled him to acquire the independent empire he had so desperately craved for when he set out from the furnace of Garmsir. Apart from southern Bihar, what remained of north-western Bengal was now under his absolute control.

The Maximum Number of Converts to Islam

A new empire needed a new capital. Bakhtiyar built it a few miles from the ruins of Gaur. He named it, unimaginatively, Lakhnauti (a corruption of Lakshmanavati). He settled down to consolidate his fairly extensive conquests, for the next couple of years. A cardinal administrative measure of this consolidation involved the demolition of the few 'idol-temples' that had still remained standing. In the typical fashion of all victorious Islamic invaders, he built mosques and madrassas on their ruins using their debris and in record time, the entire region was bursting* with *masjids, madrassas, mazhars* and *khanqahs*. His *amirs* followed his lead by sponsoring and building more Islamic seminaries and colleges. These 'praiseworthy endeavours' thoroughly endeared him to the Islamic clergy. They saw in these institutions the proof of Bakhtiyar's zeal for Islam, for converting the infidels, for Islamizing the whole of Hindustan.

A little-known fact of the Muslim history of India is that *Islam acquired the maximum number of converts during Bakhtiyar Khalji's reign.*

The contemporary Bangladeshi poet, the late Al Mahmud in his gushing work titled *Bakhtiyarer Ghora* (Horses of Bakhtiyar) paints Bakhtiyar Khalji as a great hero of the Muslim conquest of India.

---

* (1) *Masjid*: Mosque (2) *Madrassa*: School or college teaching the Islamic religion (3) *Mazhar*: A Muslim shrine or enshrined tomb (4) *Khanqah*: A building meant for the gathering of a Sufi brotherhood, where Islamic theological education and discourses are provided. These were typically sponsored and funded by Muslim kings.

That this work is written in Bengali eulogizing an Islamic fanatic who set fire to the original Sanatana culture of Bengal reflects the long-term consequences of what alien Muslim invasions have inflicted upon Bharatavarsha. Al Mahmud passed away in 2019.

Throughout Bakhtiyar's dominions, the *Khutba* and the *Azaan* replaced the mellow, soothing Vedic Mantras that had continuously sanctified these erstwhile Sanatana realms. For centuries, these divine hymns—the musical expressions of the grandest spiritual realization of the Rishis—had flowed throughout this region, like the subterranean Vedic Saraswati river. The Muslim chronicler Badauni glorifies Bakhtiyar's pious devastation of this idol-worshipping infidelity in a heartfelt couplet:

> Here, where was heard before, the clamour and uproar of the Kaffir
> Now, here is heard resounding the shouts of 'Allaho Akbar!'[64]

The inaugural ravaging of the Sanatana spiritual civilization and culture that Mahmud of Ghazni had inflicted throughout north India, reaching down to Gujarat, was replicated with greater fanaticism and ferocity by Bakhtiyar Khalji in Bengal. Unlike Mahmud, Bakhtiyar had enough leisure to sustain and savour the fruits of this ravaging.

For the next three centuries, Bengal would firmly remain in the Islamic thrall and would never regain its lost Sanatana character. At various points, the fortunes and the very nomenclature of Gaur[65] itself underwent several upheavals. But the Islamic character that Bakhtiyar had imposed on it was permanently imprinted into the state.

'His Hands Will Reach beyond the Point of His Knees'

Bakhtiyar was now a Khalji *Malik*, a solid pillar of support of Islam's eastern expansion into infidel Hindustan. In the Islamic scheme of cooking up folklore, he was apparently predestined for this glory. At least in Minhaj Siraj's perverse eulogy.

Siraj miraculously transforms the same disqualifications that had almost nipped Bakhtiyar's blood-stained career in the bud into the very founts of his blazing successes. His dwarfish stature, his ugliness and his grotesque, long arms had now become the markers of foretold divine predictions of prestige. As 'evidence', Minhaj brandishes a prophecy emanating from the unlikeliest of all sources: Hindu astrologers at Lakshmanasena's court. This is how Siraj's absurd fiction reads:

Bakhtiyar's fame…had reached the hearing of Rae Lakhmaniah [Lakshmanasena]….A number of astrologers, wise men, and counsellors of his kingdom presented themselves before the Rae, and represented, saying: 'In our books of the ancient Brahmans they have foretold that this country will fall into the hands of the Turks, and the time of its fulfilment has drawn near....'

The Rae replied, saying: 'Is there any token given in your books with respect to this man who is to subdue our country?' They replied: '*The indication of him is this, that, when he stands upright on his two feet, and lets down his two hands, his hands will reach beyond the point of his knees in such wise that the fingers will touch the calves of his legs.*' The Rae answered: 'It is advisable that trustworthy persons should be despatched in order that they may, in a proper manner, investigate those peculiar characteristics.' In accordance with the Rae's command, they sent trustworthy persons, and they made investigation respecting this matter, and, *in the external form and figure of Muhammad-i-Bakht-yar, those characteristics they found.*[66] (Emphasis added)

With great victory came greater insecurity. It was time to woo Aibak again. This time, Bakhtiyar needed Aibak's formal recognition of his authority over Bengal and Bihar. Military honours and royal robes were but superficial gestures. This was a most delicate matter. Aibak could not be allowed to grow suspicious. If he even *imagined* that Bakhtiyar posed a threat, he would immediately instigate the Muslim governors at Awadh and Kalinjara to seize Bakhtiyar's hard-won territories in Bihar and Bengal. And so, he dispatched a handsome portion of the spoils that he had looted during the heartless sack of Gaur.

Formal recognition was readily granted.

'My Good Fortune Hath Deserted Me!'

In 1206, Bakhtiyar Khalji launched his last and most ambitious conquest. This would not only shatter his meteoric career but culminate in an appalling personal humiliation. Banking on the strength and confidence of his dividend-giving recklessness, he now set his target really high. Literally.

Tibet.

With its capture, Bakhtiyar dreamed of monopolizing a new shortcut to Turkistan. It was a strategic part of the flourishing Silk Route that led to China on the other side.

Bakhtiyar was ignited by the prospect.

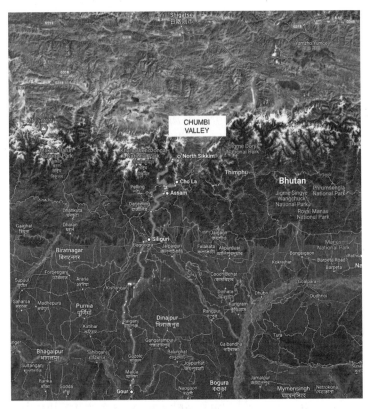

Figure 5: Route of Bakhtiyar Khalji's march to Tibet.

His northward journey began with a force of 12,000 horses that entered the treacherous terrain of Kamarupa (Assam, generally). His first raid netted a tribal chieftain named Mech, who was quickly converted to Islam and rechristened as Ali the Mech. He became Bakhtiyar's guide, leading him to a prosperous city named Bardhan-Kot[67] on the banks of the mighty Bagmati river, which was 'in magnitude, breadth and depth, three times more than the River Ganga'.[68] There was no way Bakhtiyar's army could cross it at this point. So for the next 10 days, they marched upstream along the river, the mountainous terrain growing in altitude each day. On the 11th day, Ali the Mech brought them to an ancient bridge of hewn stone and took leave of his new master. At the head of the bridge, Bakhtiyar posted two amirs, one Turk slave, one Khalji warrior, and left them behind with a small helper unit to guard it until his return.

With Bakhtiyar at the head, 'the army of Islam crossed the bridge'. He was now in the territory of the Hindu king of Kamarupa, who had already caught wind of this Turushka march across the bridge. He delivered some friendly advice to Bakhtiyar through his messengers: this is not the right time to invade Tibet. Remember that you also need to return. Go back now and come next year with better preparations. I will send my own forces to assist your revized expedition. Characteristically, Bakhtiyar did not heed the wise counsel and instead, 'turned his face towards the mountains of Tibet'. For the next 15 days, Bakhtiyar's army endured a gruelling climb up the steep hills and descended into treacherous ravines through the labyrinthine Himalayan terrain. On the 16th day, they were rewarded with the sight of the vast, open country of 'Tibbat. The whole of that tract was under cultivation, teeming with tribes of people and populous villages.'[69] This was the Chumbi Valley. But it was also a deadly trap. Bakhtiyar and his army of Islam realized this fatal truth a little too late.

That he had met with zero resistance along the whole route had not aroused his suspicion. Drunk on past victories, Bakhtiyar thought nothing was amiss and ordered an unrestrained plunder of the region. Highly unexpected and disastrous results ensued almost immediately.

The counterattack against the Turushka invaders started from … thin air. Resistance lashed out in waves. Bakhtiyar's infidel foe fought a primal war, armed with crude weapons like canes, bamboo spears, primitive cuirasses, long bows and death-dealing arrows.[70] The intense battle lasted from daybreak to sunset. By the end of the day, a substantial portion of Bakhtiyar's army was decimated. At night, he made enquiries and discovered that these wretched *but-parastans* (idol-worshippers) had been following his march for a while. They were prepared to fight, kill and win at any cost. Even worse, he learned that a reinforcement of 50,000 horsemen and archers would arrive at dawn. Bakhtiyar assembled a lightning meeting the same night. The vote of his amirs was unanimous: the Musalman troops are thoroughly exhausted, and the number of our martyrs in today's battle give us no hope. An equal number are disabled. Let us retreat now and return next year with better preparations.

Bakhtiyar immediately dismantled the camp and ordered the retreat. However, the retreat such as it was, was actually the preface[71] to a crueller nightmare. And to their lasting horror, this is what Bakhtiyar's holy warriors of Islam found:

> ….throughout the whole route [i.e., return march], not a blade of grass nor a stick of firewood remained, as they [the inhabitants] had set fire to the whole of it, and burnt it; and all the inhabitants of those defiles [a steep, narrow gorge] and passes had moved off from the line of route. During these fifteen days, not a pound of food nor a blade of grass did the cattle and horses obtain; and all the men were killing their horses and eating them.[71]

Finally, when the army reached the stone-hewn bridge across the Bagmati river, it was the beginning of a new chapter of horror. The bridge was deserted and its arches had been demolished by that accursed infidel king of Kamarupa.[72] He had tricked Bakhtiyar. Now it was simply impossible to cross the perilous river. Nor could they remain for long in this hostile country. After halting for a few days, they discovered that the only means of escape was to cross the flooded river as is. Which they attempted on horseback. But when they emerged on the other side, Bakhtiyar discovered that his original, grand army of Islam now numbered a little over a 100 men. Ali the Mech eventually reached him and accompanied him all the way to Devkot, Bakhtiyar's new capital.

Humiliated to Death

Bakhtiyar Khalji never recovered from this.

At Devkot, he slipped into depression because of the 'excessive grief which overcame him', in Minhaj's words. His authority was eroded to the point of no return. Conspiracies, dissension and treachery openly erupted in his most intimate circle but he no longer cared. The final salt on the wound was the daily torrent of imprecations hurled at him even by the lowest classes. When Bakhtiyar rode in the city streets on his regal horse, people thronged to greet him with fire in their eyes. From rooftops, at the street corners and marketplaces, women and children screamed curses at him and reviled him in the most obscene language. And the abuses never stopped. The women held him directly responsible for their widowhood and making their children orphans. They wished him to rot in hell. The dishonour and humiliation was total and it heightened his depression and shame. Bakhtiyar eventually stopped showing his face in public and confined himself to his quarters, wallowing in self-pity and composing miserable verses.

> Can any calamity have befallen the Sultan-i-Ghazi that
> my good fortune hath deserted me![73]

The Sultan-i-Ghazi was Muhammad Ghori, who had been murdered in his tent[74] by some assailants seeking vengeance, around the same time. Bakhtiyar's depression eventually morphed into sickness and he became bedridden. For three days, he lay alone and uncared for because, in his words, it is 'the way of the world which deserts one in misfortune'.

On the fourth day, Ali Mardan, 'one of Muhammad Bakhtiyar's greatest generals' arrived at Devkot and finding him bedridden, 'pulled down the sheet from his face and ruthlessly dispatched him with one blow of a dagger'.

Ali Mardan was a Khalji clansman whom Bakhtiyar had elevated to the position of the governor of Barshul province. He was yet another proof of the glaring, thematic truth of the Muslim history of medieval India: that political succession was gained through bloody betrayal and guiltless treachery.

Iltutmish Extinguishes Bakhtiyar Khalji's Empire

Bakhtiyar Khalji was the classic victim of his own hubris. His triumph and daredevilry had ultimately proven fatal. He aspired to become a sultan but real sultan-hood eluded him till the end because he did not establish a durable empire. He could not consolidate the significant extent of territory he had conquered. With Lakshmanavati (or Devkot) as his capital, the geography he controlled was spread out in this fashion:

> ....bounded on the north by a north-easterly straight line from the modern town of Purnia via Devkot to the town of Rangpur; on the east and the south-east by the Teesta and the Karatoya; on the south by the main stream of the Ganges; and on the west by the lower course of the Kosi and from its mouth across the Ganges to the Rajmahal hills.[75]

Administratively, Bakhtiyar had divided his dominions into *Sarkars* or fiefs: Tanda, Purnia, Pinjrah, Tajpur, Ghoraghat and Barbakabad. He appointed governors to each. These holy warriors of Islam who had distinguished themselves in Bakhtiyar's serial campaigns of plunder and devastation, had been suitably rewarded in this manner.

Ali Mardan Khalji, Muhammad Shiran and his brother Ahmed Shiran, and Husam-ud-din Iwaz formed the most powerful clique of this new Khalji oligarchy. Other Turkic Muslim army officers had also received their share of Bakhtiyar's bounty.

However, this administrative setup ultimately proved shaky and ephemeral because it was modelled after its stormy founder, who barely settled down at any point in his short-lived career.

* * *

After murdering Bakhtiyar, Ali Mardan went berserk with power and earned pervasive wrath both from his oligarchic compatriots and the citizens. He awarded himself the title, 'Sultan Ala-ud-din' and 'from the excessive folly and pride and arrogance of his mind, sat in Lakhnauti'.[76] He unleashed a reign of naked terror and extortion. All Muslim chroniclers are unanimous in denouncing Ali Mardan in choicest abuse. He was hypocritical, crafty, cruel, hot-headed, homicidal, bloodthirsty, bombastic, an idler, impetuous, notorious, audacious, haughty, oppressive, self-important and tyrannical.

Ali Mardan lasted two years.

His oligarchic compatriots had never forgiven him for the brazen murder of their master. However, they had tolerated him because the cushy positions and the power that they wielded, had overwhelmed their loyalty to the dead Bakhtiyar. But when Ali began reading the *Khutba*, minting *Sikkahs* (coins) in his own name and styled himself 'Ala-ud-din', they decided that things had gone too far. Yet, the impervious Ali Mardan who persisted in his tyranny, which 'exceeded all bounds', now turned against the Khalji amirs themselves.

They formed a confederacy and swiftly murdered him.

* * *

The former donkey-driver, Malik Husam-ud-din Iwaz[77] was elected the successor to Ali Mardan because like Bakhtiyar, he too, was a Khalji from Garamsir. Unlike the hot-headed and delusional Ali Mardan, he proved his mettle by consolidating Bakhtiyar's gains in Bengal. He relocated the capital from Devkot back to Lakshmanavati and built a tough fortress at Basankot.[78] Next, he embarked on an ambitious redesign and reconstruction of this ancient Hindu city. This redesign was primarily impelled by Islamic piety. Iwaz more thoroughly Islamized Lakshmanavati by demolishing whatever Hindu structures still remained, and by erecting massive Jama Masjids using their debris. He also encouraged his officials to build mosques and madrassas throughout and beyond this renovated city. He opened up his treasury and gave generous salaries to Islamic theologians, scholars, priesthood and 'descendants of the Prophet'. He regularly invited Imams and preachers from abroad to deliver Islamic discourses in his audience-hall and rewarded them with 'a large chalice full of gold and silver *Tankhas*',[79] and instructed his amirs to follow his example. He wrote commendatory letters so that when these Imams visited other Muslim dominions in infidel Hindustan, they received similar munificence.

Finally, Husam-ud-din Iwaz awarded himself the grand title of Sultan Ghiyath al-Din Iwaz Khalji.[80] Nobody complained. To the contrary, in faraway Delhi, this is how Sultan Iltutmish described Iwaz:

> What extreme magnanimity! Whenever mention of Iwaz's name chanced to arise, [Iltutmish] would style him by the title of *Sultan Ghiyas-ud Din Iwaz Khalji*. And from his sacred lips he would pronounce that there could be no reluctance in styling a man as Sultan who had done so much good [for Islam]. Allah's mercy be upon him![81]

But the same Iltutmish would prove to be Iwaz's nemesis and would extinguish his considerable empire, which had taken 14 long years to consolidate. Iwaz had committed the unpardonable crime of directly writing to the Abbasid Caliph al-Nasir, seeking an investiture from him. He had calculated it to do two things: one, to stamp his authority as sultan, and two, to act as an insurance policy protecting him from the superior Muslim power at Delhi.

It was a fatal miscalculation.

The investiture arrived in 1221-22 in the form of Caliphate honours and a *farman* declaring that Iwaz was indeed a *Nasir*, a helper of the Commander of the Faithful (i.e., the Caliph). An overjoyed Iwaz minted a special issue of coins[82] on the occasion. With that, he had declared Bengal an independent[83] sultanate, and simultaneously signed his death warrant.

The Caliph's ordination was hardly a deterrent to an incensed Iltutmish, who was busy elsewhere warding off Jalal-ud-din Mangbarni[84] and other enemies on the north-western front. Five years later, Iltutmish bulldozed through Iwaz's territories in south Bihar, effortlessly pocketing them. Then he charged towards Lakshmanavati and began battering the sturdy fortress of Basankot with his vast army. It was a decidedly unequal battle but Iwaz fought till the inevitable end. In March 1227, Iwaz, his Khalji Amir and other nobles were captured and mercilessly beheaded.[85]

This carnage not only snuffed out the fledgling Khalji Empire in Bengal but made it a lasting vassal of the burgeoning Delhi Sultanate. In less than 30 years, Bakhtiyar Khalji's independent Islamic empire in Bengal had become extinct.

No Khalji would ever sit on its throne again.

———◆◆◆———

However, what Bakhtiyar had seeded and left behind proved more enduring. Thanks to his audacious and brutal, predatory depredations, south Bihar and especially Bengal became the nurseries of Islam. Barbarians hailing from various Muslim tribes of Central Asia and Afghanistan flooded into it with extraordinary frequency. Under Bakhtiyar and his short-lived successors, Lakshmanavati became 'as happy an abode of Islam as the city of Delhi'. Iwaz, especially, 'came like a veritable blessing of Allah'.[86] If the present-day city of Gaur sports a profusion of Islamic structures—mostly mosques and dargahs—they owe their origins to Bakhtiyar Khalji and Hisam-ud-din Iwaz.

Almost nothing remains of its sacred Hindu past except its name.

A Tragic Footnote of Our Times

Unlike the other alien Muslim invaders of India, Bakhtiyar Khalji was not born a slave nor was he sold into slavery. From Sabuktigin to Balban, every invader was either a slave or the slave of a slave. Thus, while the Delhi Sultanate, till Balban's period, was a Sultanate of slaves, the Islamic territory that Bakhtiyar carved out in Bengal, by cannibalizing prosperous Hindu kingdoms, was an independent regime owing token allegiance to Delhi. However, although he styled himself a king, Bakhtiyar remained fundamentally, a mercenary freebooter and marauder. His leadership was more military than civilian.

All medieval Muslim chronicles are united in extolling him as one of the greatest heroes of the *Deen*[87] who planted the Islamic flag far and wide in infidel Hindustan. They praise his devout zealotry for spreading Islam by converting enormous numbers of infidels. They predicted that his fame would endure as long as Islam survives in this impure land of idol-worshippers.

Bakhtiyar Khalji's short-lived personal empire of Islam was the culmination of a sordid journey that had begun in sunburnt Garamsir and was littered with Buddhist and Hindu genocides. He had left in his wake industrial-scale decimation of stupas, temples, monasteries and hundreds of Hindu structures of exquisite beauty and profound antiquity. It culminated in his savage takeover of south Bihar and Bengal. Although he did not live long enough to fully savour his ill-gotten empire, he had permanently destroyed the Hindu character of these regions. His territories were large enough to equal two or three small European countries.

But in Muslim annals, Bakhtiyar had singlehandedly birthed and elevated the prestige of the Khalji tribe in Bengal and southern Bihar almost a century before the Khaljis themselves became the royalty where it really mattered: the throne of Delhi.

— · · ◆ · · —

Today, Bihar Sharif, named after Bakhtiyar's corruption of *Vihara*, is the administrative headquarters of the Nalanda district. This was once the sanctified habitat of *Bauddha Dharma* in all of Bharatavarsha. Silence, serenity and contemplation was its changeless order. There, the purpose and goal of life was the quest to attain Buddhahood. It was the home to the world's greatest university of its time. It was the noblest guide of kings and commoners—Nalanda—which Bakhtiyar Khalji heartlessly decimated with the fire and sword of Islam. Nalanda, which never rose again, which never witnessed that Buddhist tranquillity.

An hour north from Nalanda lies a city named in the honour of this gold-standard Islamic bigot: Bakhtiyarpur.

———•··•··•———

CHAPTER 1

Turkic-Muslim Tribal Chaos in Delhi

*The Shah burnt the infidel temples and destroyed the idols and thus
made a hell of paradise,
And in every ruin a treasure had been found.*

A few years before Bakhtiyar Khalji had stood before
Muhammad Ghori, an unnamed soldier had rescued Ghori
from the fatal javelin hurled by the infidel Govindaraja of Delhi
in the First Battle of Tarain. He had carried the profusely bleeding
Ghori, away to safety, on his horse. The unnamed foot soldier
hailed from the Khalji tribe, but his anonymity has found a
place in history because Muhammad Ghori eventually succeeded
in his Jihad against infidel Hindustan by defeating Prithviraja
Chahamana through treachery.

For about a century, a major chunk of the Khalji fighters who
had accompanied Mahmud of Ghazni, Muhammad Ghori and
Qutub-ud-din Aibak's serial Jihads into Hindustan had largely
remained anonymous even as their stature had grown. It was
under Iltutmish, and more prominently under Balban, that they
became a recognized class of nobility. They were titled Khalji
Maliks and received *Jagirs* and governorships. However, the
Turkic-Muslim aristocracy (see: Book 1 of *Invaders and Infidels*)
in the court of Delhi never admitted them into their coveted
inner circle for purely racist reasons. The Khaljis were regarded as
Afghans, an inferior and lowly tribe. This racism would be their
eventual undoing.

Even from this perspective, Bakhtiyar Khalji remains an oddity
who operated independently, distant from the preying eyes
of the nascent Delhi Sultanate. Bakhtiyar was respected by his

contemporary Muslim military marauders, not because he was a Khalji, but because of the holy service he had rendered to the expansion of Islam in infidel Hindustan. We are reminded of this revealing observation about the ways of the Islamic world:

> Before I was 9, I had learned basic canon of Arab life. It was me against my brother; me and my brother against our father; my family against my cousins and the clan; the clan against the tribe; the tribe against the world, and all of us against the infidel.[1]

Ironically, Balban, the 'purest' of the Turks, heralded the political destruction of his own tribe in Hindustan. In his ruthless surgery, or the purge* of the dreaded 'Turkic Forty' in his nobility, he had patronized non-Turkic Muslim bloodlines by catapulting them to various high offices.

The Khaljis were the biggest beneficiaries of this surgery.

Balban's brother, Kislay Khan as the *amir-hajib*[2] had maintained intimate relations with the Khalji amirs from as early as 1250. Balban's favourite son, Muhammad, who was slaughtered by the Mongols, also boasted of tough Khalji officers serving under him in Sind.

Apart from the Khaljis, Balban had elevated other races and tribes including but not limited to the Tajiks, Tartars, Habashis,[3] Ghuris, Seljuks and even the lowly Paiks.[4] The other notable tribe that Balban and his weak successors patronized was the Mongol. Following the upheavals in Central Asia around 1262, the Mongols had fled to as far as Egypt,[5] and forced their way into Lahore and Delhi. These immigrants comprised former military commanders, aristocrats, high-ranking officers and their respective loyalists. The influx was so copious that Balban carved out a separate *Chingizi* colony in Delhi to house them. They came in kaleidoscopic groups: some were still Mongol pagans, some Muslims, and others of uncertain religious background. But once they sought Balban's asylum, they had to convert to Islam as the

---

* For the full story, see: See Book 1: *Invaders and Infidels*

precondition. By dint of their various talents, they soon became a force to reckon with. However, the Turkic-Muslims, who enjoyed premium citizenship in Balban's 'pure' Turkic Sultanate, immediately despised them, branding them as 'neo-Muslims'. As we have seen Book 1, some of these neo-Muslims had helped in the accession of the young Kaiqubad and dearly paid for it on more than one occasion.

Wolf Eat Wolf

Balban's policy of crushing his own Turkic nobility through a cynical combination of bloodshed, terror, espionage and marginalization had proven to be a highly pragmatic strategy in the wolfish methods of sultanate politics. It was the only way he could maintain both his despotism and prevent the vapours of potential competition from rising. And it worked only as long as he was alive. His brutal devaluation[6] of his own tribe ignited far-reaching consequences. The first casualty was the Turkic Muslims. The second was the manner in which it fundamentally altered the character of early Islamic rule in northern India.

For the 80 years that culminated in Balban's death, the only accepted succession model in the nascent sultanate was this indisputable pre-qualification—the contender to the throne mandatorily had to be a Turkic *Ghulam* (slave). Other machinations mattered little. Bribery, betrayal, treachery, regicide, patricide and fratricide would eventually gain legitimacy if the new incumbent proved his mettle with the requisite heartlessness and his ability to sustain this criminality. Balban's devaluation of the Turkic 'purity' shattered precisely this succession model. It not only extinguished his infant empire, but obliterated the Turkic Muslim power in Delhi forever.

In practical terms, it was his own grandson, Kaiqubad who demolished it just three years after Balban's death. However, Bughra Khan, Kaiqubad's father, had already foreseen his debauched son's destructive propensities. He prophezied to his confidants, 'I have said farewell to my son and to the kingdom of Delhi; for I know full well that neither my son nor the throne of Delhi will long exist'.[7]

Book 1 of *Invaders and Infidels* ends with this:

> Sultan Muiz-ud-din Kaiqubad summoned a battle-hardened *sirjandar*, a noble and the governor of Samana, awarded him the title of Shayasta Khan and assigned to him the portfolio of *Ariz-i-Mumalik*, the Minister of War.

The *Ariz-i-Mumalik* was 70 years old and his name was Jalal-ud-din Firoz Khalji.

Origins

Firoz Khan bin Yaghrash Khalji,[8] like many others of his rank and stature, was Balban's creation. He had migrated into Hindustan from Afghanistan and like other Khalji fighters, served under Balban for several years. Early in his career, he had distinguished himself as a ferocious warrior and a capable leader on the battleground. His performance in the numerous battles against the Hindus, and especially against the accursed Mongols, rapidly earned him promotion and prestige. He was elevated as the *Sirjandar*[9] and awarded the governorship of the frontier province of Samana[10].

Until Kaiqubad had called him for the fateful meeting, Firoz Khalji had remained an unparalleled defender of the Delhi Sultanate's north western borders.[11] He commanded respect as a highly-valued malik. With Balban's ascent, Firoz had emerged as a power centre in his own right. Muslim chroniclers showered plaudits on Firoz because they were convinced that he was a 'man of experience and incapable of any wrong action'.[12]

But all along, Firoz had also earned the simmering wrath of Balban's Turkic nobles, who were jealous of this lowly Khalji upstart's dazzling rise to parity.

Self-scripted Epitaph

And now, Kaiqubad, the victim of his own licentiousness and addictions, had summoned the 70-year-old Malik Firoz Khalji in a desperate attempt to restore order. But the administration had already crumbled to chaos. At the end of the meeting, he elevated Firoz to a higher rank by awarding him the portfolio of war, the title of Shayasta Khan[13] and granted him the fief of Baran (present-day Bulandshahar). Two powerful Turkic nobles, Aitmar Kachhan and Aitmar Surkha were made *Barbak*[14] and *Vakildar*,[15] respectively.

It clearly was an interim arrangement but by making it, Kaiqubad had scripted his own epitaph. The immediate fallout of this arrangement was the emergence of two explicit camps: the legacy Balbani nobles and the Khalji parvenus. Swords were immediately sharpened in both camps, and the opportunity for wielding them arose when paralysis hit Kaiqubad. Doctors declared that he was beyond recovery.

The Balbani nobles moved first. With Kaiqubad's imminent death, there was a real possibility of the sultanate permanently slipping away from the house of Balban, that is, the 'pure' Turkic race. But unlike Balban, who had seized the initiative, no noble from this camp came forward to usurp the throne. The Balbani nobles were essentially schemers and slaves in the truest sense of the word. Even worse, as Barani says, they regarded each other as peers and 'could not endure that any one should rise above the rest, and should have entire command of the reins'.[16] So they did what they knew best: they found a puppet, in a nearly literal sense.

A coterie of Balbani maliks, amirs and other high-ranking officers marched straight into the royal harem and dragged out Kaiqubad's child. All of three years. They seated him on the throne and proclaimed that henceforth *he* was 'Sultan' Shams-ud-din and swore undying loyalty to the lad. They went on to award themselves all sorts of pompous titles and purloined vast tracts of land. Malik Firoz Khalji was to be the new 'Sultan's' *Naib* (deputy or regent in this case). The low-bred Khalji had finally been shown his place and 'kingship remained in the house of Balban and the Turks and did not fall into the hands of someone of another race'.

Then the Balbani nobles went for the kill.

Turko-Khalji Muslim Civil War in Delhi

With all the hot-headed overconfidence they could muster, Aitmar Kachhan and Aitmar Surkah decided to 'purify' the nobility by expelling all non-Turkic Muslims from it. Their Turkic peers naturally embraced the proposal, and a purge-list was prepared.

Unsurprisingly, Malik Firoz Khalji's name topped the list.

But the conspiracy leaked faster than it was hatched. The *Hajib*, Ahmad Chhap, a confidant of Firoz Khalji, promptly conveyed it to him. Firoz knew that it was time to make his decisive move. He immediately collected his loyalists, left Delhi and lodged himself in Baharpur,[17] a safe asylum entirely under his control. From there, he sent out lightning messages to his troops at Bulandshahar and other spots that fell in his fiefdom. Firoz's emphasis on speed, timeliness and preparedness for action yielded the desired outcome. In just a few days, he had amassed a large and impressive fighting force, ready and waiting at a striking distance from the seat of the sultanate.

On the other side, Firoz Khalji's unexpected flight from Delhi had generated another favourable result: it had broken both the Turkish ranks and their morale. The Aitmar duo had been thoroughly outwitted by this crafty old low-born Khalji. However, unwilling to admit this humiliation and fully aware of an assured military defeat if they confronted Firoz head-on, the two Aitmars lapsed into flattery. They sent him a syrupy letter addressing him as 'Sultan Jalal-ud-din', and invited him to Kaiqubad's palace at Kilughari for 'peaceful' negotiations. Firoz instantly saw through the guile. But the letter had reached him a little too late. Firoz had already received a confirmation for what he had always suspected: that Aitmar Kachhan was marching towards Baharpur with his troops. The letter was a mere decoy to lull him into letting his guard down and extract him out of his safe hideout. Kachhan's plan was to capture this old Khalji, take him to Kaiqubad's palace and murder him in front of the child-sultan.

Firoz stubbornly refused to budge. A few days after the foregoing letter, Kachhan's envoy arrived in person with this message: 'Sultan' Shams-ud-din has personally invited you to meet him. Firoz rebuffed the messenger. Then, a second messenger arrived with the same message, then a third, a fourth and a fifth and, 'in a like manner, Aitmar would send persons near Shayasta Khan, and the latter would refuse him admittance'.[18] In the end, Firoz Khalji's calculated obstinacy won. Aitmar Kachhan mounted his horse and galloped towards Firoz's *mahal*. The two rivals faced each other on horseback and exchanged courtesies befitting their status as nobles.

Kachhan opened the offensive: 'You have been summoned by the sultan himself so many times! Why didn't you honour the summons?' Aware of his own upper hand, Firoz coolly replied, 'Yes, I have received the summons. Unfortunately, some of my mounted attendants have travelled to here from faraway places and they're exhausted. Once they are fully rested, I, Malik Firoz, will personally make an appearance before the sultan with his stirrups. And his army.' The final sentence detonated Aitmar Kachhan's carefully guarded patience and he got ready to dismount his horse, signalling a veiled challenge for a duel. Firoz thundered, 'You are so vile that you think you can betray and slaughter people like sheep and then throw them in the river! You want to kill me? Come on, I'm right here!' This was a cue. Without warning, Firoz Khalji's nephew, Ala-ud-din burst on the scene and violently yanked Aitmar Kachhan down from his horse and beheaded him with one expert slash of his sword. Firoz then ordered Aitmar Kacchan's severed head to be fixed to the edge of a spear and paraded before the gates of the Kilughari palace in full public view.

A full-blown Turkic-Khalji Muslim civil war had erupted.

And Malik Firoz Khalji had the clear advantage. When his army appeared before the Kilugarhi palace with Aitmar's decapitated head, Delhi was inflamed. The Turkic nobles had not anticipated something like this in their wildest dreams. At least not from the low-born Khaljis, who were now swarming through the city like locusts. Fakhruddin, the veteran Balban loyalist and Kotwal, tried to mount the first defence. However, Firoz Khalji had pre-empted him by capturing his sons and dispatching them to Baharpur, to be held hostage. This foxy action silenced the seething Turks for an entire day. In this short-lived pregnant calm before the storm, both sides were busy hatching plans. Firoz ordered his sons to prepare for a full-blown war the next day, and appointed his second son, Arkali Khan at the vanguard of the forces. Firoz's instincts were proven right. The next day, the Balbani maliks and amirs assembled an impressive force. With Malik Nasir-ud-din, the elephant-keeper, the men and the beasts marched out towards Kilughari to meet Firoz.

But what should have been a bloody war turned out to be a hideous farce for a simple reason. Kaiqubad, the paralytic sultan, the commander-in-chief who was supposed to front the war, had atrophied long ago. He was now completely paralyzed and fully dysfunctional. It was a rather hilarious spectacle. Kaiqubad was seated under the royal canopy, now reduced to a mere cloth, a frank advertizement for the impoverishment of authority. He had been carried by two eunuchs and placed on the terrace of the luxurious palace, built explicitly for drink and debauchery. Kaiqubad's self-inflicted excesses had rendered him unfit to even mount a horse. *This* was the true face of the 'pure' Turkic-Muslim sultanate that Balban had raised. Before the first arrow could be fired, Balban's nephew Malik Chhajju, in a shameless proclamation of surrender, rushed *towards* the sultan's forces and announced loudly:

We wish to place Sultan Kaiqubad in a boat and take him to Lakhnauti. There he will reunite with his beloved father Sultan Nasir-ud-din [Bughra Khan] and spend the rest of his life in peace. We also wish for the young Sultan Shams-ud-din to continue on the imperial throne.[19]

Nasir-ud-din, the elephant-keeper, and the other maliks and amirs caved in and withdrew their forces. Malik Firoz Khalji had executed the perfect coup. Almost.

But he didn't want to leave anything to chance.

He summoned his second son, Arkali Khan and appointed him the chief of a force of 500 horsemen. In no time, this unit sped to the palace, seized the child-sultan Shams-ud-din and brought him before Firoz Khalji. Arkali Khan's unit met with no resistance. Then in a great public show, Firoz placed the kid on his lap and reaffirmed his loyalty to him. On the side, he instructed his cousin Malik Hassan to keep a close eye on the boy. But nobody was fooled.

Now it was time for real politics.

Firoz Khalji, the Shayasta Khan, the Minister of War, turned towards Malik Chhajju and said: 'This prince is like a son to you. His kingship has been reaffirmed. You be his regent. My job here is done. I'll take the entire territory from Multan, Tabar-i-Hind [Bathinda] and Dipalpur. If you grant them to me, I shall leave immediately. Take care of the prince and rule wisely.'

Malik Chhajju played along. 'On the contrary, the regency will suit *you* more than me. Even better, the sultanate itself will suit you. I shall be content to rule the territory of Kara.' Fakhruddin, the Kotwal endorsed the decision: 'The Just and the Great Allah has created You for lording over abundant wealth and Empire. Be pleased to accept Malik Chhajju's suggestion.'

Julius Caesar had to publicly refuse the crown three times, before he reluctantly submitted to the 'people's will'. Malik Firoz had to refuse once, before consenting to have royalty thrust upon him. In return for this great and grave responsibility, he presented a robe of honour to Malik Chhajju and consigned him to Kara, a vast and wealthy province that would play a history-altering role after just a few years.

Abducting a Kid

But Malik Firoz Khalji did not ascend the throne of Delhi immediately. There was still unfinished business. He ordered the child-sultan Shams-ud-din to be dispatched to Baharpur. This was another unprecedented move, which elicited another desired outcome.

Aitmar Surkah was perhaps the only surviving Turkic Balbani noble who commanded a trifling of power and influence. As his final attempt at resistance, he announced an open revolt and led a determined force to stop Firoz Khalji's child-kidnapping unit. At some distance before Baharpur, Surkah overtook the enemy and a skirmish broke out. It resulted in a hand-to-hand-combat involving Surkah and Firoz's eldest son, Ikhtiyar-ud-din Khalji. Ikhtiyar-ud-din fell from his horse and Surkah slashed him with three violent blows from his sword. But none of them caused serious damage. It gave him time to brandish his own sword. Seconds later, Aitmar Surkah's head was airborne.

Meanwhile, in Delhi, news of this shocking child-kidnap by the Khaljis had not only outraged the Turkic Muslims but others as well. With murderous retribution in mind, the Muslim population poured out from all the thirteen gates of the city and assembled at the Badaun Gate, determined to rescue the kid from the Khalji clutches. But Fakhruddin, the Kotwal stopped them. Firoz Khalji had indeed played his cards well. Fakhruddin pleaded with the blistering crowd imploring[20] that his own sons were hostages of the low-born Khalji and that it was futile to rebel and lose 'your own kith and kin'.[20] The Kotwal had reconciled with the grave situation with relative equanimity. And so, the tumultuous masses reluctantly dispersed but the hatred in their hearts for the Khaljis could not be quelled.

For the past 80 years, the Muslim population of Delhi had developed a subconscious loyalty to the Ilbari Turks. They had believed in the fantastic tales proclaiming their divine superiority that Allah himself had bestowed on this race. But now, it was becoming clear that a new, base-born race of Afghan Muslims would rule them, a prospect that brought disgust, fear and misgiving.

In fact, the Khalji revolt against the Turkic-Muslim Sultanate offers a brilliant case study into the psyche that formed and informed the medieval Muslim public opinion, both voiced and unvoiced. This specific case of the history of the Delhi Sultanate highlights the intrinsically tribal nature of Muslim rule in infidel Hindustan. This nature was preserved and it endured, almost intact, till the bloody end of the Mughal Empire. With some modifications in tenor, behaviour patterns and manners occurring over the course of time.

While the citizens prepared to reconcile themselves to the onset of the new regime, the large body of the Turkic aristocracy including amirs and maliks were at crossroads. However, consistent with their instinct for self-preservation at all costs, they cravenly defected *en masse* to Malik Firoz Khalji and placed their services and troops at his feet. Balban's imperial Turkic-Muslim army was now entirely under the command of this low-bred Khalji.

But Firoz Khalji *still* did not ascend to the throne.

———— ··· ————

Somewhere in the confines of the royal bedchamber, an 'opulent room of mirrors'[21] at the Kilughari palace, the wasted and vegetative Sultan Muiz-ud-din Kaiqubad was dying of hunger and thirst. Malik Firoz Khalji, who he had elevated as a Shayasta Khan and War Minister, had now made him a prisoner. Reminiscing his profligate life, Kaiqubad took to composing delusional poetry:

> The horse of my excellence is standing on the plain,
> The hand of my generosity is under an anvil,
> My eyes that never beheld anything less than gold mines and jewels
> Come and see today, how woefully perplexed it is![22]

Malik Firoz Khalji played his foulest card two days after the Balbani Turkic nobles had defected to his side. He summoned a man named Tarkesh whose father had served as an officer under Kaiqubad and had been killed by the dissolute and barely-sane sultan. Now, Firoz offered him the tempting opportunity he had been thirsting for: to extract vengeance with his own hands. An elated Tarkesh casually entered the Kilughari palace and slipped inside Kaiqubad's bedchamber. He stood there for a long time revelling in the pathetic sight of the former sultan writhing in disease-ridden agony. Then Tarkesh wrapped the ex-sultan in his own bedclothes[23] and began kicking him furiously. Three fatal blows to the head ended the miserable life of Kaiqubad.[24]

And then Tarkesh picked up the corpse and flung it in the Jamuna river. Its freezing currents washed away the Turkish Muslim Sultanate forever on 1 February 1290.

———•··•··•———

On 13 June 1290, Malik Firoz Khalji sat on the throne at Kilughari crowning himself as Sultanu-l Halim Jalalu-d Dunya Wau-d Din Firoz Shah Khalji.

———•··•··•———

CHAPTER 2

The Senile Sultan's Grotesque Sultanate

What is our defence of the Faith, cried Sultan Jalal-ud-din Khalji,
that we suffer these Hindus,
who are the greatest enemies of Allah and of the religion of Mustafa,
to live in comfort and do not flow streams of their blood?

Jalal-ud-din Firoz Shah Khalji was the sultan-standard freak in the bloodstained annals of the Delhi Sultanate. He was a thorough misfit for an Islamic imperialism that demanded the incessant and ruthless application of the worst of human tendencies: double-dealing, hypocrisy, despotism, treachery, mercilessness and an impulsive capacity for senseless violence even in peacetime. In short, all traits regarded as *Asuric* or *Adharmic* in the theory and practice of Hindu statecraft were mandatory in its Islamic counterpart. Not that Jalal-ud-din Khalji lacked these traits, but senility had ambushed and overpowered his fitness for sultanhood, and inevitably ruined him. The sultanate was thrust upon him by the sheer oddity of circumstances and it was not the consequence of his ambition.

Unlike Iltutmish or Balban, Jalal-ud-din was not an usurper in the strict sense of the term. If anything, Jalal-ud-din Khalji was a gold standard courtier and if left to him, he would have ideally died as one. Ironically, he became sultan in order to save the majesty and the dignity of that seat, the source of Islam's rising power in infidel Hindustan, from incompetent and petty wretches like the Aitmars. Till his miserable end, the crown sat uneasy on his head and he publicly apologized for his sultanhood. The manner in which he had taken the throne left him with lasting guilt, a sign of extreme weakness in the Islamic scheme of acquiring and wielding political power.

But on the broader plane, Jalal-ud-din Khalji had inadvertently unleashed an intra-Muslim political revolution. For the first time, the century-old Delhi Sultanate was ruled by an alien Muslim tribe of non-slave origins. Within the framework of this Muslim politics of tribalism, the Khalji revolt was a bloody and victorious uprising against the Turkic-Muslim hegemony. From Jalal-ud-din onwards, no ruler of the sultanate would seek inspiration from the Badlands of Ghur and Ghazni. The pretensions to the purity and, therefore, supremacy of the royal Muslim-Turkic blood that had existed were permanently erased with Jalal-ud-din's ascension. But it would also have more catastrophic consequences for the countless Hindus spread over wider geographies in Bharatavarsha.

———·•··•·•———

The Hindu Portrait of the Khalji Revolt

The Khalji revolution naturally had a Hindu side to it.

Around the time of Jalal-ud-din's enthronement, a good chunk of the Gangetic plain was firmly under Muslim rule, albeit facing the perpetual threat of fierce infidel resistance. Delhi and its surroundings, that is, the fabled *Indrasthaniyaka*,[1] were near-permanently trampled under the foot of the alien Turushka invaders-turned-sultans. Thus,

> ....*in the Islamic state, Delhi was not the capital of the empire; it was Quwwat-ul-Islam. The king was not the ruler of the people; he was Amir-ul-Mauminin, the conqueror of infidels and shelterer of Islam. The army was not the royal army; it was Lashkar-i-Islam. The soldier was not a cavalry man or infantry man; he was Ahl-i-Jihad. The law of the state was not any secular or humanitarian law; it was Shariat, the law of Islam. The state was not an end in*

itself, like the Greek state, *but a means of sub-serving the interests of Islam*. Conquests were made, shrines were broken, captives were taken, converts were made - all in the name of Islam. *The raison d'etre of the regime was to disseminate the Islamic faith.*[2] (Emphasis added)

The holy law of the new Islamic despotism had carved out a new class from a preexisting ancient civilizational people by branding them, the Hindus, as *Zimmis*,[3] slaves in their own homeland. For a century, these *Zimmis* had faced the cruel inevitability of forcing themselves to adjust to this new oppression that masqueraded as government. They were neither blind to, nor imperceptive of the heinous methods of political succession in this scheme of things. From Qutub-ud-din Aibak to Jalal-ud-din Khalji, they had witnessed eight sultans and one *sultana*,[4] notwithstanding the respective stature or tenure of each. The stability, continuity, peace and the intimate cultural familiarity that their forefathers had experienced under the Maharajas, Chahamanas, Devas and Samrats would never return. These had now been replaced with ceaseless and assured strife in peacetime, a state of living in constant uncertainty, all-round oppression, and a sort of spiritual and cultural degradation, the worst expressions of which they experienced in their daily lives. To them, it mattered little which Turushka ruled them. Their permanent state of persecution was a constant fuel for anguish. Almost like a force of nature. Like breathing. Nothing except death or conversion to Islam could change it. This is the overall summary of the condition of Hindus under the Delhi Sultanate:

> The frequent and quite unexpected dynastic revolutions had killed in them all sentiments of goodwill for any...dynasty. Thus the supersession of Khaljis over the Ilbaris was not of much consequence to these people....[5]

———— ◆ · · ◆ · · ————

Spoils of the Khalji Revolution

More than anybody else, Jalal-ud-din himself was keenly aware of his own unpopularity. The outrageous manner in which he had seized the throne was a wound that would not heal soon. Not only did it not heal, it was responsible for his grisly death. The pathetic child 'sultan' Shams-ud-din's 'reign' lasted all of three months. He died in Jalal-ud-din's confinement, prompting a Muslim chronicler to compose this verse:

> The wine of the sky is not unmixed with the brine of sorrow,
> The world's one employment is jugglery—naught else.[6]

More than just unpopularity, guilt also haunted the new sultan like a shadow. It was a feeling and emotion that was alien to all his predecessors and successors. Thus, while Delhi was the seat of power, Jalal-ud-din Khalji made Kilughari the seat of his government. He was both terrified of and ashamed to rule, sitting on the throne of his erstwhile master, Balban, and did not dare to enter the city for the longest time.

Jalal-ud-din Khalji completed Kaiqubad's unfinished Xanadu of debauchery and transformed it into a functional structure from where governance could be conducted. He called it *The Rocky Citadel* and decorated it with expensive carvings, paintings and inscriptions. He also built an expansive garden sporting a terraced pathway opposite the palace along the banks of the Jamuna. Then he commanded his maliks and amirs, and officers and royal household, to build a new town around Kilughari. Traders and merchants and craftsmen and experts in various professions were marched into the new town in which Jalal-ud-din had established bazars for them. He christened the town literally as *Shahr-i-nau*: new town.[7]

It was now time to divide the spoils of the revolution.

The grand durbar held for the occasion witnessed Sultan Jalal-ud-din Khalji's boundless generosity. As expected, the immediate family came first in the pecking order followed by other notables in the *dramatis personae* that had aided his capture of the sultanate.

The sultan's eldest son, Ikhtiyaruddin was awarded the title, *Khan-i-Khanan* and received some prosperous districts around Delhi as his fief.

His second son, Hisamuddin was titled *Arkali Khan.*

His third son was titled *Kadr Khan.*

His uncle, Malik Hussain received the title *Taj-ul-Mulk.*

His younger brother, Malik Khamosh was titled *Yoghresh Khan* and was allotted the war portfolio: *Ariz-i-Mumalik,* the same post that Jalal-ud-din had received from Kaiqubad.

His nephew Almas Beg was appointed as *Akhur-Beg* or Master of the Horse.

His other nephew Ala-ud-din became *Amir-i-Tuzuk,* Master of Ceremonies. Both nephews were also Jalal-ud-din's sons-in-law.

Another nephew—his sister's son—Malik Ahmad Chhap was appointed the *Naib-i-Amir-i-Hajib* or deputy Lord Chamberlain. Completely loyal to Jalal-ud-din, he would act as the fearless, truth-telling wise counsel and voice of caution.

The chronicler Yahya Sirhindi provides a detailed list[8] of these top portfolios totalling about 20.

———— ·· • ·· ————

And then, there were some relics of the Balbani nobles who received Jalal-ud-din's liberality.

The first was Balban's nephew, the craven Malik Chhajju. He was the only survivor of that bloodline—the coward who had bartered away the 'pure' Turkic-Muslim Sultanate and placed it in the hands of the lowly Khalji tribe in exchange for the fiefdom of Kara.

Khwaja Khatir retained his high office of the *Wazarat* (Chief Minister), which he had occupied since the start of Balban's regime.

Malik Fakhr-ud-din, the Delhi Kotwal, remained in the same position, not in the least because Jalal-ud-din had previously held his sons hostage.

———— · • ·· • ————

Haunted by Guilt, Overawed by Balban

Our knowledge of Jalal-ud-din Khalji's origins still remains inconclusive. Almost all Muslim chronicles simply mention him as the son of a certain Yaghresh (or Baghrash) Khalji from Afghanistan. But as a low-born non-slave who dared to capture the Delhi Sultanate with adroitness, Jalal-ud-din Firoz Khalji should have ideally been celebrated by his contemporary chroniclers in greater detail. However, even in the immediate aftermath of his ascension, 'no voice of congratulation hailed the installation of Jalal-ud-din'.[9] Comparatively, even an unaffiliated marauder like Bakhtiyar Khalji receives better treatment at the hands of his chroniclers, who retrospectively celebrate his deformity as a divine gift from Allah.

In an ironical twist of fate, the Muslim populace of Delhi forgot their reeking hatred for this aged Khalji upstart and accepted him as their new sultan with astonishing swiftness. They didn't even bat an eyelid when Jalal-ud-din changed the colour of the royal umbrella from white to red. Eliot and Dowson's perceptive observation of the temperament of this Muslim citizenry is quite insightful.

> In the course of the first year of the reign the citizens and soldiers and traders, of all degrees and classes, went to Kilughari, where the Sultan held a public Darbar. *They were struck with admiration and amazement at seeing the Khaljis occupying the throne of the Turks, and wondered how the throne had passed from the one to the other.*[10] (Emphasis added)

By the end of Jalal-ud-din's first year, their submission was unquestioning, and the old ways returned. After three years of misrule and disorder, there was now a functional government with its own power structure, cliques and factions and everybody, great and small paid homage to the new sultan.

Unlike his predecessors, Jalal-ud-din did not stamp his authority by instilling fear and terror. In fact, except on one occasion, he never quite succeeded in stamping his absolute authority at all. This trait of the new sultan was an accursed source of discomfort, fury, pathos and frustration for his tyranny-loving aristocracy. In their eyes, this was a bizarre and unseemly quality, ill-befitting a sultan. In fact, it was a lethal flaw. Even worse was that Jalal-ud-din showed no guts to rule directly from Delhi.

After he became sultan, the fight had pretty much gone out of Jalal-ud-din Khalji. He now wanted *love,* not fear, from both his aristocracy and citizens. It seemed incredible that this was the same hardened warrior who had spilled the blood of infidel Hindus on countless occasions and had heroically battered the dreaded Mongols. The sheer heartlessness with which he had kidnapped a mere child, and had murdered a dying and helpless Kaiqubad appeared to be the deeds of a different man. In his new avatar as sultan, he had become a feeble pacifist, often showering undeserving generosity on absolute wretches and ingrates.

> ....his generosity and devotion [to Islam] gradually removed the aversion of the people, and... hopes of grants of land assisted in conciliating, though grudgingly and unwillingly, the affections of his people.[11]

At 70, Jalal-ud-din spent most of his time contemplating his inevitable death, and with each day, became more Allah-fearing. Old age had also intensified his remorse, and despite repeated warnings from his genuine well-wishers, he continued on a suicidal course, hurtling from blunder to blunder. His ultimate desire was to be known as a pious Muslim, for his sultanate was a speck of dust before the unity of the *Qaum* (Muslim community) and the *Ummah* (global Muslim brotherhood).

Jalal-ud-din Khalji's guilt at becoming the sultan was also fueled by a profound psychological reason. Till his death, he had remained incurably in awe of Balban. It took him more than a year to summon the courage to formally enter the city of Delhi. Accompanied by his close confidant, Malik Chhap, Jalal-ud-din entered Delhi with great pomp and then stood before Balban's magnificent Red Palace. The splendour of the whole setting overwhelmed him. It was not the first time that he was seeing the Red Palace but the inexpressible feeling that gushed up from within was new. And surreal. Suddenly overcome with emotion, Jalal-ud-din dismounted his horse at the outer gate and bowed in obeisance at the structure. He prostrated himself twice on the threshold of the palace, walked inside, and ascended on the dias and sat on the throne. His face showed visible discomfort. He raised his eyes and hands up to the heaven beseechingly, looked around his court and confessed his guilt aloud: 'How shall I ever be able to acquit myself of the gratitude I owe to Allah for these great benefits? He who has raised me to this throne, before which I have been accustomed all my life to bow down, and who has preferred me to this dignity, while my peers, many of whom are equally, and even more deserving, stand around with their arms folded before me, in token of obedience.'[12] Then he got down from the throne, took his seat among his former peers, removed his turban and wept bitterly.

The whole episode was a candid broadcast of weakness. His courtiers were simultaneously aghast and delighted. While they admired his piety, they also felt sorry for him.

Later, in private, Malik Ahmad Chhap reminded Jalal-ud-din Khalji of his stature: 'The palace now belongs to you, Your Highness. Your behaviour was rather unbecoming.' At which Jalal-ud-din once again burst into tears and chided him: 'You know that nobody among my ancestors has ever been a king. I have not inherited the pride and dignity of that kingship and have no right over it. Sultan Balban sat here on the throne and I served him. The awe and dignity of that monarch has not left my breast. This palace had been built by Balban while he was sultan and it is his property and that of his sons and relatives.' While Jalal-ud-din's intensely heartfelt reply silenced Ahmad Chhap, it was another reminder that the old sultan had lost his bearings on so many fronts.

What Jalal-ud-din had failed to realize was that Balban himself belonged to no royal descent: he had treacherously usurped the sultanate from his own son-in-law.

Jalal-ud-din had also forgotten a key canon of the Islamic state: *there was no such thing as private property.* As long as the sultan was alive, everything in his dominion solely and ultimately belonged to him in the sense of chattel. Past ownership, inheritance and maintenance were disposable principles, kept or discarded at the whim of the reigning sultan. There was no separation between the sultan's private property and the public exchequer. Fiefdoms and high offices and salaries and perks could be crushed at will as Balban had demonstrated so ruthlessly in his purge of the dreaded 40. However, Jalal-ud-din Khalji[13]

> ...hardly ever punished a fault among his dependents, and was never known to lay violent hands on the property of his wealthy *Amirs*, as is too often the case with despotic monarchs. He was in the habit of associating familiarly, even after his accession, with his former acquaintances, and joining their parties, and drinking wine...with them, the same as before.[14]

Jalal-ud-din's admission of weakness soon yielded its logical consequences. In Balban's regime, the aristocracy would suffer instant death penalty if they were found drinking alcohol and throwing lascivious parties. But Jalal-ud-din Khalji had opened both these floodgates wide and personally chaired these enjoyments. However, the parties separately organized by his depraved and ungrateful nobles quickly became hubs of intrigue with the explicit aim of dethroning Jalal-ud-din, the coward and weakling who didn't deserve to be sultan. Even the lowliest official began to abuse him in choicest language and escaped unpunished. Each time he received reports of such intrigues, Jalal-ud-din would summon the offenders to his court, chastise them, and weep openly: 'What wrong have I done to you that you must plot against me?' And instead of meting out punishment, he would mollycoddle them by drinking with them 'to remove all cause of misunderstanding'. In K.S. Lal's perceptive character-sketch,

> Never was a man more unsuited to wear the crown than the founder of the Khalji dynasty. To him, kingship was a fraud and its magnificence a few days' unstable splendour. He actually

cursed his enemies not so much for plotting against him as for compelling him to strive for the throne.[15]

In Jalal-ud-din's own words, this was how the aforementioned curse sounded:

> May God confound the house of Aitmar Kacchhan, and Aitmar Surkha, who, by aiming at my life, compelled me, from motives of self-preservation, to adopt these measures. Had this not been the case, had I still been in my former rank, and Allah knows how distant that was from the throne of Delhi! I was content to have passed away my life with the title of Malik or Khan.[16]

Jalal-ud-din Khalji's forgiveness and misplaced magnanimity also spilled over to the feared *Thags*[17], a class of professional highway bandits and murderers. On one occasion, when his officers captured a 1,000 *Thags,* the sultan, instead of punishing them, put them in boats and shipped them off to faraway Lakshmanavati. The chief reason for their wholesale deportation was Sultan Jalal-ud-din's Islamic piety: a good chunk of the *Thags* were infidels who regularly spilled Musulman blood through their bloody depredations. They would now become the headache of the Muslim ruler at Lakshmanavati.[18] Vincent Smith's unsparing condemnation of Jalal-ud-din is worth recounting. 'He adopted the imbecile plan of putting them into boats and transporting them to Lakhnauti (Gaur)....That piece of folly probably is the origin of... thuggee in Bengal....'[19]

Jalal-ud-din Khalji's choice of Lakshmanavati was not accidental but a continuation of the Delhi Sultanate's conscious policy of treating that region with contempt. Since Iltutmish's time, Lakshmanavati was regarded as a distant nuisance, tolerated merely because the rulers out there were also Muslims.

> ....nothing shows better the contempt in which the king of Bengal was held at Delhi than Jalaluddin's mode of disposing of the dacoits captured in the Delhi territory....He sent them by shiploads into Bengal, where he let them loose....That Bengal was completely severed from the Delhi empire is clear from

the omission of the Bengal Balbanis from the lists of imperial commanders which [the chronicler] Barani gives in the beginning of the reigns of the Khaljis.[20]

Unlike Jalal-ud-din Khalji, both Iltutmish and Balban had shown that these upstart Bengali Muslim rulers could be pulverized at will.

———•••••———

Embers of Vengeance at Kara

At Kara, 700 kilometres from Delhi, Malik Chhajju received regular reports about the upstart Khalji sultan, whom he despised passionately. Not Jalal-ud-din, but he was still the rightful heir to his uncle, Balban's, imperial throne. His prior surrender to Jalal-ud-din and his choice of this faraway fiefdom was a tactical ploy to bide time and marshal resources. The reports were consistent and they affirmed his growing confidence that Sultan Jalal-ud-din had turned soft, sentimental and weak, and had become the butt of filthy humour amidst his own courtiers.

The timing was perfect.

In September 1290, Malik Chhajju declared independence by raising the white canopy and had the *Khutbah* read in his name. With the same haste, he also minted coins in his name and awarded himself the title, 'Sultan Mughis-ud-din'. It was an audacious declaration of revolt.

Chhajju had support both from the simmering Balbani nobles and dedicated Jalal-ud-din haters. Malik Ali Hatim Khan, the powerful *Sarjandar*[21] of Awadh, headed this support group. Other powerful amirs such as Malik Tajuddin Kuchi, Malik Muhammad Qutlagh Khan and Malik Nusrat lent their might. This cabal was further strengthened by the Rawats, Ranas and Paiks who whiffed a faint chance to carve a niche for themselves. It is also evidence of their power and indispensability that Chhajju was compelled to enlist their services. They were distinctively fabled for the competence of their *piyada* (infantry) and the prowess of their *dhanuks*[22] (archers). In an elaborate ceremony of flattery, Chhajju invited these Hindu chiefs and offered them *paan-supari* (betel leaves and nuts), a solemn symbol of friendship and loyalty and did them other honours.

Such attempts of Hindus at making the most of internecine Muslim battles is a common theme in the history of medieval Muslim rule in India.

Amir Khusrau,[23] the poet, courtier, fair-weather loyalist, flatterer-laureate and one of the world's greatest self-servers, was also a favourite of Jalal-ud-din Khalji. He displays extraordinary feats of exaggerated sycophancy while describing Chhajju's revolt. His narratives are case studies in cheerful servility, and give us the impression that *he,* more than Jalal-ud-din himself, was in high dudgeon at Malik Chhajju's betrayal. While Khusrau's friend and fellow-chronicler Barani shows restraint when he plainly writes that 'Malik Chhaju, nephew of Balban, raised the white canopy in Kara', Amir Khusrau's uncorked pen goes wild:

> ....the faithless Chhajju....Pride had inflated his brain with wind, which extinguished the light of his intellect.... Neither fear nor hope was able to inform [him] that a particle cannot contend with the sun....
>
> [The Sultan], outrageous like a male lion, ...exclaimed, in the violence of his anger, 'Bravo! Is there any man in the world who dares to raise dust in my plain? What weakness has that wretch seen in me, that he dares to peer where my arrow can penetrate? If he has not seen the splendour of my sword, he must have heard its renown from afar....How I have issued orders for the shedding of the blood of my enemies, who have become like worms, when they hear the whizzing of my Kirmani blade; how...from the heads of the Mongols, I have filled my cup with blood, and stuck their inverted skulls upon the top of my standards.... The Hindus themselves cannot conceive how full I have made hell of them. What did that ignorant thoughtless man imagine, that he dared advance his foot into my territory?'[24]

Confident in what he thought was overwhelming support, Malik Chhajju marched with a sizeable force towards Delhi. He also harboured the delusion that the people of Delhi were waiting with open arms to welcome this redeemer and restorer of the old Balbani regime. In Barani's words,

> Many of the inhabitants of Delhi heard of his approach with satisfaction and joy, and recognized him as the rightful heir to the throne; for they said that no Khalji had ever been a king, and that the race had no right or title to Delhi.[25]

Malik Chhajju sincerely believed these tales.

But he had fatally miscalculated. It was true that Sultan Jalal-ud-din Khalji had become lax and was rapidly losing his former acuity. However, news of this traitor's mutiny immediately rekindled the semi-barbaric instincts he had honed so well over the course of his battle-hardened journey from Afghanistan to the throne of Delhi. He would give Chhajju a personal taste of what a frontal war with him truly meant.

Jalal-ud-din appointed his eldest son, Ikhtiyaruddin, as vice-regent, to guard Delhi and personally marched with a large army. After crossing the Jamuna, he divided his troops. An advance contingent numbering 12,000 was put under Arkali Khan's leadership and Jalal-ud-din himself led the command of the other contingent, following behind at a distance of 12 *Kos* (about 21 miles). By forced marches, Arkali Khan reached the banks of the Kali Nahar river.

Malik Chhajju had already encamped on the opposite bank and had complete possession of all the boats stationed there. Undaunted, Arkali Khan opened the offensive by crossing the swollen river with his army, prepared for bloody retribution. Chhajju's advance guard comprised the forces of the 'Rawats and Paiks who had flocked around him like ants and locusts'.[26] All Muslim chroniclers describe the slaughter of these 'rice-eating Hindus' with special relish. In Barani's words, the 'spiritless rice-eating Hindus made a great noise, but lost all their powers', when they saw the sultan's valiant warriors of Islam rushing towards them with drawn swords. Amir Khusrau's hatred for these 'Hindu thieves' attains full poetic venom when he says that 'the earth was dyed with the blood of the evil-disposed crowd of these Hindu *sipahis* without any religion'.[27]

It took less than a week for Malik Chhajju to realize the full extent of his clumsy expedition. For two whole days, Arkali Khan plundered and devastated Chhajju's camp but Chhajju didn't give him a direct fight. Amir Khusru delights in Chhajju's misfortune, writing that this 'stony-hearted rebel in the depth of the night, oppressed with grief, fled towards the hills, leaving his camp on the bank of the river'.[28] Chhajju dodged and evaded with some skill, but a determined Arkali Khan eventually overtook him and compelled a direct military engagement at Chupala, near Badaun. It was completely one-sided. By this time, Chhajju's forces had been scattered and he had lost his nerves. Yet he put on an impressive show in a desperate day-long battle during which 'the sword knew no rest'. In stark contrast, Arkali Khan had built up a solid formation: he commanded the centre. Two wings of the battle array in the front were helmed by the formidable Qutlagh Tighin, who could 'split a spear with an arrow', and by the intrepid Ala-ud-din, who exceeded his mettle in this fight. Malik Chhajju was severely hammered but somehow managed to hold his ground at the end of the day. At night, the infidel chieftain of Aligarh, Bhima Deva Kotla[29] visited Chhajju's camp with deadly news: Sultan Jalal-ud-din was slated to arrive the next morning with his massive rear-guard force. The moment he heard this, Malik Chhajju's instinct for self-preservation kicked in. He wrote an impromptu script for a craven drama in the dead of the night. Accordingly, war drums were continuously beaten, sounding a cacophonic message of intimidation to the enemy: I am preparing for a severe engagement tomorrow morning. Be prepared! But using this as a diversion, Chhajju had stealthily slipped away from his camp. In the morning, his soldiers belatedly realized that the great leader of this revolt had quietly thrown them before Arkali Khan's bloodthirsty wolves. They offered unconditional surrender. However, Arkali Khan turned his wrath against the infidel Bhima

Deva. He retraced his steps to Kali Nahar, crossed it and attacked Aligarh. Bhima Deva gave a valiant fight but was hopelessly outnumbered and 'dispatched to hell'. Chhajju's co-conspirators and other Balbani nobles including Malik Masud Akhurbeg, Malik Muhammad, Malik Amir Ali, Malik Alghachi and Malik Tajvard were captured, chained and thrashed mercilessly with wooden bludgeons and iron rods.

Malik Chhajju had vanished without a trace. But an unrelenting Jalal-ud-din Khalji pursued him. It was soon discovered that Chajju had sought refuge in a small fortress in the vicinity.

The chieftain of that fortress betrayed him to Jalal-ud-din.

The whole episode was a prestigious triumph, primarily for Arkali Khan, and he readily exploited this career-altering achievement. But first, the accursed rebels had to be humiliated appropriately. Arkali Khan fastened heavy yokes around their necks, bound them in massive metallic chains and ordered them to be paraded before Sultan Jalal-ud-din Khalji who had convened a special Durbar to decide the fate of these traitors. Barani quotes his close friend, Amir Khusrau about what happened next:

I, the author of this *Tarikh-i-Firuz Shahi*, heard from Amir Khusrau, who was an attendant of the Court, that when the rebellious *Maliks* and *Amirs* were brought before the Sultan, he held a public Durbar. Malik Amir Ali, Sarjandar, Malik Ulughchi, and other nobles were conducted into his presence, riding upon camels, with yokes upon their shoulders, their hands tied behind their necks, covered with dust and dirt, and their garments all soiled.[30]

The courtiers in the Durbar waited with lusty anticipation to cheer the ensuing fulfilment of their bloodthirst. As was customary in all such cases, the sultan would devize innovative methods to humiliate and punish these wretched rebels. They would be paraded throughout the city in this degraded state. Perhaps, people would be ordered to spit on them or hurl footwear or rotten vegetables and eggs and dung. Or like

Muhammad Ghori had done, they would be made to carry heavy bushels of horse gram around their neck. The macabre possibilities were endless.

But the moment the sultan saw them fettered and bound, wounded and bleeding, limping and dirty, their heads bowed low in shame, his senility slapped him and flung him on a ludicrous course. In open view of the Durbar, he took out his handkerchief and wept profusely. These wretches were rebels. But they were also men of former rank and distinction who had enjoyed stately honours throughout their lives. They were fellow-Mussulman warriors and aristocrats. Jalal-ud-din cried out in a loud voice, 'What is this horror!' and ordered them to be unshackled at once. The maliks, amirs and other high officials were parted from other rebels and sent to separate tents where the sultan's personal attendants gave them a luxurious bath, perfumed them and dressed them in splendid clothes. Meanwhile, the sultan had gone to his private apartments and made arrangements for an extravagant wine party. Soon, the former rebels were transformed into his esteemed guests. At the party, the sultan's kindness and compassion flowed like the riverine wine consumed that night. In an act of extreme forgiveness, *he* apologized for *their* rebellion: 'in drawing your swords in support of your old benefactors at the house of Sultan Balban, you have taken an honest rather than a dishonest course'. The ungrateful rebels were 'so overwhelmed with shame that they kept their eyes fixed on the ground and did not speak a word'.[31]

More horrifying than the wine party itself was what Jalal-ud-din did next: he *rewarded* Malik Chhajju's treachery by granting him the fiefdom of Multan where he spent the rest of his life in unimpeded luxury. His erstwhile governorship of Kara went to the sultan's favourite nephew, Ala-ud-din.

Malik Chhajju breathed his last in February 1291, forgotten and ungrieved.

However, for Jalal-ud-din's nobles, this was conclusive proof that this doddering sultan had to go. *Now.* In a revealing comment on the ethics-free impulses of this aristocracy, Firishta, the chronicler notes: 'Clemency is a virtue which descends from *Khuda*; but the degenerate nobles of that age did not deserve it.'[32] Indeed, the undying loyalist of Jalal-ud-din, Malik Ahmad Chhap conveyed the exact sentiment to his sultan. It was a mixture of sermon and warning.

> A king should reign and observe the proper rules of Government or be content to relinquish the throne. This action is highly unworthy. When Malik Chhajju escaped punishment for the worst of all political offences, how could it not be expected that other rebellions would not break out? The punishments awarded by kings are warnings to men. Sultan Balban, who never forgot his dignity and power, visited rebellious and political offences with the greatest severity, and how much blood he shed! If the Sultan and his followers were to fall into [the rebels'] hands, no name or trace of the Khaljis would be left in Hindustan![33]

However, the sultan's reply once again reflected how thoroughly he was decreed by his senility:

> Oh Ahmad! I know better than you what sultans in the past have done to rebels. But I am an old Musalman now and am not habituated to shedding the blood of the Musalmans. I am now past seventy and have not killed a single *Muhadi* [believer in the Oneness of Allah]. A short life remains before me now. At this stage, do I act against those principles of Muhammadan law and place Musalmans on the chopping block? On the other hand, if I spared the lives of these rebels, and if they are true Musalmans, they will be ashamed before Allah. However it be, I cannot reign by shedding the blood of Musalmans. I would rather renounce this throne for I cannot endure the wrath of Allah.[33]

Once more, Jalal-ud-din Khalji had proclaimed how badly he had lost his grip over the psyche required to operate a sultanate. He was indeed a pious Musulman in that sense. But he was a pious Musulman in that accompanying sense as well: of harbouring permanent hatred towards the infidels of Hindustan and punishing them for the mere accident of being born as infidels. It would reveal itself on several occasions in his short-lived reign.

Casual Hindu Massacre as Ordained Damage

The quelling of Malik Chhajju's revolt was one such occasion. Even as Arkali Khan was leading the charge against Chhajju, Jalal-ud-din, in the rear guard, had marched into Bhojpur (in present-day Farukkhabad district). There, he crossed the Ganga and ripped through Rohilkhand, mercilessly razing and plundering and despoiling hundreds of Hindu villages en route. He bestowed special attention upon the eastern districts[34] bordering the Sarayu river. The infidels living here were falsely accused of helping Chhajju. The chief of Rupal was humiliated and made to cough up a heavy tribute. However, the other infidel chief at Kahsun offered resistance. His territory was plundered and devastated. Amir Khusrau's violence-laden description[35] of the Rohilkhand carnage gives us a mere glimpse of the horrors suffered by the Hindus there. In one poetic stroke, he transforms Sultan Jalal-ud-din Khalji into a collective embodiment of an Islamic saint who emitted light, a warrior, an artist, a robber-baron and a redeemer of the *Deen*:

> ....he departed towards Bhojpur, and his light illumined the banks of the Ganges... for when he arrived at the Jumna and Ganges, by the power of his art he constructed a bridge over both those rivers. He collected gold from the *Rais* of the Ganges, for he had the power of crossing the river at his pleasure.... When the Shah [Sultan] arrived at the land of Kabar, a contest ensued, and the Musalmans made their swords rusty with the blood of the Hindus.... *Whatever living Hindu fell into the king's hands was pounded into bits under the feet of elephants. The Musalmans, who were Hindis (born in Hindustan), had their lives spared, and were distributed amongst the chiefs as slaves.* (Emphasis added)[36]

As we shall see in greater detail, Jalal-ud-din Khalji, too, was following a familiar scriptural ordination: Hindus who had been forcibly converted to Islam continued to enjoy a status slightly higher than that of a Kafir. Even a high-ranking official like Imad-ud-din Rihan,[37] a former Hindu, had been so rudely shown his place and then dispatched to hell by Balban for the singular crime of being a low-bred 'Hindi'.[38]

A Royal Joke

The reward that Malik Chhajju had received for his brazen military revolt radiated waves of ambition in the topmost echelons of the sultanate's power structure. More than anything, it was a reassurance that an enterprising, crafty and ruthless malik or amir could actually succeed where Chhajju had failed. Especially since there was no downside to such a treacherous enterprise because failure would not bring punishment but reward.

The frequent orgies of wine and degeneracy thrown by Jalal-ud-din Khalji's nobles had now become flagrant venues for hatching insidious plots. Although the details varied in these parties, the action point was settled: the dethronement of the sultan. Who would occupy that seat was the subject of heated drunken debates and bravado. But the sultan, characteristically, ignored these dangerous tidings, which never stopped coming. His advanced senility readily manufactured excuses on their behalf: men often drink too much, and then say foolish things; do not report drunken stories to me. But the drunken stories were real because the ambition that bred them was real.

Tajuddin Katchi,[39] a long-time drinking buddy of Jalal-ud-din Khalji, once threw a wine party at his mansion. As usual, *pyaalas* (wine goblets) were passed around thick and fast and the heady liquid loosened tongues. Barani narrates the scene.

'Tajuddin, you are fit to be a king, not Sultan Jalal-ud-din.' This and similar absurdities they uttered. All who were present promised to aid Tajuddin in acquiring the crown. One of them said he would finish the Sultan with a *Nim-Shikhari* [hunting knife], and another drew his sword and said he would make mince-meat of Jalal-ud-din.[40]

When Jalal-ud-din Khalji heard this news, he understood that the matter was indeed grave, and summoned the entire gang of the drunken nobility. Before the Durbar, he verbally humiliated them, his voice rising with each stream of obscenity that flew from his mouth. Finally, he drew his sword, flung it on the ground and roared, 'Ah you filthy drunken negroes! You brag together in the privacy of your parties. One wretch boasts of killing me with just an arrow, another of slaying me with a sword! Here, I'm right here! I sit before you! Is there one among you who is man enough to take this sword and fight it out fairly with me? I'm ready for him, let him come on!'

Nobody spoke for a long time. Then, Nusrat Sabah, the chief inkstand bearer and Jalal-ud-din's veteran drinking partner stepped forward and toyed with the sultan's mind: 'Your Majesty knows that topers who drink deep from their wine-cups typically speak nonsense. Does His Majesty, in the depths of his compassionate heart, seriously believe that we can actually kill a Sultan who cherishes us like sons, as you do? Where O Sultan, can we ever find so kind and gracious a master?' He paused and then delivered the knockout: 'Neither will you kill us for our absurd drunken ravings, because you will never find other nobles and gentlemen like us.'

Sultan Jalal-ud-din Khalji immediately ordered wine for all of them. He personally led the bacchanalia. Nusrat Sabah received a special cup of wine and became the sultan's special male guest for the night.

The conspiracies flourished with greater vigour and frequency, and the cycle of warning and forgiveness was repeated. The maximum punishment that Jalal-ud-din inflicted was a threat: Behave yourself or I will unleash my second son, Arkali Khan upon you. Aware of Arkali's ferocious temper and cruelty, the conspirators chose discretion over bluster[41] for some time.

Sultan Jalal-ud-din Khalji had become a royal joke.

Sidi Maula or the Lasting Curse of the Islamic Clergy

Barely weeks after Malik Chhajju's treason had been crushed, fresh trouble erupted from a highly unlikely but an extremely delicate source. This definitive slice in Jalal-ud-din's brief reign clearly reveals who, in reality, held the reins of the Muslim community's psyche in a typical Islamic state.

In a niche of pious Islamic exclusivity in Delhi, the dervish Sidi Maula had been carefully observing the futile bluster of these drunken louts who passed off as the sultan's nobility.

Originally from Persia, Sidi Maula had landed in Delhi sometime during Balban's reign. He had earned his spurs as an Islamic preacher and saint at the feet of the Sufi, Shaikh Fariduddin Ganjshakar[42] at Ajodhan.[43]

In the Sufi annals, Fariduddin was one of the pioneers of the widely familiar tactic of present-day Christian evangelism of imitating and appropriating Hindu practices and customs in order to convert them into Islam. Like his[44] master, Shaikh Hamiduddin Sufi, Fariduddin imitated the modes and lifestyles of Yogis in order to lure unsuspecting Hindus into his fold. For a practical and devious reason. The methods of the sultans and maliks and amirs and ghazis were violent and crude and provoked immediate retaliation and lasting hostility from the Hindus. Although the full extent and success of Fariduddin's conversion of Hindus[45] is questionable, he certainly travelled extensively in eastern Uttar Pradesh, Bihar, Rajasthan and Punjab on these evangelical campaigns. The most celebrated disciple of Fariduddin was Nizamuddin Auliya whose influence on at least three Delhi sultans was considerable.

Early on, Fariduddin had offered a highly practical counsel to his disciple, Sidi Maula, on how he should conduct himself in Delhi:

> I give thee a bit of advice, which it will be well for thee to observe. Stay away from *maliks* and *amirs* and regard their intimacy as

dangerous; there is no dervish in history who cultivated such an intimacy and in the end, found it disastrous to himself.[46]

However, Sidi Maula had decided to explicitly woo that particular strain of disaster. But the manner in which he went about it is interesting. It is also a familiar technique in contemporary marketing parlance—he deliberately created curiosity about his own persona through bizarre and unusual methods. For a dervish, Sidi Maula was truly weird. As a Muslim holy man, he followed all the Islamic religious norms: he religiously kept up the Namaz, observed fasts and other prescribed disciplines during festivals. However, he never visited the Jama Masjid and did not pray in congregations. He maintained neither maidservants nor slaves and it was rumoured that he was celibate; in Barani's measured words, 'he indulged no passion'. Like Yogis, Sidi Maula observed severe austerities and ate frugally. However, his Khanqah exhibited the exact opposite picture. It was a distinct Islamic monastery, but it was housed in a sprawling mansion, open to everyone at all hours. Muslim pilgrims and travellers of all sects could find assured accommodation there. Akin to the contemporary Sikh *langar*, his Khanqah complex housed an enormous dining hall the size of a small stadium—open to everyone at all hours. Prodigious quantities of food were served 'twice a day which no khan or malik could furnish'. In Firishta's[47] estimate, the typical Sidi Maulan daily menu comprised about '1,000 *maunds* of flour, 500 maunds of mutton, 200 maunds of sugar, besides rice, oil, butter, ghee, vegetables, and other necessaries in proportion'.[48] For an ostensible monastery, this scale of expenditure exceeded even the proverbial princely sum.

To all of Delhi, it appeared that this self-denying, pious man, somehow had an endless stream of funding, because he also unfailingly paid every vendor, merchant and shopkeeper who supplied goods of such monstrous quantity. Sidi Maula never kept dues. More puzzlingly, he did not accept anything in cash or kind from anyone as donation. Overall, this mysterious dervish was a true giver. Businessmen who came to collect payments would go around the city, gushing with excitement, about how this devout man had a 'queer way of telling [them] to take the exact amount they were owed from under a brick or a coverlet and the *tankas* they found there looked so bright as if they had been brought from the mint that very moment'.[49] Their stories corroborated with with those narrated by other folks: Sidi Maula's extravagant spending and limitless charity had convinced Delhi that he was well-versed in the art of *Kimya va Simya,* alchemy or magic or both.

Naturally, Sidi Maula's Khanqah quickly became a magnetic nerve-centre attracting amirs, khans, maliks and assorted nobles. Over time, it became the latest and the most sought-after venue for elite parties. Under Balban's absolute despotism, Sidi Maula had not dared to raise his head. He had kept up the pretence of being a pious Muslim dervish. Now, he began lavishing as much as 5,000 or 10,000 gold *tankas* upon these nobles.

Sure enough, word reached Sultan Jalal-ud-din Khalji. It was said that one night he went to the Khanqah in disguise and witnessed the whole scene with his own eyes. It became instantly clear to him that the kind of money which this monk-Maula was splurging, exceeded even the amounts his spies had reported.

Jalal-ud-din's worst suspicions were confirmed.

Sidi Maula had carved out a parallel Government right under his nose. And his influence was bulging each day.

Eventually, the source of his endless funding was discovered—the sultan's eldest son, the *Khan-i-Khanan* himself. The growing clout proportionately escalated Sidi Maula's confidence. He now began to publicly address the *Khan-i-Khanan* as 'my son'.

Sidi Maula's other funding sources also came to light: the remnant of the Balbani Turkic faction who could never forgive this lowly old Khalji for occupying the throne.

Then there was Mir Mohsin, the *kotwal* who had joined the Maula.

Hathiya Paik was a once-reputed but now-disgraced wrestler seeking vengeance, which the Maula promised.

The *qazi* (judge), Jalal Kashani had been purchased for a lavish sum, and he spent three nights and days with the dervish. It was whispered that Kashani was a dangerous man, a skilled intriguer, highly malicious and manipulative. He had managed to brainwash Sidi Maula into believing that this man of God was rightfully entitled to the sultanate. For months, Kashani had patiently worked on the dervish's mind and 'having obtained the entire confidence of Sidi Maula, began to inspire in him views of ambition'.[50] And Sidi Maula allowed himself to be convinced that

'....the people looked on him as sent from God to deliver the kingdom from the tyranny and oppression of the Khaljis, and to bless Hindustan with a wise and just government.

Sidi Maula suffered himself to be deluded, and privately began to bestow titles and offices upon his disciples, and to assume a tone and manner sufficiently indicative of his design on the throne[50].

This sinister game of thrones had fluid but intertwined limbs, each willing to cut off the other if necessary. Sidi Maula's chief benefactor, the *Khan-i-Khanan* or Ikhtiyar-ud-din Khalji wanted the influential support-base of this crafty dervish against his younger and more ruthless brother, Arkali Khan. The latter had clearly seen through Sidi Maula long ago. But now, Sidi Maula himself aspired for the ultimate prize.

All the conspirators were assured that the 70-plus-year-old sultan would die within weeks.

There indeed was a subtle reason behind Shaikh Fariduddin's cautionary counsel to Sidi Maula years ago: he had astutely judged his disciple's true character and ambition.

⟶•··•··•⟶

Sidi Maula made the first move.

One night, the dervish summoned his co-conspirators and indicated that hour had arrived for concrete action. Sultan Jalal-ud-din would be assaulted and murdered at the Jama Masjid when he went for his Friday prayers. Sidi Maula would then be crowned and titled as *Khalifa*[51] and would be married off to the daughter of (the deceased) Sultan Nasir-ud-din. *Qazi* Jalal Kashani would get the title, *Qazi Khan* along with the *Jagir* of Multan. Other conspirators would be similarly rewarded.

The visionary plan reached Jalal-ud-din's ears within hours, and barely minutes after that, the entire cabal was arrested and brutally thrashed and paraded before Jalal-ud-din with 'ignominious treatment of all kinds, bound in fetters and chains'.[52] The Muslim citizenry was horrified at the sight of the pious dervish Sidi Maula who was now looking like a wreck... bleeding, bruised, his clothes tattered and he was treated worse than a *janwar* (brute). Jalal-ud-din Khalji issued a straightforward command: confess your crimes voluntarily, we will show leniency. This too, was a significant departure from the former Delhi sultans. Iltutmish or Balban wouldn't have blinked before subjecting these traitors to extreme torture to extract confessions. But Jalal-ud-din at this late stage in life was scared of Allah and the Judgement Day. So he asked the dervish: 'Why should a dervish make himself busy with the affairs of the Empire, or the business of Our Realm?'[53] Sidi Maula was defiant even in these perilous circumstances. He coolly denied the charge and with a pious smile designed to infuriate the sultan, sang one of his favourite couplets:

> In the kitchen of love, they slay naught but the good;
> The weak-natured and evil-disposed they kill not;
> If thou art a sincere lover, flee not from slaughter,
> He whom they slay not is no better than a corpse.[54]

With one verse, Sidi Maula had reduced the sultan's serious trial to a pathetic farce. Apart from his co-conspirators, there were no witnesses to the plot to assassinate the sultan. However, still unwilling to inflict torture, Jalal-ud-din ordered an ordeal by fire,[55] a patently Hindu practice of jurisprudence. The scene now shifted to the vast plains of Baharpur. An open court. The entire nobility, ulema and citizens of Delhi gathered there to witness the public ordeal. A massive pile of dried wooden logs was raised up and a circle was drawn outside which the citizens stood. Then the pyre was set afire. Jalal-ud-din turned again to Sidi Maula and said, 'let's now test your fabled powers of working miracles. Sit on the pyre. If you emerge unhurt, you're free to go.' The ulema and the Islamic jurists were horrified at this order. They emphatically argued that this was a *Kaffir* practice,[56] illicit in Islamic law: 'the quality of fire is to burn and it makes no distinction between guilty and non-guilty', they said.

But this pious sanctimony only pushed Jalal-ud-din off the cliff. The plot to assassinate *Him*, the sultan, was a confirmed truth and here, this Islamic clerical crew was repeatedly, deliberately making him look like a grand old fool in public. He turned towards the *Qazi* Jalal Kashani and mocked him: 'Only a person who is intelligent, a man of true eminence is raised to the rank of a *Qazi*. And you want to raise to greater dignity than *this*?' The *Qazi* retorted: 'This is a false accusation. By Allah! This is a false indictment brought by my enemies! I am innocent!'

At this, the sultan's fury was finally breached. Still, unwilling to kill a *Qazi*, his rage turned against Hathiya Paik the wrestler. A commander charged against him with an iron mace and smashed his head killing him on the spot. Other co-conspirators were banished from Delhi and their property was confiscated. Jalal-ud-din Khalji transferred the *Qazi* to Badaun[57].

Only the infernal Sidi Maula remained.

Slashed to Death with a Sack-maker's Needle

Sidi Maula was thrown into prison for some days and then paraded before Jalal-ud-din's Durbar again, bound in painful chains. The very sight of this holy schemer infuriated the sultan once more. Looking around the court, he addressed Shaikh Abu Bakr Tusi, the chief dervish of the order of Haidari Qalandar Sufis, tauntingly: 'O dervishes, who among you has the courage to avenge me?'

The moment those words escaped his lips, a Qalandar named Bahri leapt up from his seat, rushed towards Sidi Maula with a razor[58] and began slashing him indiscriminately. Even as blood gushed from the Maula's body, the pitiless Bahri dragged the dervish around the court by his whiskers and then chopped off his beard with a knife all the way up to his chin. His rage still unsated, he took out the sack-maker's needle and repeatedly skewered the Maula's sides. As Sidi Maula lay bleeding on the ground, other Qalandar dervishes sprang into the fray and began pounding his head with his own prayer-beads, made of stone. It was a hideous spectacle of unrestrained primal barbarism.

Jalal-ud-din Khalji relished the gruesome sight from the loftiness of his throne. Sidi Maula, in his dying breaths directly addressed the sultan:

> Be more expeditious in sending me to Allah. Indeed, I am rejoiced that you have thought of putting an end to my life; yet it is sinful to distress the pious and the innocent; and be assured that my curse will lie heavy upon you and your unfortunate posterity.[59]

At this, Arkali Khan signalled to the elephant-rider to put a decisive close to the matter. The elephant stomped all over Sidi Maula and tore his body to pieces.

And brought everlasting infamy upon Jalal-ud-din Khalji in the annals of the history of Islam in Hindustan written by Muslim chroniclers.

The Absolute Psychological Grip of the Ulema

Every medieval Muslim chronicler from Ziauddin Barani onwards reserves varying levels of severity in condemning Jalal-ud-din Khalji's grisly execution of Sidi Maula. Their denunciation is completely blind to the fact that this alleged saint actually plotted the assassination of the head of an Islamic government. On the contrary, their gushing sympathy for Sidi Maula, in a perverse fashion, holds *Jalal-ud-din* guilty for the unforgivable crime of executing a man of God.

This notable incident serves to illustrate and confirm the truth that there is no separation between 'political' Islam from 'religious'

Islam. Touching a member of the ulema and killing him in this dastardly manner, invited immediate and universal outrage and opprobrium even if you were the sultan. In a more contemporary context, Arun Shourie brilliantly analyses this frightening power of the ulema over the Muslim community:

> ....it is actual power which has enabled the ulema to bury every reformist impulse. To start with, there was the pattern that was set during the Prophet's own life: from the time he acquired control of Medina, *Islam became indissolubly linked with the state.* Subsequently, states far and wide came to be captured in the name of Islam. The rulers—often dissolute, often tyrannical—needed the ulema to provide rationalizations for their rulership.... As agents and allies and rationalizers, they continued to have a key role, and, from that role to acquire great power. *The ulema... came to have great say in applying the law: they assessed evidence, they decided which rule of law was applicable, they decided whether the accused was guilty or not, they decreed what punishment was to be inflicted on the guilty.* Such power over the daily life of the individual, naturally gave them great power over the community, as distinct from merely the court, in the countryside as distinct from merely the capital....To this day, no Muslim who speaks out against the ulema can afford to forget this lethal potential....
>
> The ulema control the mosques, they control the madrasahs and *maktabs*. They control every seminary: it is not just that they thereby control the mindset of those who will control the community in different geographical areas...[all these] give the ulema an unequalled capacity to ignite the entire community.[60] (Emphasis added)

Thus, Barani writes in a measured tone that while Jalal-ud-din was a 'most humane' king, his order to slaughter Sidi Maula broke the 'prestige and sanctity' of the lineage of the Khaljis. The historian and scholar, K.S. Lal also notes how the 'death of Sidi Maula was too much for an orthodox Maulana like Ziyauddin Barani to stand. He had visited the Shaikh a number of times and had had the privilege of dining at his mansion'.[61]

But Barani's guarded tone had an otherworldly, vengeful side to it. As Jalal-ud-din's contemporary who lived in Delhi when Sidi Maula was executed, and fully conscious of his own station, Barani was powerless to physically avenge Sidi Maula. He therefore invokes an Allah-inflicted textual curse upon Jalal-ud-din:

> I, the author, well remember that on the day of the Sidi's death, a black storm arose which made the world dark. Troubles afterwards arose in the State. In the same year there was a scarcity of rain, there was dearth [i.e., famine] in Delhi, and grain rose to two *jital* [copper coin] per *seer*. In the Siwalik also the dearth was greatly felt. The Hindus of that country came into Delhi with their families, twenty or thirty of them together, and in the extremity of hunger drowned themselves in the Jumna.[62]

By writing this, Barani had set a pioneering template which subsequent Muslim chroniclers faithfully followed and embellished.

Here is Firishta writing, 300 years after Barani, with the self-assured authority of an eyewitness.

> ....immediately after the death of Sidi Maula, a black whirlwind arose, which, for the space of half an hour, changed day into night, and drove the people in the streets against one another, so that they could scarce grope their way to their own habitations....
>
> The prosperity of the King began visibly to decline; for every day new factions and disputes arose, which greatly disturbed his administration. Domestic calamities also pressed hard upon him....[63]

Next is Badauni, Firishta's senior contemporary, adding generous literary flourishes and retrospective embellishments to an incident he had no way of witnessing.

> ....on the very day of [Sidi Maula's] murder, a whirlwind black with dust arose, and the world was darkened; there was a scarcity of rain in that year, and such a famine occurred that the Hindus, from excess of hunger, went in bands and...threw themselves

into the River Jamuna, and became the portion of the alligator of extinction…the rest of the world took these signs and events as proofs of the verity of Sidi and as evidence of his sincerity.

God has never cursed any nation
Until the heart of a holy dervish has been grieved.[64] (Italics added)

In hindsight, and entirely consistent with the psyche of the typical medieval Muslim chronicler, Sidi Maula posthumously emerges coated with the unstained gold of Islamic piety.[65] In the words of Yahya Sirhindi,[66] he was 'that pure-souled and generous-dispositioned Shaikh, on whom be Allah's mercy and forgiveness'.[67]

CHAPTER 3

The Indomitable Defiance of Hammiradeva

The prince would make the whole earth wet with the blood of the enemies of this country, the Mohammedans.

About a month after the disgraceful affair of Sidi Maula, Sultan Jalal-ud-din Khalji embarked on a familiar course of action: that of extending Islam's borders in infidel Hindustan. The repulsive Hindu ruler at Ranasthambapura[1] had reared his head again and was gobbling up territories at an astonishing pace. Around this time, Jalal-ud-din's eldest son, Ikhtiyar-ud-din, the *Khan-i-Khanan*, had died due to an illness.[2] The occasion elicited a poem from Amir Khusrau who expressed the sultan's grief in proxy:

> What day is this that I see not the sun shining,
> If night has come why do I not see the brilliant moon?
> Since two days my sun has remained behind the clouds,
> So that in my eyes I see nothing but clouds and rain.
> The stone of the royal signet is hidden as a stone in the mine.
> My heart has turned to blood like the colour of ruby for I see
> him not.
> Lo! there is the King, seated on his throne, with his courtiers
> standing round him on all sides,
> All are there, but still I do not see Khan-i-Khanan.
> When I saw fortune blinded, I asked the King, Dost thou wish for sight?
> He replied, What could I do with sight, since I cannot see the
> Khan-i-Khanan?[3]

But Firishta attributes Ikhtiyaruddin's death to Allah's divine vengeance for the gruesome execution of Sidi Maula:

Domestic calamities also pressed hard upon [Jalal-ud-din], among which was the illness of his eldest son Khan-i-Khanan. Medicines were of no avail; and the distemper gaining ground, that Prince fell a victim to the disease in a few days.[4]

———•··•··•——

On 22 March 1291, Jalal-ud-din Khalji amassed a large force and marched towards the impregnab le fortress of Ranasthambapura. He nominated Arkali Khan as the *Naib* of Kilughari to take care of the regular affairs at the capital in his absence.

The blighted infidel ruler of Ranasthambapura was Hammiradeva, who had now grown formidable enough to menace the sultan himself.

———•··•··•——

Prithviraja Chahamana's death had shattered the federated network of a united and undaunted Hindu defence throughout north India, a century ago. In its catastrophic aftermath, the expansive and rugged geography of Rajputana—the land of limitless Hindu heroes—had emerged as the strongest hub of Sanatana defence, lodged so close to Delhi. It would prove a permanent headache to every sultan, until Akbar used his special brand of guile and subjugated them through a mixture of war, diplomacy, deceit, divisiveness and appeal to the ego.

Ajayameru or Ajmer, which had been the seat of Hindu power under Prithviraja, had been swallowed by the Delhi Sultanate. However, its grip was fraught with the clear threat of slipping back into Hindu hands. Successive Muslim rulers following Muhammad Ghori and Qutub-ud-din Aibak had failed to definitively crush the undying spirit of defiant resistance of these infidels, who kept a tight watch on the power politics of Delhi. Whenever the sultanate weakened due to internecine warfare or succession battles, this Hindu *Kshatra* or warrior-spirit, surged forthand blasted out phoenix-like, and succeeded in reclaiming their lost territories. Only to lose them again. It was a prolonged

saga of the Hindu civilizational seesaw, which characterized much
of medieval Indian history.

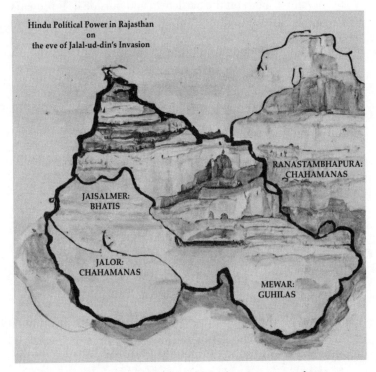

Hindu Political Power in Rajasthan
on
the eve of Jalal-ud-din's Invasion

RANASTAMBHAPURA:
CHAHAMANAS

JAISALMER:
BHATIS

JALOR:
CHAHAMANAS

MEWAR:
GUHILAS

*Figure 6: Political quadrangle of Hindu power in 13th-century
Rajasthan. Representational map. Not to scale.*

On the eve of Jalal-ud-din Khalji's march towards
Ranasthambapura, Hindu political power in the broad vicinity of
Delhi had already been consolidated for about half a century in the
southern and western parts of Ajayameru, under powerful Rajput
dynasties. The Rajput power now formed a doughty political
quadrangle that included the Chahamanas of Ranasthambapura,
the Guhilas[5] of Mewar, the Chahamanas of Jalor and the Bhatis
of Jaisalmer. As we sadly recall, the unifying force that could
forge them together under a consolidated Hindu umbrella had
permanently ended with the death of Prithviraja Chahamana.
This had terminally impaired their vision of independence. They

were rendered incapable of fathoming the precise nature of the
alien enemy lodged in Delhi. It became a primary cause for their
recurrent failures both on the battlefield and outside it. It presents
a sorry scene.

> But [the Raputs'] vision of independence was narrow and they
> always sacrificed the national cause for dynastic interests. As this
> warrior class among the Hindus was individualistic to the core,
> their dynastic rivalries never allowed them to be organized under a
> single banner to oppose the foreign foe. Consequently, *even nearly*
> *a century's alien rule in Delhi could not produce political unity in*
> *Rajasthan,* and different centres of power sprang up to hold their
> own, individually against the forces of Islam, newly planted in
> Hindustan.[6] [Emphasis added]

In this political quadrangle, Hammiradeva of Ranasthambapura
presented perhaps the most formidable threat. Rightly so.

A Flashback of Revenge

The story of Hammiradeva begins with the *Jauhar* of his uncle,
the heroic Hariraja, who in one final burst of valour, had wrested
Ajmer back from the 'hated Muslim whose face he had vowed not
to see'.[7] This was a vow to avenge the treacherous murder of his
dear brother, the great *Samrat,* Prithviraja Chahamana.

The immediate aftermath of Muhammad Ghori's visceral
capture of Ajayameru had not only thrown the various Rajput
clans into disarray but had created unprecedented dissensions,
which would take nearly half a century to heal and settle down.
A pronounced feature of this great drama was the singular
wound that Ghori had inflicted upon the Kshatra pride of the
Chahamanas and their loyalists. This phenomenon would
repeatedly express itself both on the battlefield and outside it.
Deprived of the unity and protection that Prithviraja Chahamana
had provided, the whole of Rajputana, spilling over to the borders
of Madhya Pradesh and Gujarat, was soon transformed into
mutually warring Hindu powers.

It all began with Hariraja.

After Prithviraja Chahamana's death, Muhammad Ghori had allowed his son Govindaraja IV to retain Ajayameru after extorting a massive tribute. The last great Hindu Empire of North India was thus reduced to a vassalage of an alien Turkic Muslim invader. However, on Govindaraja's part, it was pure pragmatism, a resigned acceptance of a degraded reality. A continued fight against Muhammad Ghori's army would mean the obliteration of whatever was left of Ajayameru. Subordination would allow him to retain the ancient Dharma of his land and prevent further Turushka incursions. Govindaraja IV chose to live to fight another day. In hindsight, it was a wise policy.

However, his own uncle Hariraja, saw it as a betrayal, a sentiment passionately shared in several quarters. They viewed Govindaraja's peace-buyout as an act of cowardice, something that was deeply unpatriotic. Govindraja had wreaked a two-fold disgrace by allying with the unclean Turushka. He had sullied the dignity of the Chahamana clan and besmirched the very ornament of the Rajputs: *valour.*

No sooner had the Ghori force departed from Ajayameru, Hariraja sprang from the hills of Alwar with a strong contingent comprising the loyalists of Prithiviraja and expelled Govindaraja from the capital. Elsewhere in Hansi, another Chahamana chieftain launched an all-out war against the Muslim presence there. It was simply not in the Chahamana blood to submit to the Turushka.

Govindaraja IV fled to Ranasthambapura and sheltered himself in its formidable fort.

—•——•—•—•——•—

Hariraja justly deserves a separate chapter dedicated to his honourable accomplishments. From 1192 or 1194, he launched a series of daring exploits to wrest back the lost Hindu territories and incessantly harass the alien Muslim forces in the general

region. In fact, Muhammad Ghori had coincidentally provided
the opening for him. Along with Qutub-ud-din Aibak, he
was busy in another prolonged campaign[8] that witnessed the
hideous ravaging of Kanauj, Varanasi, Asni and Kol.[9] Seizing
the opportunity, Hariraja dispatched his intrepid commander
Jaitra to recapture Delhi. The terror that he struck in the Muslim
forces stationed there was so intense that the chronicler Hasan
Nizami grudgingly admits how

> [Jaitra] supported by an army, hastened to the borders of Dehli,
> and the people were suddenly caught in the darkness of his
> oppression and turbulence, and the blood and property of the
> Musulmans fell into danger and destruction.[10]

However, Qutub-ud-din Aibak ultimately defeated Jaitra after a
ferocious battle, which has been described in Book 1 of *Invaders
and Infidels*.

Meanwhile, Hariraja had opened up another front. With
Ajayameru once again under Hindu control, he sought to
reconquer Ranasthambapura to punish his nephew, Govindaraja
IV, the coward who had compromised with the Turushka.
However, Qutub-ud-din Aibak's resident intelligence officer
named Ruh-ud-din Hamza acted first. He sent an urgent message
to Aibak, the 'sublime court'. This is how it read:

> [Hariraj] has turned his face towards the siege of the fort of
> Rantanbor. The son of Pitaura [Prithviraja Chahamana], who is
> living under the protection of the Sublime Court, is in a state of
> extreme danger.[11]

Aibak's swift action was in itself a measure of his alarm at the
increasing audacity of Hariraja. He personally marched towards
Ranasthambapura, an event which hurls the chronicler Nizami
into poetic raptures. Aibak is described as a 'wild ass' whose 'army
of Islam' passed over 'hill and desert'.

Hariraja was clearly outnumbered. After mounting token
resistance, he decamped to Ajmer with his army.

At Ranasthambapura, Govindaraja IV expressed his gratitude towards Aibak by giving him an abundant treasure and three gold kettledrums, which 'with extreme ingenuity had been cast in moulds like the full moon'.[12]

Figure 7: Representational sketch of kettledrums.

An astounding sidelight of history emerges from Govindaraja's expensive gift. Elated at yet another victory for Islam against the infidel Hariraja, Qutub-ud-din Aibak sold one of the kettledrums as an offering of his piety. The sale proceeds were enough to fund the construction of the Great Mosque of Herat[13].

Aibak also bestowed a robe of honour upon Govindaraja IV. He then turned his attention again, towards Hariraja. The accursed infidel had to be completely and conclusively crushed in his own stronghold at Ajmer. The tragic story of how the isolated

Figure 8: Jumah Mosque of Herat, Aghanistan.

Image Source: https://commons.wikimedia.org/wiki/File:Herat_Congregational_ Mosque_-Afghanistan.jpg. Copyright: DidierTais

Hariraja ascended the funeral pyre and burnt himself along with his family, to avoid disgrace at this unclean Turushka's hands, has been narrated in Book 1 of *Invaders and Infidels*.

However, Hariraja's death while heroic, also marked the ultimate closure of a great epoch of unbroken Hindu valour lasting half a millennium. From the 300 odd years that the alien Muslim invaders had taken to establish themselves in Delhi and another 200 to crush the Chahamana power in Ajayameru. This is how the learned scholar and historian of Rajasthan, Dasharatha Sharma describes the melancholic end:

> Thus with Hariraja… ended the kingdom of Sapadalaksa after a continued existence of nearly five centuries. It had on the whole, a glorious history, and *the Indian bard still gets eloquent and rhapsodical, as he sings of the brave deeds of the mighty Bisala and the gallant Prithviraja, the last Hindu Emperor of Delhi.*[14] (Emphasis added)

If Prithviraja Chahamana's defeat and death forms a fulcrum that altered the course of the Hindu civilisational history in the north for the worse, the entirely avoidable clash between his biological son and brother reflects its psychological facet. Today, we have the luxury of hindsight to speculate on hypothetical scenarios of the different epochs of this history[15]. However, all such speculations also teach us vital lessons.

Haririaja and his loyalists were motivated by pure vengeance and the call of honour—admirable traits, doubtless. However, Govindaraja IV had opted for temporary respite to salvage the ancient Dharma of the truncated empire of his father. In both cases, it was the nature of the response that made all the difference, since they were faced with an existential crisis of the most primal kind. Haririaja's thirst for retribution had clouded his wisdom and Govindaraja's desperate struggle for survival had pushed him closer into the hated Turushka's embrace. In the Kautilyan sense, both parties were flummoxed regarding the most appropriate usage of *Sama* (conciliation, diplomacy), *Daana* (gift, compensation), *Bheda* (trickery, dissension) and *Danda* (war, punishment).

> One can lose a war as easily as one can win.
> War is inherently unpredictable.
> War is also expensive. Avoid war.
> Try *Upayas* (four strategies).
> Then try the *Sadgunyas* (six forms of non-war pressure).
> Understand the opponent and seek to outwit him.
> When everything fails, resort to military force.[16]

Had the uncle and the nephew talked it out in a calm fashion, there was every opportunity for unifying their forces, recouping their strength and then dislodging the Turushka from Delhi. Instead, the hot-headed Haririaja chose a rash course. He allowed his prized generals like Jaitra to be isolated and vanquished in direct confrontations with Aibak until no supporter was left alive. However, it was the sacred region of *Brahmavarta* and *Aryavarta* that ultimately suffered the destructive consequences of such myopic politics of war—from the undatable Vedic geography of Pushkar to the whole of the Gangetic plain sanctified by *tirthakshetras* such as Prayaga, Kashi, Mathura and Ayodhya.

———◦—◦·◦·◦·◦—◦———

The extinction of the Sapadalaksha lineage[17] of the Chahamanas birthed the Ranasthambapura branch, which, consistent with its roots, radiated a similar trail of glorious valour.

Its founder was the same Govindaraja IV.

The remainder of his reign, which lasted till 1215, was quite placid. During this time, the only change that occurred, did so in Delhi—the treacherous usurping of the Delhi Sultanate by Iltutmish in 1211. On his part, Govindaraja showed the same allegiance to this new Turushka sultan. Perhaps, the greatest credit owed to Govindaraja is for the subdued manner in which he preserved Hindu power in Rajputana, broadly speaking. He magnanimously gave refuge to the dead Hariraja's loyalists who had fled from Ajayameru. He appointed them to high offices. Thus, instead of allowing Hindus to be completely overrun by the Turushka menace, Govindaraja IV consolidated the remnants of his father's former empire. His descendants eventually led the charge of spirited and sustained resistance against successive Delhi sultans. In fact, Aibak's annexation of Ajayameru had actually proven precarious. That region remained a permanent theatre of Hindu resistance[18] beating back even the semi-barbaric sultan, Balban at the height of his tyranny.

Govindaraja IV was succeeded by his son Gadhapati Vallanadeva (or Balhanadeva), who continued his father's policy of vassalage to Iltutmish. He further consolidated the new Chahamana power and built up a prosperous economy through a variety of measures.

The Magnificent Mangalana Stepwell

Vallanadeva's reign is noteworthy for quite an extraordinary event whose wellspring draws from the unbroken tradition of Hindu charity.

His *Mahamandaleshwara* or chief feudatory was Jaitra Simha, a Kshatriya descended from the Dadicha[19] *gotra*. Apart from being a gallant general, he deeply cared for the welfare of the people in his dominions. An illustrious son of his illustrious father, Padmasimhadeva, Jaitra Simha was pained to observe the plight of his people suffering from water scarcity in this *daumara-bhumi*. The word in the Marwari dialect for water scarcity is *dumara*. Indeed, the word 'Marwad'[20] itself means 'land of the desert'.

To remedy the situation, Jaitra Simha ordered the construction of a large step-well in the Mangalanaka region so that its inhabitants would never fall short of water again. Today, Mangalanaka is the nondescript Manglana village, lying eighty kilometres north of Ajmer. A straight line, 115 kilometres westwards from Jaipur leads to this forgotten village.

Jaitra Simha did not levy a fresh tax to meet the capital expenditure for funding the step-well construction. However, once it was complete, he formulated a separate class of cess for its maintenance, known as *Dharmartha* or charitable levies. The people of Mangalana willingly paid the levies for they recognized where Jaitra Simha's intentions emanated from: the *Dharmartha* would provide food and water to the hungry traveller, wayfarer, mendicant and pilgrims. The night-traveller would also be supplied with lamps and lanterns to illumine his way. Jaitra Simha instituted a management board which would ensure the perpetuity of this noble institution.

The Mangalana stone inscription inscribed in 1215 records the whole ennobling event in detail. The inscription should ideally count as one of India's enduring civilizational and cultural treasures. The insight it shines on the exalted complex of the unbroken Hindu administrative system is a lasting beacon of guidance for contemporary and future bureaucratic procedures.

In the city of Joginipura [or Yoginipura or Delhi], there ruled an emperor named Samasadana [Shams-ud-din Iltutmish] of the Gora [Ghor] family, lord of Garjana [Ghazni] and bearing the title of Hammira [Amir]. At that time, Vallanadeva held sway over the fort of Ranastambhapura [Ranthambhor]. Under him, there lived in Mangalanaka, the great Rajput [*Maharajaputra*], the *Mahamandalesvara* Sri Jayatrasimhadeva of the Dadhicha family, son of Padamasimhadeva and grandson of Kaduvaraja. He caused a step-well to be built in the *Daumara-bhumi*...nearly four miles from Mangalana... the step-well was constructed by the *Sutradhara* [mason] named Asala, and the stones were worked and shaped by the mason Jahada. The *prasasti* [inscription] was composed by Kayastha Suhada of the Naigama lineage.[21]

The inscription composed to consecrate this step-well befittingly ends with an invocation of the sacred rivers of Bharatavarsha that include the *Deva-Nadi* Ganga, Kshipra,[22] Vetravati,[23] Sarasvati, Mahanadi, Gandaki and Purna, and prays to the three seas to bestow their fruits upon this step-well. In other words, to keep its water always filled to the brim.

———————

On his deathbed, Vallanadeva appointed his eldest son Prahlada as his successor. His younger son Vagbhata became prime minister. Prahlada was killed in a hunting expedition a few years after his coronation, and his minor son, Viranarayana became king. While Vagbhata had every opportunity to usurp the throne, he chose to remain the regent, safeguarding Ranasthambapura and guiding his young nephew.

When he reached adulthood, Viranarayana's wedding was fixed with the princess of the Kacchawaha chief ruling from Jayapura (Jaipur). Accordingly, he journeyed towards Amarapura (Amber), and en route, met with a sudden attack from Iltutmish's forces. The Turushka sultan in Delhi had launched the offensive against his own vassal for no reason. Viranarayana countered the attack with heroic vigour and returned to Ranastambhapura with the Muslim army hot on his heels. His home turf provided him with immense advantage. The fierce battle which raged on for days sent an unambiguous message to Iltutmish: the infidel fort of Ranastambhapura would simply not yield. It seemed to have an infinite capacity to withstand the severest of Musulman onslaughts. Iltutmish would eventually learn of its fabled unimpregnability, which in Minhaj Siraj's description runs as follows:

....the fort of Rantabhur, which, for its exceeding strength, solidity, and impregnability, is famous and notorious throughout all Hindustan. They have narrated in the Chronicles of the people of Hind in this manner, that seventy kings and more had appeared [at various times] at the foot of its walls, and not one of them had been able to reduce it.[24]

Unable to counter Viranarayana with military might, Iltutmish beguiled him with a sugary invitation to partake of his fabulous hospitality in his palace at Yoginipura (Delhi). The Turushka envoy who brought him the invitation said:

Your Highness the Prince and Sultan Iltutmish are the sun and the moon in the surrounding starry heaven of kings and that my master, extremely pleased with your gallantry in the late war seeks your friendship. If both live in harmony, how strong both would be by this alliance of friendship, which would be like the union of wind with fire. Sultan Iltutmish now looks upon Viranarayana as his brother and called upon the Almighty to witness if there was any deceit in his heart. On behalf of my Sultan, I invite the Prince to be his esteemed guest in his capital. Or, should your Majesty have any objection to accept Sultan Iltutmish's hospitality, the Sultan himself will come to Rantambhor and pass a few pleasant days with you.[25]

This naked flattery transported the blithe Viranarayana into ecstasy. The envoy's message was the surest proof of admission that Iltutmish had been humbled. However, sage counsel and a dire warning immediately came from his uncle, the ever-dependable Vagbhata.

I disapprove of your alliance with the wicked Muhammadans. *An enemy like this is never your friend no matter what he says, no matter how loyally you may serve him.* If you really wish to live and govern this kingdom, you must listen to the well-meaning counsel of your teachers and elders. You must immediately avoid having aught to do with Iltutmish and the Muhammadans.[26] (Emphasis added)

Predictably, the advice didn't penetrate Viranarayana's flattery-addled mind. Incensed, he humiliated his wise and farsighted uncle, with undisguised contempt: 'Old age has enfeebled your mind. It is best you stop thinking about the affairs of the state. I am more than equal to the task of government. Mind your own business or retire. I shall henceforth do and act as I please. Remember, *I* am the King.'

Dejected and disgusted, Vagbhata immediately vacated the palace and left Ranastambhapura.

Viranarayana travelled to Yoginipura. To meet his death. The *Hammira-Mahakavya* narrates what happened in Delhi.

> The wily Muslim came out to receive him, and treated his guest apparently with the greatest respect. The prince was delighted with the reception and became much attached to Iltutmish. After a few days' hospitality, however, the prince was poisoned and died.
>
> The joy of the Muhammadans at this event was excessive. They exclaimed that now the whole tree was prostrate at their feet, and they could help themselves with any part of it.[27]

Viranarayana had wooed his own doom, and this deplorable episode is not only similar to but is actually characteristic of the psyche of a sizeable number of Hindu kings of north India after the fall of Prithiviraja Chahamana. Overconfidence in their infallibility and a fatal myopia regarding the patented art form of ethics-free deception which in turn was characteristic of Muslim kings.

And now, with both Viranarayana and Vagbhata out of the way, Ranastambhapura was easy meat for Iltutmish, who marched towards the leaderless city and captured it in 1226. It was the first ever Muslim conquest of this ancient and unassailable fort.

Then he trained his sight on the accursed Vagbhata who was still roaming free, and therefore posed a threat.

After departing from Ranastambhapura, Vagbhata and his loyalists had found a safe harbour in Malwa. And now, the Hindu ruler[28] of Malwa received a direct threat from Iltutmish: kill Vagbhata or face my wrath. However, news of the Turushka's intimidation also reached Vagbhata who fired the peremptory shot by murdering this frightened Hindu king, and sat on the throne of Malwa. The daring feat transformed him into a great hero in the eyes of the 'distressed Rajputs', according to the *Hammira-Mahakavya*. They quickly rallied around him as did the various other victims of the despicable Turushka sultan. They had been patiently waiting for such a solid leadership. Vagbhata, now 'possessed of a country and an army', would ultimately reclaim his fond homeland, Ranastambhapura. For now, he wisely bided his time because he was still ill-equipped for a head-on confrontation with Iltutmish.

Meanwhile, Iltutmish was distracted by the growing threat in Bengal created by the wretched Husamuddin Iwaz, the upstart who had dared to obtain ordained robes from the Caliph. Once Iwaz was neutralized, other conquests beckoned him in Bihar, Punjab and Sindh.

Vagbhata was forgotten.

For Vagbhata, the hour of his wrath arrived after Iltutmish died. His weak successor Rukn-ud-din Firoz inaugurated a series of revolts, a story that has been fully narrated in Book 1 of *Invaders and Infidels*. And so, even as Iltutmish's fledgling empire was ablaze in all directions, Vagbhata poured the hot oil of Hindu reclamation into it. With the combined force that included his new allies, he marched towards Ranastambhapura and vigorously invested the fort for several months. Shorn of assistance, the Turushkas were trapped within and eventually began to run out of provisions. But Vagbhata was unrelenting.

Meanwhile in Delhi, Rukn-ud-din was murdered in a palace coup and Raziya became the new sultana. When reports reached her about the half-starved warriors of Islam encaged in Rantambhor, she ordered a blundering expedition. She dispatched a malik named Qutub-ud-din Hussain to assist the panicked Musulmans out there and to repel the infidel. Hussain reached Ranasthambapura, mounted a garrison and began preparing for a siege. Weeks passed but the accursed fort was sturdier than he had anticipated. Hussain eventually realized the futility of the whole exercise and ordered the amirs and their troops to withdraw. But before leaving, he destroyed the garrison, dismantled the fortifications, broke up the siege-equipment[29] and returned to Delhi empty-handed. In effect, the Musulmans were evacuated in a retreat operation and the magnificent fort remained untouched.[30] The *Hammira-Mahakavya* extolls the victory: 'Vagbhata...reduced the Muslim garrison to such a plight that they vacated the fort *en masse*. Thus, Vagbhata and the Rajputs once more became masters of Ranathambhor.'[31]

———•—•—•——

Vagbhata's regime flourished from 1237-53. It is notable for his remarkable foresight in safeguarding this great bastion of Hindu power in one of the toughest terrains of north India. During the period of the bloody succession battles raging in Delhi following Iltutmish's death, Vagbhata was instrumental in reconquering numerous Hindu territories lost to the Turushkas. His vision, valour, statesmanship, and his overall legacy, deserves a detailed retelling. Indeed, the very fact that his name—like hundreds of other such forgotten Hindu stalwarts—has been eclipsed in the mainstream histories of India is rather unfortunate. In many ways, Vagbhata resembles Jayapaladeva, the last frontier Hindu hero who mounted such a spirited and sustained defence against the Ghaznavi raiders, Sabuktigin and Mahmud. Like him, Vagbhata too, accurately grasped the intrinsic nature of the Turushkas and beefed up Ranastambhapura's defence in an unprecedented fashion. He also had first-hand knowledge of Muhammad Ghori's slimy victory over the great Prithviraja Chahamana and had learned invaluable lessons from it. The Turushka could not be trusted on any count. Vagbhata identified all the vulnerable points in his dominion and stationed large military contingents and secured his frontiers. The deterrence worked not only in his lifetime but for the better part of half a century. It is to Vagbhata's lasting credit that he made the perilous landscape of Ranastambhapura more impregnable than before.

In fact, a backhanded compliment testifying to his prowess emanates directly from the enemy's mouth. The Muslim chronicler Minhaj Siraj calls Vagbhata as Bahar Deo Rai (a corruption of 'Vagbhata Deva Raja'), and in a rare act of condescension, praises him as 'the greatest of the Rais, and the most noble and illustrious of all the princes of Hindustan'. The occasion that elicited this compliment was a military campaign that Balban launched in 1248-9 against Ranastambhapura, Bundi and Chittorgarh: a straight line stretching southwards from Delhi. This campaign occurred when Balban was still christened Ulugh Khan. He was not the sultan but the father-in-law of Sultan Nasir-ud-din Mahmud and the chief conspirator of the dreaded forty. His botched Rantambhor campaign would teach him not to mess with Vagbhata. Minhaj Siraj downplays the outcome[32] of this fierce battle for obvious reasons but it is clear that Balban's vast army of holy Islamic warriors met its match in Vagbhata.

> ....the Khan's [Balban's] soldiers showed great courage and sent many valiant infidels to hell, and secured great spoils...They then returned safe with their booty to Nagor...in...Ulugh Khan's presence.[33]

Two elements stand out in this episode. One, Balban's soldiers were bested and had to return without capturing Ranastambhapura. Two, Balban had stationed himself at Nagor and it appears that he did not directly participate in the battle. However, he had learned his lesson: the infidel Vagbhata was a dangerous and powerful enemy and Balban's preparation had been inadequate.

For five more years, Ranastambhapura remained an eyesore for Delhi and in 1253, the last year of Vagbhata's reign, Balban returned with an even greater force. And met an even worse fate. The clobbering was more severe, leading to enormous losses on the Muslim side and one of Balban's chief maliks, Baha-ud-din Aibak and a *khwaja* (a Sufi) were killed by Vagbhata's soldiers.

Balban never looked in the direction of Ranastambhapura again.

Vagbhata remains one of the greatest beacons of defiant Hindu resistance against the Delhi Sultanate in an era where other Hindu kings were falling like ninepins throughout northern India. Till the end of his life, he held his own against Iltutmish and Balban.

In fact, the history of the aforementioned Hindu political quadrangle in Rajputana during the sultanate period merits an independent volume.

———•—••—•—••—•———

'Hira Devi Was Possessed with a Desire to Bathe Herself in the Blood of the Muslims'

Vagbhata was succeeded by his son Jaitra Simha[34] in the same year, 1253. He sadly proved unequal to his father and spent much of his career[35] harassing other Hindu kings and chieftains in the vicinity. Balban's son-in-law, Sultan Nasir-ud-din took advantage of this and sent a large force under the leadership of Malik-un-Nawab Aibak in 1259. Jaitra Simha was defeated in the battle and had to cough up[36] a hefty tribute.

> Thus, within a short span of eleven years (1248-59), Ranthambhor had to be invaded thrice. It was the third attempt that bore some fruits.

Jaitra Simha's son is the fabled Hammiradeva who succeeded him in 1283.

———•—••—•—••—•———

Hammiradeva deservedly rubs shoulders with the greatest warriors and patriots in Hindu history, and his fame has remained abiding. He is lionized for his gallantry, celebrated for his extraordinary hammering of the Turushkas, and glorified for being a just, liberal and generous ruler. His marvellous Sanskrit biography titled *Hammira-Mahakavya* authored by the Jain poet Nayachandra Suri in the epic narrative style is heroic, inspirational, vivid and evocative. Other notable works in the Indian literary annals eulogizing his eminence include *Surajana-Charita, Prakruta-Pingala, Sharngadhara-Paddhati, Hammira-Raso* and *Hammira-Hatha*. For centuries, generations of bards and wandering minstrels in Rajasthan have sung poems and ballads extolling Hammira's valour, his standard of honour, his sense of justice and above all, his staunch adherence to Dharma, for which he paid the ultimate price.

The price was entirely avoidable as we shall see in Book 3 of *Invaders and Infidels*.

The *Hammira-Mahakavya* uses a charming and steely brush to paint an eulogistic, prenatal portrait of the circumstances of Hammiradeva's birth. This is entirely consistent with the Sanskrit literary tradition of ascribing valiant, exalted and virtuous qualities to the protagonist[37] who is typically born to noble descent. He is a protector and upholder of Dharma, and if he dies in its defence, his death is celebrated in a rather divine fashion.

The contrast between such corpuses of heroic Indian literature and Muslim chronicles is sharply glaring. In an overall sense, every Muslim chronicler[38] has a twofold objective: (a) to eulogize the glory, victories and expansion of Islamic political power in infidel lands and (b) to brazenly flatter his patron and paint the patron's appalling barbarism and loathsome brutality as acts of piety rendered in the service of Islam.

Heroic Portents

The *Hammira-Mahakavya* describes Maharani Hira Devi carrying Hammiradeva in her womb in words that portend heroic auspiciousness:

> In course of time, Hira Devi was found to be with child. Her cravings in this condition presaged the proclivities and greatness of the burden she bore. At times she was possessed with a desire to bathe herself in the blood of the Muslims. Her husband satisfied her wishes, and at last, in an auspicious hour, she was delivered of a son....The astrologers predicted...that the prince would make the whole earth wet with the blood of the enemies of his country, the Muhammadans.[39]

The epic poem is highly reflective of the mood and psyche of the Hindus of the era. If, on one side was the continuous bouts of Turushka depredations from Delhi, it was the other side that really indicated this mood: defiling the honour of Hindu women and Brahmanas, cow slaughter, prolific temple destructions and epic slave-taking even of children. It was akin to an unending soap-opera of fanaticism, armed with sword and fire. Unsurprisingly, the literary, social and other spheres of the period mirrored this mood[40].

After being crowned, Hammiradeva strengthened his administration and trained and outfitted his military with remarkable speed and focus. The illustrious Vagbhata had not conducted any notable campaigns of conquest for reasons of preservation and consolidation. As we have seen, he had spent most of his reign curdling up Ranastambhapura's defences and repelling the Turushka armies.

One of the first things Hammira did after enthronement was to undo his father's practice of paying tribute to the Delhi sultan. But before that, he had to prove his mettle by launching a *Digvijaya* or expedition of conquest.

His unstoppable blitzkrieg began in 1286 and it was extraordinarily successful. Hammira pocketed[41] all the neighbouring Hindu principalities: Malwa, Mandalakrita-Durga,[42] Dhara, Ujjaini, Chittor, Mewar, Arbudadri,[43] Vardhanapura,[44] Changa, Pushkar, Shakhambari, Medhata, Champa and Karauli. In one expansive sweep, he had the entire south-eastern Rajasthan and western Malwa tightly in his thrall.

When Hammira returned to Ranastambhapura in 1290, the capital exploded in jubilation. His chief minister, Dharma Singh, trailed by the top officers of the state were waiting to honour him with a magnificent procession. 'Loving subjects, eager to get a glimpse of their monarch'[45] lined the streets decorated with multi-coloured buntings, festoons, and auspicious artefacts. Chants of victory soon morphed into a commotion of riotous joy.

—◆·‡·◆—

On 22 March 1291, Jalal-ud-din Khalji marched towards Ranasthambapura.

———⋅⋅◆⋅⋅———

Although the infidel Hammiradeva had not openly revolted, he had stopped paying tribute to Delhi. To Jalal-ud-din's eyes, this was the definitive omen of rebellion. Even worse, there was no force to check his escalating power. And, to further scrape this insult with more abrasiveness was another humiliation. Jalal-ud-din's vassals, the other infidel chieftains around Ranastambhapura, had now become openly recalcitrant, secure in the protection afforded by Hammira. To Jalal-ud-din, his was nothing short of an insurrection.

The 22 March 1291 campaign began with a stately durbar held in the Siri Fort. In a great display of pomp and majesty, Jalal-ud-din Khalji showered robes of honour, conferred red umbrellas, distributed *durbashes* (ceremonial batons) and other royal insignia to two of his most confidential and trusted nobles. Rukn-ud-din Ibrahim was elevated to special favour. The nobility reciprocated the sultan's profusion by raining a shower of gold coins upon his crowned head.

Jalal-ud-din Khalji departed from Siri at the head of a massive army, crossed Lohravat'[46] reached Chandaval[47] and encamped there for a few days. Then in two forced marches, he reached Rewari, covering a distance of 50 miles. Another rapid march of 33 miles south-west took his army to Narnaul.[48] This began the final leg of the expedition to Ranastambhapura. Turning south-east from Narnaul, Jalal-ud-din's military train entered the viperous sands of Rajputana. It was the harbinger of a fortnight-long nightmare, which Amir Khusrau describes in severe language:

'Thence the march was to Beohan,[49] where the people had their mouths shut through thirst. The earth was dry, and in it not a blade of grass had sprung up anywhere, through drought. The *Sipahis*, whom a river would not have satisfied, how could they procure enough water from two or three wells?' A hundred camels, however, were here laden with water, to satisfy the necessities of the army.[50]

Unmindful of his army's desperate plight, Jalal-ud-din Khalji indulged in a merry sport of hunting tigers. He also took out time to leisurely admire the rugged elegance of the mountainous landscape. It appeared as though an entire forest of peacocks had supplanted the foliage that blanketed the crooked undulations of the hills and crags on either side of the route.

For Jalal-ud-din's beleaguered force, the hellish ardour of the two-week march finally ended in relief in the vicinity of a town named Jhain, a strategic frontier post. It was the gateway to the infidel Hammira's kingdom. Encamped on its outskirts, Jalal-ud-din began preparations to besiege Ranastambhapura. He first dispatched a reconnoitring party of armed horsemen to collect intelligence. Then he opened a parallel front of brutality. Accordingly, his Jihad-and-plunder hungry warriors of Islam stormed into the neighbouring villages and hillside like packs of feral wolves, killing innocent men, women and children, pillaging and burning everything in sight. In an act of wanton cruelty, his soldiers used poisoned arrows to slaughter unarmed villagers and non-combatants. A thoroughly delighted Amir Khusrau gives us the final tally: '[All] Hindus were killed or enslaved, as far as within four *parasangs* [roughly thirteen miles] of Jhain.'

But that was just the appetizer.

The Rape of Jhain

A short, straight line from Sawai Madhopur that abruptly swerves right and then slopes down along a serpentine south-west path before cutting right again, finishes its descent in the obscure village now known as Chhan. It is one of those numerous unremembered towns in the long historical geography of India, now flung into near-permanent oblivion. It is a geographical carcass still awaiting our rediscovery. Thirty-five kilometres from Sawai Madhopur.

Jhain.[51]

The site of several battles of Hindu resistance lasting more than a century. Once, the home to a royal granary.

———◆··◆·◆··◆·—

The unrestrained slaughter of infidels in the vicinity of Jhain emboldened Jalal-ud-din Khalji to launch a determined raid to capture the town itself. As a pilot mission, he sent a unit of archers under the leadership of Karri Bahadur to the hilly ravines of Jhain. A troop of 500 Hindu warriors, who spotted the Turushkas, mounted a severe offensive. The skirmish left casualties on both sides. Jalal-ud-din's soldiers employed the same poisoned-arrow strategy which claimed 70 Hindu lives and 40 wounded warriors. Although reinforcements arrived, the Hindu side strategically elected to retreat into the oblivion of the hills sensing that there was more to this archery unit than met the eye. The sultan's unit returned to camp and reported the incident to Jalal-ud-din.

The aged and vacillating but battle-hardened sultan intuitively knew that Jhain was now primed to receive the message of Islam, which he would deliver through fire and sword. He formed a contingent of a thousand men, dividing it among Karibak, Malik Khurram Ariz Malik, Malik Katlagh-tigin, Azam Mubarak, Ahmad Sarjandar, Mahmud Sarjandar, Ahmad the chief huntsman, Anku and Abaji Akhurbeg. This army of Islam left the next morning, advancing at full speed until it was within two *parsangs* of Jhain, and entered a narrow pass in the hills.

The news spread like wildfire in Jhain. Hammiradeva immediately dispatched his fearsome general, Gurdan Saini, an experienced general who had in the past helped wrest several territories in Malwa and Gujarat for his master. The engagement was extremely intense and evenly matched but Saini met a heroic death. His retreating men were slaughtered and those who were captured alive were tortured, converted and enslaved. In his patented style, Amir Khusrau goes overboard with his blarney, glorifying Jalal-ud-din's army of the holy warriors of Islam. According to him, only *1* Muslim soldier was merely *wounded* in this severe battle against *10,000* Hindu warriors. The historian, A.K. Srivastava records his disbelief at the extent of Khusrau's ruddy exaggeration:

> This is rather strange that in a severe battle, large number of soldiers including the commander were killed on one side while on the other only one man was wounded. This is obviously one of the innumerable instances of the partialities of Muslim historians towards their co-religionists in their wars against the Hindus.[52]

The Hindu chieftain of Jhain and the surviving soldiers of the vanquished army decamped to the intestines of the Ranastambhapura mountains.

Jalal-ud-din's victorious troops returned to the sultan's camp, loaded with booty. Among other items, they piled before him a large amount of jewellery, precious metals, armour, swords, horses and the heads of the infidels they had chopped off. Then they presented a 'string of *Rawats* with their hands bound' and reduced to abject humiliation, which 'the infidel fully deserved'. The old sultan, now in the advanced stages of his Islamic piety was naturally overjoyed. He not only allowed his holy warriors to retain the entire booty but distributed gold and robes of honour from his own kitty.

'The Sultan Made a Hell of Paradise!'

Three days later, Jalal-ud-din Khalji personally marched into Jhain and discovered that it was an exceptionally beautiful town. Like any other infidel city, it was suffused with rich, ornate and large temples, bedecked with exquisite sculptures, carvings, and ornamented with elaborate gold and silver work. At noon, he barged into the Raja's dazzling palace and forcibly occupied his private apartments. The whole spectacle that Jalal-ud-din witnessed in Jhain took his breath away and Khusrau gives us a flavour of its beauty:

....he admired the exquisite colours and carving on the stone, on which the figures were so beautifully cut, that they could not be exceeded in wax. The plaster was so beautifully made, that it reflected the image of the person looking at it, and the mortar was mixed with sandal. The woodwork was all of aloe-wood.[53]

The sultan rained hell upon Jhain the next day.

Figure 9: Representational sketch showing Jalal-ud-din's sack of Jhain.

Jalal-ud-din took an elaborate tour of the infidel temples once again and admired their splendour, elegance and artistry. And then, in the familiar tradition of Mahmud of Ghazni, Muhammad Ghori, Qutub-ud-din Aibak, Iltutmish and Balban, ordered their wholesale devastation. It is difficult to equal the naked violence in Amir Khusrau's graphic exultation of the all-encompassing rape of Jhain:

Next day, the sultan went again to the temples, and ordered their destruction, as well as that of the fort, and set fire to the palace, and thus *made a hell of paradise. The foundations of Jhain were so destroyed,* that the army of the sultan was enriched by the discovery of burnt treasures, and so much gold was laden upon elephants, that who could tell its amount? This enormous wealth made rich men of beggars, for *in every ruin a treasure had been found.* While the soldiers sought every opportunity of plundering, *the sultan was engaged in burning the temples, and destroying the idols. There were two bronze images of Brahma, each of which weighed more than a thousand maans.*[54] *These were broken into pieces, and the fragments distributed amongst the officers, with orders to throw them down at the gates of the Masjid* on their return to Delhi.[55] [Emphasis added]

Abdul Isami, a later contemporary of Barani and Khusrau, supplements[56] this horrifying episode with even more ghastly details. Fully conscious of the fact that these infidel idols seized and shattered during the rape of Jhain were the objects of great veneration for the filthy Hindus, Jalal-ud-din Khalji ordered them to be permanently hammered into the threshold of the Jama Masjid in Delhi so that Muslims would trample upon them when they went for *Namaz.* But the accursed idols were far too numerous for the threshold of just one mosque to contain. So the remaining idols were scattered around the Badaun Gate in Delhi, 'in order that the passers-by should walk over them. In that passage, the Hindu idols should always be trampled upon by all, high and low.' Isami concludes his heartless narrative: 'after some years I saw that these idols were so trampled upon in that passage that they were completely defaced, and each was reduced to dust'.

Jhain never recovered from this.

* * *

Under the leadership of Mahmud Sarjandar, Jalal-ud-din's bloodthirsty army of pious Islamic warriors, marched from Jhain towards Malwa. It crossed the Chambal and Kuwari rivers and 'shed the blood of the false religionists'. By Amir Khusrau's own admission, the bacchanal of plunder and slaughter of the infidels was so enormous that 'it is beyond my power to describe'.[57] When words fail Khusrau's otherwise fecund pen, it is left to our imagination to visualize the horror that Jalal-ud-din inflicted upon the Hindus.

Following the time-honoured Islamic tradition of piety, large-scale temple destruction occurred in Malwa as well. Mahmud Sarjandar's party returned and met Jalal-ud-din on the banks of the Chambal river with a bigger haul of loot and shattered infidel idols.

The old sultan's confidence soared. If Jhain itself had been pummelled so thoroughly, the Ranastambhapura fort was not so impregnable after all. His confidence was further bolstered when he observed that the 'Rais and Muqaddams[58] and their families shut themselves up in the fort and prepared to stand a siege'.[59]

Figure 10: Jalal-ud-din Khalji's siege of Ranthambhor.
Representational image.

The siege proved to be enormously painstaking. Construction activities began at a feverish pace. A *Sabat* (tunnel) was sunk, leading to the fort. A *Pashib* or a long earthen ramp meant to escalade the fort walls by bypassing moats began to be raised.[60] Three siege-engines of varying capacities were erected: (a) *Arrada*, the small but nimble and powerful catapult; (b) the *Gargach* or stone-throwing machine and (c) the ever-dependable *Manjanik* or traction trebuchet, which also had a deeply religious significance[61] among the soldiers of Islam. Even as these activities went on apace, Jalal-ud-din paid a personal reconnaissance visit to inspect the site of the siege.

Then he returned to Jhain that evening and announced the verdict of his recce to his stunned officers: it is impossible to take this wretched fort without substantial losses on the Musulman side. Let's go back to Delhi. In one line, the sultan had doused their fire for war with the cold wind of withdrawal. He was openly admitting defeat before the siege had even begun. His angry generals and commanders bristled and Jalal-ud-din understood their sentiment and tried his best to quieten the murmurs of protest and disbelief ensuing from these war-hungry warriors. When no amount of persuasion worked, he unleashed his trump card: a large number of our soldiers would be killed even while raising the *Pashib* and I cannot waste the lives of so many Musulmans. I do not value even 10 such forts above a single strand of hair of a Musulman. Once again, the faithful Ahmad Chhap emphasized his dissent:

> Whenever a conqueror has determined on some expedition, no consideration had deflected him from attaining his objective. If Your Majesty returns without taking this citadel, the infidel Raja of this place will become proud and your kingly dignity will be lowered in the breasts of men.[62]

And once again, the counsel not only fell on deaf ears, it elicited a furious tongue-lashing from Jalal-ud-din.

> I have often told you that being now on the brink of the grave, I am unwilling to entail the curse of widows and orphans upon me

in a reign of a few days. Even if I took the place and plundered it after the slaughter of many Muhammadans, these curses would turn the spoils of war into bitterness. I am an old man. I have reached the age of eighty years, and ought to prepare for death. My only concern should be with matters that may be beneficial after my decease.

According to the 16th-century Muslim chronicler, Nizam-ud-din Ahmad, Jalal-ud-din composed a couplet to signal his reproach:

The empire of the world, by my manliness, I swear,
    Doth not deserve that a drop of Musulman blood on the earth should fall.[63]

In Zia-ud-din Barani's angry assessment, nothing would change the non-virile sultan's shameful abdication. The whole episode culminated in a battle-less retreat from Rantambhor and it only spiked the rage of his courtiers, nobles and generals. Jalal-ud-din Khalji returned to Delhi on 3 June 1291.

Barani's fanaticism is at least honest in that he openly chastens Jalal-ud-din Khalji's un-Islamic action of botching up the occasion to plunder and punish the infidel Hammira at Ranastambhapura. But Amir Khusrau's eye is unblinkingly fixed on the money. There is not even a whiff of criticism against the sultan's self-admitted failure at capturing Ranasthambapura. Amir Khusrau's narrative directly skips to Jalal-ud-din's leisurely return journey to Delhi, an occasion which he finds much to flatter the sultan about. The sultan's army was 'so encumbered by booty, that it could not proceed more than a mile a day'.[64] And when he reached Delhi at last, he celebrated the second anniversary of his coronation on an unprecedented scale on *Jumada al-Akhirah*[65] in the Siri palace. Khusrau describes the spectacle: 'Each bride who witnessed the procession from the housetop, when she gazed at the countenance of the king, tore up her marriage settlements in love and despair-imbued longing.'[66]

Jalal-ud-din Khalji was 72 when these brides of Delhi were allegedly love-struck with him. But Khusrau crowns his mountain of sycophancy with the radiant jewel of self-deception: 'When I commenced this history, I thought of writing falsehoods, but truth seized my hand and restrained me.'[66]

In reality, Jalal-ud-din Khalji had returned to Delhi only to face another humiliation.

———◆··◆··◆——

It typhooned in from the northwest the very next year. Its name was Abdullah, the grandson of the accursed Hulagu Khan, the infidel burner of the Muslim world who had permanently smashed the so-called golden age of Islam, centred in Baghdad. Like his grandfather, Abdullah was the full-blooded inheritor of the Mongol gene committed to the destruction of Islamic power in the world.

Medieval Muslim chroniclers across the Islamic landscape reserve unanimous contempt for and violently denounce the Mongol race, starting with the very man who so thoroughly demolished Islam at a time when its march seemed unstoppable— Genghis Khan. Their contempt also stemmed from a deep-seated fear and generational memory of humiliation at the hands of these dwarfish Mongol fiends.

Like his predecessors, Abdullah arrived with an enormous military train comprising 10 or 15 *Tumans,* each *Tuman* consisting of 10,000 seasoned warriors. He camped across the Sindhu river at Sannam.[67]

Jalal-ud-din Khalji immediately departed from Delhi to meet this fearsome challenge to his authority. His substantial army comprising 30,000 horsemen occupied the opposite bank at Sannam. For five days, neither party declared war but engaged in pirouettes of skirmish, testing the waters, and trying to advance each other's posts bit by bit. The losses on either side were evenly matched, and the deadlock finally broke on the sixth day, when the enemies met on a large, open plain, making a formal order of battle. It was a truly intense one, lasting hours and claimed thousands of casualties on both sides.

In the final outcome of the battle, we once again observe the trademark owned by medieval Muslim chroniclers: of downplaying or distorting the reverses suffered by their sultans. Barani, Firishta, Badauni, et al., describe the battle of Sannam as a great victory. However, they don't explain why Jalal-ud-din Khalji sought an unilateral truce from the Mongols if he had emerged triumphant. More so when, according to the chroniclers, the enemy was completely vanquished and a 1,000 Mongol officers and commanders of high rank were taken captive. K.S. Lal puts the battle in perspective:

> The narrative of Barani leaves the impression on the reader's mind that the Mongols lost against [Jalal-ud-din] and were granted a treaty by the king. *But the fact is that Jalal-ud-din had not dared face the 150,000 Mongols in a major encounter and had hurried to make a settlement, giving the Mongols very favourable terms...* in his old age he had lost all vigour and virility and during the seven years of his rule he was an extreme pacifist.[68] (Emphasis added)

Iltutmish, with no credit to his prowess, had narrowly escaped Genghis Khan's wrath because that world-burning Mongol had abandoned the plan of a full-fledged invasion of Hindustan. But Jalal-ud-din Khalji actively sought to mollify Genghis Khan's descendant through flattery and inducements, to escape a similar Mongol wrath. Emissaries of goodwill flew back and forth between the two camps and finally, they met face to face and exchanged expensive gifts. The aged sultan addressed Abdullah as 'my son', a fact that drives Barani to rage: 'Abdullah, grandson of Hulagu, the accursed', was addressed in this servile fashion by none other than the sultan. The negotiations stretched over several days and Barani describes the real nature of these exchanges when he says, 'buying and selling went on between the two armies [and] Abdullah departed with the [Mongol] army'.[69] The clinching evidence for Jalal-ud-din's unvoiced capitulation before the Mongol force is the betrothal of his daughter to Abdullah's son, Alghu Khan who decided to stay back in Hindustan after being assured that he would receive a treatment befitting the sultan's son-in-law. Barani ejects venom on Alghu as well, calling him the grandson of 'Changiz Khan, the accursed'.

Jalal-ud-din Khalji kept his word. Alghu Khan and his 4,000 strong retinue comprising nobles, commanders, centurions and their wives and children were granted exclusive colonies in Ghiyaspur near the tomb of Nizam-ud-din Auliya, and in Kilughari, Indraprastha and Taluka.[70] Together, the whole area was called Mughalpura named after the Mongols—the term 'Mughal' was a corruption of 'Mongol'. But this grant of colonies came at a fundamental cost: the Mongols had to convert to Islam and read the *Kalma*. The sultan renewed their allowances for a couple of years but by then most of them had had enough. This country was new. The climate was unsuitable. Their homes were built in a strange fashion and the people spoke a strange tongue. And so, a large batch departed from Delhi back to their home country. However, some remained and eventually mixed with the local Muslim community and formed various alliances but their identity was firmly marked: they were 'new Musulmans' or neo-Muslims or neo-Mughals. Inferno would visit them in just a few years.

Mandor Gets Its First Mosque

With the Mongol threat successfully bribed over, Jalal-ud-din Khalji now turned his attention to administrative matters. He appointed his son Arkali Khan, the governor of the frontier posts of Lahore, Multan and Sindh. Stability was largely restored in the sultanate and the sultanwas in an elated mood. The chronicler Isami describes the mood: 'When the generous and forbearing king was freed from anxiety about the aggressive hordes [i.e., Mongols], he gave an order to the chiefs to arrange the payment of dues to the army.'[71]

But this bout of generosity was also motivated by conquest. The infidel fort at Mandor[72] had to be plundered and reduced to submission. Without wishing to repeat the earlier blight at Ranastambhapura, Jalal-ud-din carefully outfitted his cash-flushed army and made thorough preparations. After personally inspecting the readiness, Jalal-ud-din led the campaign from the front.

When he reached the fort, he ordered a complete encirclement. Although it wasn't as impregnable as Ranastambhapura, it was still imposing and the infidel Rajputs simply wouldn't surrender. They had doggedly holed up inside and withstood the siege, which lasted for four excruciating months of intense fighting. In the end, Jalal-ud-din's resolve won. Isami describes the bloody climax:

> The Khalji army devastated the place completely and enriched themselves by plunder. A large number of booty including women and children fell into the hands of the victors.[71]

But the bloodlust that followed the victory was even worse. Furious at the resistance the infidels had given, Khalji's army ravaged the whole region burning and wrecking everything in sight. Before leaving for Delhi, Jalal-ud-din Khalji built a mosque in Mandor and engraved the pious tidings of Islam's victory on a slab inside it.

——•—•—•—•——

Meanwhile, emboldened by Jalal-ud-din's retreat from Ranasthambapura, the infidels had raised their impure heads again at Jhain. The wretch Hammiradeva had recovered and transformed it into a hub of idolatry once more. Ahmad Chhap had been proven right: the sultan's decision to withdraw from the siege had resulted in this humiliation.

Jalal-ud-din launched a campaign of vengeance and wrecked Jhain for a second time. However, he returned to Delhi without attempting to capture the Ranastambhapura citadel. Yet again. In the final assessment,

> Hammira paid no attention to the threats of the Sultan. *This shows that the ruler of Ranthambhor had become so powerful that he held the imperial army in contempt.* The second invasion was also, at the most of the nature of a plundering raid and was confined to Jhain

only. It had practically no effect on the might of the Chahamana
ruler of Ranthambhor.[73] (Emphasis added)

The brutal conquest, destruction and handsome plunder of
Mandor flung Jalal-ud-din Khalji into the throes of ecstasy. He
threw a lavish party in his palace in Delhi to celebrate this superb
victory over the infidels. Liquor and licentiousness flourished
nonstop for about a day and half. In a telling gesture, the sultan
seated himself right in the middle of his favourite slaves and
courtiers and ordered these two quatrains to be composed, giving
us an unerring revelation of his literary tastes:

> I wish not thy afflicted ringlets to be entangled,
> I like not that the pomegranate-face of thine be dried up,
> For this night, I like to have thee bereft of thine skirts on my lap,
> Oh yes! I utter these words in my loud voice and wish it not to
> be concealed![74]

However, the conquest of Mandor and his renewed sack of Jhain
simultaneously inaugurated the blood-soaked sunset of betrayal
on the aged sultan's grotesque career as a reluctant monarch.

CHAPTER 4

The Embers of
Treachery at Kara

'But for the want of money, Malik Chhajju would have succeeded.
The crafty suggestions of the Kara rebels made a lodgement in
Ala-ud-din's brain.'

The engulfing waves of Mahmud of Ghazni's holy Islamic fanaticism, which had netted its prized catch in the heartless demolition and plunder of the Somnatha Temple, claimed other victims as well. As Book 1 of *Invaders and Infidels* narrates, it swept the fertile land and ravaged the smiling fields of the Gangetic plain leaving hundreds of wrecked temples and and lakhs of Hindu dead bodies and slaves in its wake.

Mahmud's nephew, Salar Masud took his uncle's permission to invade Hindustan to further extend the empire of Islam in this infidel land. Salar Masud was all of 16. After a series of successful raids, Masud encamped at Satrikh[1] and dispatched separate contingents to reconnoitre Bahraich, Varanasi and Gopamau. The powerful Hindu chieftains in the region were rudely awakened to this unclean *Mleccha* upstart and tried to reason with him on friendly terms. Accordingly, the chieftains and groups of *Raees*[2] from Manikpur sent a barber to Salar for negotiations. The barber was also a scout and spy. As expected, the Jihad-crazed Masud refused to listen to reason. At this, the barber used a poisoned nail-cutter and injected a small dose into Salar Masud's finger. Masud did not suspect anything and let him go unharmed. The poison eventually worked and it took several days for Masud to recover. The news of his recovery according to his enamoured chronicler Abdur Rahman Chishti,[3] greatly dismayed the infidels.

Some days later, Masud's men seized three Hindu spies on the banks of the Sarayu river and discovered that two were Brahmanas carrying 'sorceries and enchantments'[3] to the Rajas of Kara and Manikpur. The third was the aforementioned barber. Masud tortured the Brahmanas and confiscated everything they had and then released them. The barber met a ghastly death. Among the belongings of the Brahmanas were some confidential letters written by the Rajas of Kara and Manikpur addressed to other Rajas in the vicinity of Bahraich. Masud had them read aloud: 'A foreign army is encamped between you and us. You draw out your army on your side, while we attack them on ours, and thus we shall destroy the Musulmans.'[4]

Clearly, the alert Hindu kings and chieftains of the region had begun to assemble a confederacy to vanquish and drive out this alien Turushka. However, the unwitting capture of the spies proved fatal, especially for the Hindu kings at Kara and Manikpur. Abdur Rahman Chishti describes the consequent episode with his pen dipped in the acid of bigotry. According to him, Masud's army

> ....proceeded that night to the head-quarters of the ill-fated unbelievers, and, dividing his army into two bodies, sent one division against Kara, and the other against Manikpur. The brave Musulmans quickly surrounded each place, and the heathen came out to battle; but the forces of Islam prevailed, and, putting thousands of unbelievers to the sword, they took the two Rais [Rajas] alive...and put chains about their necks, and dispatched them...to Masud....Kara and Manikpur [were reduced]... and plunder and slaves to a great amount fell into the hands of the army.[5]

Masud now turned his attention to Bahraich and we get a fascinating episode from this expedition.[6] It offers several sidelights into the sacred geography of the Gangetic plain and once again, reveals the intrinsic character of Islamic raids and conquests in India.

Salar Masud's biographer Abdur Rahman Chisti, author of *Mirat-i-Masudi* (Mirror of Masud), mentions a place named Suraj Kund in the vicinity of Bahraich, which housed a magnificent Sun Temple. It was a *tirthakshetra*, a sacred pilgrimage site visited

by thousands of Hindus round the year. Near it was an enormous
Mahua tree which was regarded as equally sacred. The soothing
shade it emanated was a sight and an experience to behold. The
British archaeologist, Alexander Cunningham who surveyed the
region in 1862-63, identified[7] the temple and the *Mahua* tree as
lying between Ayodhya and Gonda.

Chisthi describes Masud's incursions into the region in these
words:

Masud hunted through the country around Bahraich, and
whenever he passed by the idol temple of Surajkund, he was wont
to say that he wanted that piece of ground for a dwelling-place.
This Surajkund was a sacred shrine of all the infidels of India.
They had carved an image of the sun in stone on the banks of the
tank there. This image they called Balarukh, and through its fame
Bahraich had attained its flourishing condition. When there was
an eclipse of the sun, the unbelievers would come from east and
west to worship it, and every Sunday the heathens of Bahraich
and its environs, male and female, used to assemble in thousands
to rub their heads under that stone, and do it reverence as an
object of peculiar sanctity.

*Mas'ud was distressed at this idolatry, and often said that, with
Allah's will and assistance, he would destroy that mine of unbelief and
set up a [mosque] for the worship of Allah, the Nourisher of the Universe
in its place, rooting out unbelief from those parts.* Allah was pleased to
prosper the undertaking, and the light of the true faith there is now
brighter than the sun, and clearer than the moon.... On the eighth
day [Masud] returned towards Bahraich. As the weather was warm,
and he had come a long journey, he rested for some time under
a Mahua tree on the bank of Surajkund, at which time he said,
'The shade of this tree is very refreshing; and this spot is pleasing to
me.... Here I will often come, till the crowds of unbelievers, and the
darkness of unbelief, be removed... *Until this place be cleansed from
idolatry, it is impossible for the faith of Islam to spread in the land of
India. If it please Allah, I will...destroy the worship of the temple.'*... He
passed orders then and there that the ground should be levelled, and
all the old trees cut down and removed quickly, with the exception
of the Mahua tree... [Later], When [Masud] went to visit [the place]

… he would sit under the Mahua tree where they had built a fine large platform. The tree was close to the Surajkund, with the idol Balarukh on its banks, and in its waters the unbelievers were wont to bathe before offering it their worship. *Masud grew angry whenever his eyes fell upon that tank and idol.* Miyan Rajab, who knew well his lord's thoughts, one day presented the following petition: 'My lord, now that your lordship has completed this garden, and made it your constant place of worship and resort, the spot has become sacred to the faith of Islam. If you give the command, I will remove this idol and its temple.' The Prince replied, 'You do not consider that Allah is without equal…. In a short time the angels shall, by the order of Allah, remove the darkness of the unbelievers, and sprinkle upon them the true light of Islam.'[7] (Emphases added)

Alexander Cunningham justifiably calls this the 'mad expedition of Salar Masud'. The expedition culminated in Masud meeting his beloved Allah in a fierce battle against the celebrated Hindu warrior Suhel Dev, sometime in 1033.

Salar Masud's Bigotry Sanctified

Salar Masud occupies a special place of reverence in the Islamic annals which celebrate him as a true *Ghazi,* a pious Musulman soldier who fought till his fanatical end to extend the borders of Islam in infidel Hindustan. Chisti goes into raptures of ecstasy describing his unprovoked and unnecessary battles against Hindus, 'the unbelievers'. He repeatedly calls Salar Masud 'the Prince of Martyrs' and 'the Prince of the Faithful'. In the typical style of Muslim chroniclers, Masud's victories become the victories of Islam; his reverses and defeats become fearless desires for 'nothing as much as martyrdom' and an intense 'longing for union with Allah'. On numerous occasions, Chisti indulges in passionate literary flourishes when the armies of Islam are routed:

Perfect is the love of the moth;
it cares for nothing but to burn.
[Masud's] sun-like countenance became

pale as the new moon;
All the servants of Masud lay scattered
like stars around that moon[8];

Abdur Rahman Chisti is inconsolable at his fond *Ghazi's* fatal death. In a fit of denial and irreconcilability, he even invents a Brahmana historian and makes him utter the open falsehood that the slain Salar Masud appeared in Suhel Dev's vision and threatened the infidel king: 'You have killed me. But do you think you can escape me?'[9]

However, the epilogue to *Mirat-i-Masudi* contains the real history. For all his *Ghazi*-exploits, Salar Masud met a truly miserable death and Hindus recovered their ancestral territory in this ancient region sanctified by their Divine Mother Ganga. Chisti also adds a corollary that reveals[10] the real extent of Muslim loss[11] even outside the Gangetic region:

> The unbelievers drove [Muslims] from Ajmer, and re-established their idols; and idolatry again reigned over the land of India. Things remained in this state for 200 years.

The First-ever Turushka Province in Awadh

Muhammad Ghori's deceitful victory over Prithviraja Chahamana worsened this state for Hindus in North India. As Book 1 of *Invaders and Infidels* narrates in detail, Prithviraja's death was followed by the death of Jayachandra belonging to the powerful Gahadavala Dynasty in a battle as significant as the Second Battle of Tarain. With that, the glorious ancient Hindu Empire of the fabled Kanyakubja (Kannauj) was extinguished. Ghori's favourite slave and commander, Qutub-ud-din Aibak, who accomplished this pious feat for Islam, ravaged and defiled the entire region.

Indeed, Muhammad Ghori had succeeded where Mahmud of Ghazni and Salar Masud had failed: he had carved out the first-ever Turushka province in the sacred land of Awadh[12] in 1194. From then on, it ceased to belong to Hindus for many centuries. In this specific case, it was the province of Manikpur. Qutub-ud-din

Aibak ejected its chief Manik Chand[13] who fled to the Vindhyas. This was the same Manikpur whose Raja had sent a letter to Salar Masud through the aforementioned Brahmanas and the barber.

The next province that Qutub-ud-din Aibak captured was Kara, about 85 kilometres north of Manikpur.

Figure 11: Painting of the remnants of the old fort of Kara.
Image Source: *https://rarebooksocietyofindia.org/photo_archive/196174216674_10151408034091675*

The conquest of Kara and Manikpur proved history-altering as far as medieval Muslim rule of India is concerned. It eventually came to be called Kara-Manikpur, an important seat of Government of the Delhi sultans, all the way till the end of the Mughal regime. Situated on opposite sides of the river, both Kara and Manikpur commanded strategic and commercial value of extraordinary proportions. Both cities had been prestigious strongholds throughout the long and distinguished history of successive Hindu Empires ruling from Kannauj.

Following Ghori's decimation of Jayachandra, all subsequent Muslim sultans grasped the farsighted wisdom of the infidel rulers in selecting this strategic tract. In one stroke, this region commanded sway over a wide geography that included such thriving and filthy infidel cities as Prayag, Varanasi, Jaunpur, Bahraich, Gonda and Ayodhya. The region was also an inexhaustible treasure trove that supplied the perennial revenue for a perpetually ravenous Delhi Sultanate. The 14th century chronicler Abdullah Wassaf in his list of the 'most celebrated cities and tracts' of Hindustan says,

> On travelling from Delhi…you proceed in this wise—'Iwaz (Awadh), Badaun, Kara, Manikpur, Bihar, Lakhnauti. Each of these places comprises several subordinate villages, and there are strong forts and towns and other inhabited spots, which cannot be noticed in this narrative on account of their great number.[14]

Needless, a Kara governorship was highly coveted.

———•··•··•———

Kara was also the city that launched the ship of Ala-ud-din Khalji's vaunting ambition, and the Kara-Manikpur riparian bivouac was precisely where he realized it through unapologetic treachery.

———•··•··•———

Balban's nephew, the coward and the ingrate Malik Chhajju had caved in before Jalal-ud-din Khalji's vengeance-seeking march into Delhi and he had meekly accepted the governorship of Kara as mentioned earlier in this book. In a year, he had revolted against the aged sultan, which ultimately cost him this fief but not his life.

In 1291, Jalal-ud-din Khalji had granted Kara to Ala-ud-din Khalji as a reward for his services in suppressing Malik Chhajju.

By doing so, the old sultan had unwittingly replaced a weak rebel with a lethal one.

———•··•··•———

Ali Gurshasp or Ala-ud-din Khalji was 25 when he became the Governor of Kara. By then, he had already distinguished himself as an outstanding warrior and had consistently demonstrated guts and ruthlessness on the battlefield and showed unquestioning loyalty to his uncle and father-in-law, Jalal-ud-din. Exposed to the cannibalistic political life of the Delhi Sultanate from an early age, Ala-ud-din had carefully imbibed the cancerous lessons it had taught him but he had locked those lessons up in his secretive, scheming mind. He would have ample time to execute them in cold-blood. One lesson at a time.

Kara was the greenfield that provided him the maiden opening.

As its new governor, Ala-ud-din Khalji surveyed the scene first and to his delight, found the niche he was looking for: discord.

Malik Chhajju had been ousted but his officers, friends, nobles and amirs—indeed, the entire chunk of the old conspirators of the botched rebellion was still seething against the superannuated weakling, Sultan Jalal-ud-din Khalji. His magnanimous pardon of Chhajju and others hadn't thawed their hearts hardened by habitual treachery. However, the more egregious among these traitors had either been imprisoned or deprived of their lucrative offices.

Ala-ud-din decided to thoroughly milk the situation.

First, he lent a sympathetic ear to the plaints streaming from these disgruntled nobles. Then he freed the imprisoned and disgraced amirs and enlisted their services. The message was clear as daylight: these nobles would henceforth pledge their loyalties exclusively to Ala-ud-din Khalji. But almost immediately, they showed their true colours. In Barani's blunt language,

> These disaffected persons began at once to suggest to Ala-ud-din that it was quite possible to raise and equip a large force in Kara, and through Kara to obtain Delhi. Money only was needed: but for want of that Malik Chhajju would have succeeded. The crafty suggestions of the Kara rebels made a lodgement in Ala-ud-din's brain.[15]

Ala-ud-din never forgot the two key takeaways from these counsels of treason. The first was the unquestioned supremacy of money as a psychological force and the greatest source of political power. Only an absolute suzerainty over money would ensure absolute despotism. The second takeaway eventually culminated in formulating a stony policy towards amirs and aristocrats of all stripes.

This required careful planning and sustained and error-free execution. But above all, it required time, and Ala-ud-din Khalji had befriended patience of the most excruciating sort.

————•••——•••——

Even as Jalal-ud-din was basking in Delhi in the lull of relative stability after his raid against the infidels at Mandor, his nephew was making discreet inquiries at Kara. He incessantly sought out travellers, merchants, Sufis and 'men of experience' to find out the details of the *mulks* (countries) in Hindustan that housed enormous amounts of wealth. His ears were simultaneously wide open to news from Delhi, and what he heard only spurred his ambition onward. In Delhi, it was murmured that the old sultan 'knew nothing about government'. Jalal-ud-din lacked the two critical qualities befitting a real sultan: the first, a lavish spending on the princes and boundless liberality towards the nobles, and second, the dignity, severity and awe, which alone struck terror in the hearts of the enemy and the rebels alike. Clemency, humanity and kindness would destroy not only the sultan but the empire of Islam itself in infidel Hindustan. Ala-ud-din soaked himself in these tidings, which eventually became a deluge flooding Kara.

Within a year of Ala-ud-din's governorship, Kara had been transformed into a hot rendezvous of malcontent maliks and amirs and bands of shady intriguers from various parts of the sultanate. The self-servers and rumour-mongers found a willing and understanding receptacle in Ala-ud-din, and their stories increasingly took on airy wings aimed at flattering and provoking this promising governor. They said that the old sultan had inflicted lasting disgrace upon the proud Khalji blood. His control over Delhi itself was not absolute. He neither had the will nor the guts to punish rebels. His loyalists were not rewarded generously enough. His drinking parties had become boring. His craven retreat from the infidel hub of Rantambhor was a blot on Islam itself. But the mother of all insults to the fair name of Islam's power and prestige was giving his own daughter in marriage to Alghu Khan, the accursed Mongol.

The taunts worked on Ala-ud-din's fertile mind, willing to be convinced. His uncle-cum-father-in-law had morphed into a thorough coward at this late stage in his life. Outwardly, Ala-ud-din betrayed no emotion. Unlike Malik Chhajju, who had candidly voiced his frustration and paid for it, Ala-ud-din was well-versed in the dark arts of his amirs. He doggedly kept his own counsel with them but reaffirmed his obedience and loyalty to Jalal-ud-din, the just and benevolent sultan. This was his changeless stance in both public and private meetings with the amirs.

In late 1292, Ala-ud-din Khalji launched his first manoeuvre.

Aware of Jalal-ud-din's deep and genuine affection for him, Ala-ud-din wrote a highly reverential letter requesting the sultan's permission to pillage the prosperous infidel city of Bhilsa. Flushed with the victory and plunder obtained at Mandor, the sultan readily sanctioned it. His fondness and affection for Ala-ud-din, no doubt, played a big part in giving this sanction.

When the *Kalma* Replaced Kalidasa in Vidisha

Bhilsa.

Vidisha.[16]

The ancient *tirthakshetra* sanctified by lineages of Rishis. The flourishing city gifted by Sri Rama himself to his youngest brother Shatrughna. The immortal megapolis overflowing with wealth and happiness, teeming with people from various countries. The paradise populated by large, ornate mansions and grander, more exquisite palaces. The home of the finest jewels on earth. The abode of every Vedic, Jain and Buddhist sect. Invoking its very name brought prosperity, joy and radiance.

The Puranas never tire of extolling Vidisha's glory and lauding the spiritual merit of bathing in the sacred waters of the Vetravati[17] river, on whose banks it is situated. The *Skanda Purana* recommends the pilgrim to visit Vidisha and take a dip in the purifying waters of Vetravati after visiting Somnatha in Gujarat. The annals of sacred Buddhist literature too, elevate Vidisha to a pristine pedestal. Countless Buddhists spread over centuries contributed substantial sums to build various Buddhist shrines in the city.

Ashoka prized it. Pushyamitra Sunga regarded Vidisha as one of his most important cities along with Pataliputra and Ayodhya. It was his eastern capital. The Greek ambassador, Heliodorus, who joyously embraced Sanatana Dharma and became a Bhagavata, built the fabulous Garuda pillar at Vidisha. The Gupta Empire treasured Vidisha as one of its most precious jewels. Chandragupta II made it his capital for a while before shifting to Ujjayini.

Figure 12: Heliodoros the Greek embraces the Vaiṣṇava Pantha.
Painting by Asit Kumar Haldar.

As a commercial powerhouse, Vidisha and its surroundings were renowned over the centuries for a stunning variety of industries, trades and businesses. It was a thriving cotton hub, and manufactured and exported various grades of cotton. Vidisha was also famed for its exquisite ivory work, sculptural and architectural talent. It produced some of the finest swords, which were in huge demand throughout Bharatavarsha. If this was not enough, Vidisha's pre-eminence derived from its physical location itself: it occupied a median position on the commercial route between the seaports on the West coast and Pataliputra in the East. It was also the halting place on the *Dakshinapatha* (route to Southern India).

Above all, Vidisha has been immortalized by the Emperor of Poets, *Kavikulaguru* Kalidasa in his elegant narrative poem, *Megadhuta*. Kalidasa, through the *Yaksha* (a demigod) instructs the cloud-messenger to soar over the majestic Vindhya peaks to witness the gurgling Narmada breaking into brilliant rivulets on its rocky side after which the cloud would arrive at the *Dasharna Desha*. Kalidasa wields his poetic brush to paint a fantastic panorama of this *Desha*:

> ....the Dasharna country will have the hedges of its gardens coloured white with the *Ketaka* flowers opened at their apexes; the sacred trees of its villages will be disturbed by the nest-making of the domestic birds; the *Jambu* forests that skirt this country will be dark with their ripe fruit; swans will halt there for some days.
>
> O Cloud, when you reach its capital Vidisha, famed throughout all lands, you will immediately obtain the entire fruit of your lovemaking since you will drink the sweet water of Vetravati with its undulating ripples, its face full of the knitting of eyebrows, in a charming manner on account of your thundering on the borders of its banks.[18]

Indeed, Vidisha was a geographical expression and a miniature of the panorama of Sanatana Dharma itself: ageless, eternal, gorgeous, soothing, soulful and elevating. It is one of those ancient civilizational and cultural nuclei of the Hindu people that has survived continuously till our own time. Defaced over the centuries, yet unbroken. Its environs exude its profound history, akin to a tangible object. For a better part of two centuries, the amount of research that has gone into excavating its full history is nothing short of staggering.

The Majestic Bhayillasvamin Sun Temple

On the eastern bank of Vetravati opposite Vidisha was its twin, Bhilsa,[19] a bustling commercial town. From the post-Gupta era onwards, Bhilsa[20] had largely eclipsed the splendour of the ancient Vidisha. By the 9th century, the eclipse was near-total with the unstoppable ascendance of Bhilsa as an important *Surya-Kshetra*, thanks to the grand Sun Temple of Bhayillasvamin[21]. Bhilsa derives its name from that temple. Its deity, Surya, was known as *Bhayila*[22] or *Bhailla*.

One of its greatest patrons and devotees was Krishna III, the monarch of the pan-Indian Rashtrakuta Empire, who transformed Bhilsa into an important city in his dominions in Malwa. At the peak of its glory, Bhilsa not only became a magnet for pilgrims throughout Bharatavarsha but the deity Bhayillasvamin inspired the construction of scores of Sun temples in the Malwa region. One such notable temple was located in Siyadoni in the contemporary Jhansi district.

Writing in 1030, Alberuni too, testifies to the enduring prestige, splendour and sanctity of Bhilsa in his famous travelogue.

> If a man travels from Mathura to Ujjain…he comes to a large village called Dudahi; thence to Bamahur…and thence to Bhailsan [Bhilsa], a place most famous among the Hindus. The name of the town is identical with that of the idol worshipped there.[23]

By any measure, Bhilsa was also a flourishing economic nerve centre with large marketplaces or *Vithis*, where each *Vithi* was dedicated to trade in a specific class of goods. The crowning glory of its prosperous commerce was its sanctity as a place of pilgrimage. A moving inscriptional record[24] narrates how Bhayilasvamin himself directed and regulated trade, commerce, justice and piety in Bhilsa. A *vyavastha* or system of jurisprudence was made in the city whereby judicial decisions flowed from the 'deity and his attendants and not from any judicial or administrative authority'.[25]

·——·—·+——·+·—·—·

More than two centuries after Alberuni's visit, Bhilsa had its virgin, savage encounter with the bloodthirsty and expansionist sword of Islam in the form of Iltutmish's bigoted army of holy warriors.[26] In 1232, Iltutmish had marched against the formidable fort of Gwalior, then under the control of the Paramara feudatory, 'Milak Deo, the accursed son of Basil,[27] the accursed'.[28] After a resolute siege, lasting almost a year, he finally starved it into submission. And then,

> During the night, the accursed Milak Deo evacuated the fort and fled and about seven hundred *Gabrs* [infidels or Hindus] were directed to be brought to public execution before the entrance of the Sublime Pavilion [Iltutmish's tent].[28]

Elated with this victory, Iltutmish led another campaign into Malwa in 1234 and claimed Bhilsa as his first victim. Bereft of the steely protection of an imperial dynasty like the Guptas or the extraordinary Paramara monarch, Bhoja Raja, both the fort and the city of Bhilsa succumbed to Iltutmish's army. With that, the grand Paramara Empire, which had sustained its glory for nearly 500 years, hurtled towards extinction. Its present ruler, Devapala, having already lost Gwalior, had to face this additional humiliation.

As expected, the magnificent Sun Temple of Bhayillaswamin was demolished. Minhaj Siraj estimates that this 'idol-temple, which took 300 years in building, [was] in altitude… about 100 ells [one ell is about 45 inches]'.[29]

The Bhayillaswamin Temple was rebuilt a few years after Iltutmish left, that is, when Muslim control once again weakened over Malwa. This was a phenomenon akin to the restoration of the Somnatha Temple in Gujarat after Mahmud departed. The scene in Malwa and Bhilsa in the aftermath of Iltutmish's raid looked like this:

> The Paramara government thus received rude shock, which no doubt, accelerated its decline and downfall. The storm of the Moslem invasion passed away as quickly as it came, leaving desolation in its wake. The upheaval was tremendous, but Devapala succeeded in restoring peace and order.[30]

However, this renewed glory was just a presage to its total eclipse.

Shattering the Gateway

Ala-ud-din Khalji had chosen Bhilsa with immense care and calculation. Its wealth would supply him with the seed capital needed to fulfil his long-term ambition. The expedition would also not arouse Jalal-ud-din's suspicion for several reasons. First, Bhilsa was not fully incorporated into Delhi's dominions because it was still infested by the infidels, and Ala-ud-din was determined to subdue them. The prospect naturally appealed to his uncle, the sultan. There was also an important geographical dimension in Ala-ud-din's calculations. While Rajputana was situated southwest of Delhi, Kara lay to the southeast. Thus, Kara and Rajputana stood almost face to face. Bhilsa was roughly equidistant from both. The sultan in Delhi commanded both Kara and parts of Rajputana. And Ala-ud-din was keenly aware that his uncle was focused almost entirely on maintaining his stranglehold over Rajputana, the chief source of his frequent troubles.

Ala-ud-din Khalji had indeed studied Bhilsa (or Malwa in general) quite thoroughly.

Even on the eve of Iltutmish's invasion, Malwa had become a sorry mess. In fact, it was this mess that had actually spurred the Turushka's raid. Devapala had squandered away most of his reign in waging pointless wars against his neighbouring Hindu rulers, and they in turn, against him. His successors were equally myopic and foolish. Each war not only shrunk their territories and bled their treasuries, but had paved the way for the self-inflicted extinction of this once-grand Hindu Empire, one of the greatest ever to rule northern and central India.

Thus, by the time Ala-ud-din Khalji embarked on a renewed Turushka assault, Malwa had been ravaged by other *Hindu* kingdoms including but not limited to the Chalukyas of Gujarat, Sevunas of Devagiri, the Vaghelas of Gujarat and Hammiradeva of Ranastambhapura. In fact, a direct evidence testifying this internecine Hindu warfare flows from Wassaf, the 14th century Muslim panegyrist. Writing in 1300 CE, he describes the situation in Malwa:

> And it may be about thirty years previous to my laying the foundation of this book that the king of Malwa died, and dissension arose between his son and minister. After long hostilities and much slaughter, each of them acquired possession of a part of that country. In consequence of these disturbances, every year incursions are made into it from most parts of Hind, much property and wealth, and captives, and fine linen (*Kirbas*) are carried off, and as yet no change (for the better) has taken place.[31]

In early 1293, Ala-ud-din Khalji marched from Kara armed with the sultan's permit and a sizeable force. The route to Bhilsa passed through one of India's most important centres of Jaina-Dharma— Chanderi. It was an ancient and well-traversed route, which terminated at the renowned Ujjaini. Ala-ud-din's marauding army 'cleared the entire road of vile infidel wretches',[32] a euphemism for Hindu genocide, wanton pillage and destruction, before reaching the ill-fated Bhilsa. The Turushka's rude advent predictably shook the defenceless city to its foundations. Its infidel inhabitants though, had prior experience of a Turushka invasion, but all they could do now was salvage whatever they could and flee towards safety.

Ala-ud-din engorged himself on a feast of rapacity. His plunder-hungry army wasted the city with abandon, wrecking its abundant temples and stupas and smashing the offending infidel idols on an epic scale. The Bhayillaswamin Sun Temple was pounded to the ground, never to rise again. Muslim chroniclers uniformly refer to Bhilsa as *Bhailasan,* a corruption of *Bhayillaswamin.* The most important part of the salvaging efforts of the Hindus was to cart off their sacred *murtis* to safety. They concealed a good number of Murtis in the bed of the Vetravati river. But as a testimony to his immeasurable bigotry, Ala-ud-din drew them out and shattered them. Among these were two enormous 'brass idols which had been the object of the worship of the Hindus of those parts'.[33] He loaded them on a special cart and gave a familiar order—they should be sent to Delhi and smashed at the Badaun Gate so that the Muslim faithful could trample upon the pieces.

Figure 13: Ruins of Bhilsa. A 19th-century British artist's sketch.

Judged solely on monetary terms, the Bhilsa expedition was a wild success. Like a hardened bandit, who is also heartless and bigoted, and equipped with a kindred army, Ala-ud-din handsomely rewarded himself after chewing up Bhilsa to a carcass. The pilfered booty travelled on hundreds of horses and carts and included cattle, precious metals, pearls, rubies, gems, and the 'inevitable idols to be trampled under the zealot's feet'.[34] While this raid did provide him with the seed capital, Ala-ud-din's stratagem now underwent a change. Unlike the normal Islamic

practice where the underling gives a fifth of the war spoils to the
sultan, Ala-ud-din furnished a prodigious portion of the booty
looted from Bhilsa to Sultan Jalal-ud-din Khalji. There was also
the additional act that earned him Islamic merit—of breaking the
infidel idols.

The old sultan was overwhelmed. Exactly as his astute nephew
had calculated. Ala-ud-din Khalji received two substantial
rewards. The first was the grant of the highly lucrative *Iqta*
(fief) of Awadh. The second was his promotion: he was now
the prestigious *Ariz-i-Mumalik,* Minister of War. The same
office which Jalal-ud-din had received at the hands of Sultan
Kaiqubad just a few years ago.

However, while Ala-ud-din had surrendered the wealth of
Bhilsa, he had concealed what would eventually be the sultan's
undoing—information and intelligence.

Even as his soldiers were busy wrecking Bhilsa, Ala-ud-din had
used his time there to collect precious intelligence. What he
learned only heightened the flames of his treachery.

Downwards from Bhilsa was the fabulous fort city of Deogir or
Devagiri, capital of the powerful infidel kingdom of the Yadavas
or Sevunas. It was bursting with unlimited wealth. It was also
the gateway to the *Dakkhan,* or Dakshinapatha, a vast geography
swarming with formidable infidels. For nearly three centuries, this
region was not even in the realm of the Delhi Sultanate's fantasies.
But in Ala-ud-din Khalji's judgement, his lucrative sack of Bhilsa
had suddenly hurled the *Dakkhan* into the realm of possibility.
On the broader plane of Hindu destiny, his pivotal conquest of
Bhilsa meant this:

> The wound first inflicted [on Malwa] was widened by the
> successive attacks of the numerous Hindu chiefs, who were its
> enemies, until at last, the Moslems descended upon its weakened
> power, and finished the work of destruction. With its fall the
> barrier of the Deccan was broken; there was none to stem the

tide of the Moslem armies, before which were swept away all the Hindu sovereignties of the south.[35]

———•·•·•·•———

Vidisha and Bilsa, the ancient, sacred Hindu cities had been permanently extinguished by the Turushka. Henceforth, the foreign noises of the *Kalma* would drown out the profound rhapsody of Kalidasa.

CHAPTER 5

A Fatal Bait

Ala-ud-din Khalji's one idea was to keep away from the two shrews.

Avarice was ruling Jalal-ud-din Khalji when he received a humble submission from Ala-ud-din, who had returned to Kara. This request came shortly after his visit to the sultan's court in Delhi for placing the looted wealth of Bhilsa at his imperial feet.

> I beg the Sultan's favour…Chanderi and its neighbourhood are free from payment of revenue and are heedless of the army of Delhi. If it be your pleasure I shall employ new troops and retainers with the revenues of my fiefs so as to attack these places and bring countless booty…and deposit everything in the Sultan's Imperial Treasury.[1]

This was Ala-ud-din's second and final gambit. His surrender of the booty from the Vidisha expedition had immeasurably endeared him to the aged sultan, whose sense of judgement had been irretrievably eroded. It was also compounded by that distinctive hallmark of all Muslim rulers of infidel Hindustan: an insatiable, lifelong lust for wealth. However, Ala-ud-din's plea didn't stop at that. He added an audacious clause: would the sultan grant me, his humble slave, the benevolence of postponing the deposit of *fawazil*—the revenue from my *Iqtas*—so that I can use that money to raise additional troops for invading the infidel territory of Chanderi where 'peace and security reigned?'[2] Ala-ud-din gave a vivid and mouth-watering description of the abundance and riches that the infidel Rajas at Chanderi had piled up. He concluded his submission: the sultan's imperial treasury will not only swell but this is another opportunity for this humble servant to rise higher in the estimation of the Supreme Sovereign.

As the master manipulator Ala-ud-din had anticipated, the sultan swallowed this shiny bait. The nephew was granted remission of the revenues of Kara and Awadh.

He was also given permission to pillage Chanderi.

Jalal-ud-din's well-wishers and close advisors were horrified. In fact, the closest person who sounded the trumpet of alarm was the sultan's own wife, the *Malika-i-Jahan,* queen of the Delhi Sultanate.[3]

> The *Malika-i-Jahan* had gotten scent of [Ala-ud-din's] ambitions and kept a close watch upon him. She warned her old and vacillating husband about Ala-ud-din's alleged intentions of establishing an independent principality in some remote corner of the country.

However, Ala-ud-din's subterfuge prevailed. He had unerringly grasped the floundering sultan's psyche: no matter what the detractors said, Jalal-ud-din interpreted his nephew's request to raid Chanderi as a further demonstration of his fealty. And no one could change his mind. Barani analyses the sultan's psyche as follows:

> The Sultan, in the innocence and trust of his heart, thought that Ala-ud-din was so troubled by his wife and mother-in-law that he wanted to conquer some country wherein he might stay and never return home. In the hope of receiving a rich booty, the Sultan granted the required permission, and postponed the time for the payment of the revenues of Kara and Oudh.[4]

The episode reveals two important sidelights about the medieval Muslim history of India. First, it has a parallel with a similar request that al-Hajjaj had sent to the Caliph about 600 years ago: please grant me permission to plunder the infidel country of Hind and plant the victorious flag of Islam there. The Caliph had finally granted the permission owing entirely to the greed that had overpowered him. From the first flows the second—a defining character of an Islamic kingdom was that it was acquired by savage and ethics-free war and sustained by endless plunder and extortion, and was a government whose head had no notion of retirement.[5] As such, the foundational purpose of a Muslim State was not governance but despotism sanctioned by Islamic theology. Every act of tyranny had a justification if not endorsement in the Islamic scripture.

In direct contrast, the Hindu precept and practice of statecraft (Rajadharma) was consonant with the profound fourfold framework of *Ashrama Dharma*, which applied to the common citizen and the monarch alike. *Ashramas* can generally be understood as stages of life. These are respectively:

I. *Brahmacharya*: Studenthood, devoted to studies and strict practice of celibacy.
II. *Gruhasta*: The stage of the householder or family life, in general. The purpose is to earn an honourable living and beget children who are groomed to become respectable citizens first and everything else afterwards.
III. *Vanaprastha*: Literally, 'leaving for the forest'. Or retired life in general, where the husband and wife voluntarily relinquish family duties to lead a life of spiritual contemplation, social service, etc.
IV. *Sanyasa*: Renunciation from all worldly bonds. While a Vanaprastha can maintain ties to his family, a Sanyasi should renounce even that.

Thus, a Hindu monarch who was as old as Jalal-ud-din Khalji would ideally fall in the Vanaprastha stage. He would have typically vacated office of his own volition after appointing a worthy successor and would have retired to a life of quietude and meditation. In hindsight, an eminent case can be made for the sultans of Hindustan in this regard. Had they cared to learn the profound values that inspired and guided the lives of some of the exalted infidel kings of their time, perhaps, they wouldn't have wasted their own ephemeral lives chasing the illusion of unlimited wealth and unbridled debauchery.

For example, Mahmud of Ghazni's senior contemporary, the exemplary Chandela ruler Dhanga,[6] embarked on a series of yatras to different *tirthakshetras* in the final years of his life. He retired at Prayaga, where he transformed himself into a regal Sanyasi. As Dhanga's renunciation matured and ripened, he entered the sacred waters at the Triveni-Sangama and closing his eyes, fixing his thoughts on Shiva-Rudra, he abandoned his mortal body.

Figure 14: An artist's impression of a contemplative Dhanga:
Hutchinson's Story of the Nations.[7]

Another example is Mahmud's junior contemporary, the infidel Kalachuri king Gangeyadeva[8] ruling from Tripuri.[9] He too, retired to Prayaga and attained *Mukti* after meditating for many years under the *Akshaya Vatavruksha* (the Indestructible Banyan Tree). In fact, the voluminous annals of Hindu history contain a rich haul of such truly renunciate and enlightened Rajas.

Clearly, none of the sultans had cared to learn any of this because anything other than Islam was by default false knowledge which had to be exterminated. In this context, but on a different topic, the historian and scholar, Dr. Quanungo's observation is quite insightful:

'In order to understand a Muslim, one must understand Islam, and *the key to Islam lies with Islamic history…[studying the nature of] Islamic history and culture outside India…might do justice to Aurangzeb who was much less an individual than an ideology that had inspired the Muslim community* at every critical period.'[10] (Emphasis added)

For all his pretensions that he had a short life before him, which he would dedicate to the service of Islamic piety and his claim that he would renounce the throne than stray from the path of Allah, Jalal-ud-din Khalji's rapacity had remained intact. Even as he was pushing 80.

The Untameable Shrew

All Muslim chroniclers unanimously and unequivocally condemn Ala-ud-din Khalji's wife as the principal fount of his miseries. She was Jalal-ud-din Khalji's daughter, a position she never let her husband forget: he was the beneficiary of her father's largesse. And when Jalal-ud-din became sultan, Ala-ud-din's home became hell. Her inherently overbearing nature now revealed itself in full technicolour. She was openly vain and contemptuous of Ala-ud-din. However, aware of his own debt to Jalal-ud-din, he tolerated her dominance and smarted under her humiliation, but did not report her disobedience to the sultan. The *Malika-i-Jahan,* the Queen, actively encouraged her daughter's impudence and taught her new devices to humiliate Ala-ud-din, her own son-in-law. She also took individual initiative by regularly poisoning Jalal-ud-din's ears against his ambitious son-in-law and nephew. On one occasion, Ala-ud-din's wife caught him red-handed while he was amorously cavorting in his garden with his second official wife, Mahru.[11] Thoroughly enraged, she began thrashing Mahru with her sandal. Ala-ud-din had reached the end of his patience and in a fit of violence, took out his sword and grievously assaulted the sultan's daughter. The matter was duly reported to Jalal-ud-din who duly ignored it.

However, the matter cut on both sides. Ala-ud-din was by nature cold, fierce, unfeeling, short-tempered, unforgiving and vindictive. His first and only love in life was absolute power and things like marriage were nuisances to be tolerated or obstacles to be overcome. As long as he was in Delhi, he had to grind his teeth and bear the humiliation. When Kara was offered to him, it came as the perfect opportunity for the freedom that he was desperately longing for.

Two analyses provide the full picture of Ala-ud-din's situation. The first:

> At Kara Ala-ud-din breathed a sigh of relief. Here he was away from the indifference of the Sultan, the dominance of the Malka-i-Jahan, and the priggishness of his imperious wife. He began to ponder over his past and to plan out his future. *His one idea was to keep away from the two shrews.*[12] (Emphasis added)

The second was:

> [Ala-ud-din] had grown up…with an ambition which he found constantly thwarted by his haughty, sharp-tongued wife and his mother-in-law. But domestic misery only increased his thirst for avenging himself on the family and his unsympathetic critics by deeds that would free him from the galling family tutelage and ensure him an independent, perhaps glorious, existence.[13]

However, domestic trouble was just one of the causal factors in Ala-ud-din Khalji's extraordinarily brutal career and life. A close reading of history reveals that even if his marriage had been happy, he wouldn't have turned out any different.

———•–•••–•———

On 26 February 1296, Ala-ud-din Khalji marched from Kara with an 8,000-strong cavalry and 2,000 foot soldiers. A substantial body of these troops had been freshly recruited from the surplus revenue from both Kara and Awadh. It was the same money that Ala-ud-din had withheld in lieu of his promise to bring enormous booty from Chanderi for the sultan.

However, the destination was not Chanderi but Devagiri, the doorway to Dakshinapatha.

The march would alter infidel India's destiny for the worse and forever. A fact that Ala-ud-din Khalji had no way of knowing when he began his southward campaign of mercenary extortion.

CHAPTER 6

Dakshinapatha in Disarray

Geography has laid down some inexorable laws for the time and manner of conducting military operations in our country.[1]

To the inherited Hindu civilizational consciousness, the sacred geography of Bharatavarsha is broadly divided into two parts: *Uttarapatha* and *Dakshinapatha*. A geography primarily unified by a shared spiritual culture. Political boundaries have played an insignificant part in forging this unity.

In general, *Uttarapatha* signifies the entire region north of the Vindhya Range, which included the whole of Pakistan and Afghanistan. *Dakshinapatha* was the whole region lying south of the Vindhyas. The topographical layout of *Uttarapatha* and *Dakshinapatha* are distinguished more by dissimilarity than resemblance.

Uttarapatha

Three features in the geography of *Uttarapatha* stand out in a pronounced fashion.

The first is the federated network of towering mountain ranges crowned by the familiar natural fortress of the Himalaya, the guardian of Northern India from the dawn of its civilization. The Sulaiman Range closes the Himalayan bracket on the north western frontier sloping down to the mouth of the Sindhu river, which empties out into the Arabian Sea. Running roughly parallel to this range and well within India is the dwarfish Aravali Range that overlooks Delhi at its northern end. A freefall from the Aravali Range lands the fortunate soul atop one of the peaks of the mighty Vindhya Range, the scarped blanket that covers Central India from west to east *and* divides the Indian peninsula. This is the natural separator of Bharatavarsha into *Uttarapatha* and *Dakshinapatha*. Its southwestern tip, separated by the fertile and gorgeous Narmada Valley, is where the Satpura Range begins and expands eastwards into an enchanting lushness, until it is rudely cut off at the Baghelkhand Plateau.

The second feature is the collection of hostile playgrounds of nature strewn with deserts, plateaus and interminable stretches of hard, bare rocks and scorching treeless terrains, all of which fall under the suzerainty of these mountain ranges. The *Marusthali* or the Thar Desert running directly parallel to the Aravali Range, and the barren Rann of Kutch to its southwest have sustained their inhospitable infamy. The Madhya Bharat *Pathar* (plateau) situated at the western opposite of the Vindhyan Range is a rugged terrain dotted by boulders and scarps and brutal ravines.

The third and the most important feature in the geography of *Uttarapatha* is where the cradle of the Sanatana civilization birthed itself, to borrow a philosophical maxim from Vedanta. The Sanatana culture and civilization emerged as the refined fruits of the eons of philosophical contemplation carried on in the quiet and undisturbed caves and crevices of the Himalayan Range. From a contemporary perspective, this is the vast arc and a magnificent geographical umbrella that shelters and nurtures a 3,300-kilometre expanse, from Calcutta in the east to Karachi in the west. The journey which begins at Calcutta rises upwards, reaches Patna, moves west, touches Varanasi, Prayaga, then travels further northwest passing through Agra, and then reaches Delhi and from there, climbs upwards to the northwest and stops at Lahore. From Lahore, it slopes downwards to reach Multan before culminating in Karachi. This is the Great Indian Fertile Plain, the home[2] of the maximum number of sites venerated in the Hindu civilizational memory.

It includes the hallowed *Aryavarta*.

It was home to the largely forgotten but glorious *Sindhu-Sauvira Desha*.

It is the *Ganga-Kshetra*.[3]

It is the pocket of the celebrated *Pancha-Nada Kshetra*.[4]

It retains its pre-eminence as one of the most ancient civilisational locales in a continuously flourishing condition.

Indeed, the near-precise recognition of the boundaries of *Aryavarta* is an eternal testimony to the prestige and genius of the ancient seers and rishis who recognized the vitality and soul of this geography and bequeathed its knowledge to hundreds of generations in an era characterized by an absence of modern technology.

Dakshinapatha

The southern limit of *Aryavarta* (or more broadly, the *Uttarapatha*) is the Vindhyan range. 'Vindhya' literally means 'to obstruct'. Like its more imposing and majestic brother-rival Himalaya, it has a paramount salience in the annals of Hindu sacred literature. Like Himalaya, Vindhya too, is a stern but highly accommodative mountainous monarch who places his lofty pedestal obediently at the feet of the devatas and rishis. If Himalaya gave his daughter Parvati (daughter of *Parvataraja*) in marriage to Shiva, Vindhya[5] respectfully agreed to dwarf his growth at the command of Rishi Agastya. The 'modern' mind unthinkingly discards an ocean of values embedded in such stories based on undefined notions of realism. One such value—on the practical and realistic plane—is the fact that for more than a millennium, these tales constituted an entire education system that taught the nuances of our geography right down to the last illiterate man, without the boredom induced by contemporary 'geography lessons'. And our ancestors gladly learned them without formal education, kept them in memory and happily transmitted them to future generations out of a sense of discharging a debt to this sacred geography. The medium was the story. The language was sanctity. Indeed, the sacredness ascribed to our geography was what preserved their beauty and prevented their destruction.

While the Great Plain of North India is continuously hydrated by a complex web of rivers, the huge region to the south of the

Vindhya is walled by a chain of imposing mountain ranges and harsh passes, treacherous ravines, arid plateaus and deceptive rivers. This broad layout of *Dakshinapatha* (or simply, *Dakshina*), the original word for 'Deccan',[6] has an uninterrupted historical record dating back to the 3rd century BCE.[7] The Deccan is further cut up into three major slices:

I. The Northern Deccan Plateau comprising the Maharashtra Plateau, located south of the Satpura Range.

II. The Eastern Plateau that includes the Telangana and Rayalaseema regions running parallel to the East Coast.

III. The Southern Plateau comprising the northwestern regions of Karnataka, sandwiched between the Northern and the Eastern Plateaus.

The lengthy natural fortress of the Western Ghats lying parallel to the Arabian Sea safeguards the entire plateaued region of Maharashtra and Karnataka while the Eastern Ghats running parallel to the East Coast affords a similar protection to the Telangana Plateau.

This complex geography is further complicated when we survey its zigzagged riverine networks. All three major rivers, Godavari, Krishna and Kaveri originate as streams in the Western Ghats and as they stretch and spread, they collect rain from the bordering hills before branching out into scores of tributaries, finally emptying out into the Bay of Bengal. From one perspective, the civilizational history of *Dakshinapatha* is the history of its river-cities. Similarly, the mercantile routes that led to and commercially mapped South India from time immemorial followed the course of its rivers.

From a historical perspective, Jadunath Sarkar paints a captivating portrait of *Dakshinapatha:*

> Thus Nature has cut the Deccan up into many small isolated compartments, each with poor resources and difficulty of communication with its neighbours. Hence, invading armies are slowed down in their march in such a terrain and usually starved out even when they have penetrated to any of these nooks.... A north to south advance is impossible in most parts of the Deccan

[where] ... long parallel mountain chains... run west to east, cutting the country up into isolated districts, and an army [could] ... reach any city in the south only after painful climbing up and dismounting from several parallel hilly barriers on the way.[8]

Sarkar's brilliantly detailed observation comes alive when we examine the particulars of Ala-ud-din Khalji's inaugural campaign of plundering Devagiri.

The Cradle of Brilliant Hindu Empires

Despite the hazardous landscape and nature-enforced obstacles, *Dakshinapatha* incessantly birthed some of the most remarkable Hindu empires in Indian history. The fables of their power, the prowess of the vast military and the prosperity of the sprawling cities of these empires reached the scorching badlands of Arabia and echoed in the citadels of Christian Europe.

The earliest of these is undoubtedly the Satavahana Empire ruling from Andhra from the 2nd century BCE to the 3rd century CE. Other notable empires that followed include the Vakataka, Pallava, Chola, Kadamba, Ganga, Chalukya, Rashtrakuta, Pandya, Chera, Western Chalukya, Hoysala, Yadava, Kakatiya, Musunuri Nayaka, Reddi, Vijayanagara, Maratha and Mysore. The timeline continuously occupied by these empires totals roughly up to 2100 years.

As the 13th century was racing towards its end, a major Hindu empire located bang at the doorway of *Dakshinapatha* was hastening towards extinction.

The Yadavas on the Edge

The Sevuna or Yadava[9] empire continues to suffer the misfortune of being almost blotted out in the historical annals of great Hindu Empires. The misfortune plummets to the status of ignominy given the truly spectacular peaks it attained in a relatively short span. Perhaps, a major portion of this historical amnesia is due to its tragic fate at its first brush with the Turushka invader from the north. People generally weep shortlived tears at how the mighty have fallen but the same psyche that produces the tears also seeks to erase the memory of the tragedy. But in the overall reckoning, the relative paucity of historical literature about the Sevuna Empire is baffling. More so when its equally illustrious contemporaries, the Hoysala, Kakatiya and Gujarat Chalukya kingdoms have been widely written about.

The origin and phenomenal success of the Sevunas is the proverbial story not of rags to riches, but rags to an empire.

Its founder was Dhridhaprahara (literally, 'firm attacker') who flourished in mid-9th century and is credited with the founding of the Chandwad[10] town, about an hour from Nasik.

His son and successor was Sevunachandra, after whom the dynasty is named. Sevunachandra quickly distinguished himself as a dependable feudatory of the Rashtrakutas, then at the zenith of their power. By 950-70, the political status of the Sevuna dynasty had risen through a matrimonial alliance with the indomitable Rashtrakutas. The daughter of the younger brother of the Rashtrakuta monarch, Krishna III was married to a Sevuna chieftain. With the eclipse of the Rashtrakuta power, the Sevunas permanently shifted their allegiance to the rapidly ascendant Kalyana Chalukya[11] dynasty. The foes of the Chalukya became the foes of the Sevuna. This kindled a lasting and ferocious enmity with the Paramaras of Malwa, the Gujarat branch of the Chalukyas, the Kakatiyas in Telangana, and the Hoysalas in Dwarasamudra.[12] It was a saga of multi-cornered generational wars in which every single dynasty imploded in the brutal climax at the hands of the alien Turushka.

For the next century and half, the fortunes of this lineage of feudatories severely vacillated but in 1187, Bhillama V ejected the Hoysala King Ballala II from Kalyana[13] and declared himself a sovereign.

And because this newly-minted sovereign needed his own capital, Bhillama carved it out afresh in Devagiri. His reign was marked by rapid conquests in all directions. He wrested a series of forts on the Konkan Coast, raided southern Gujarat as well as the Paramara territory in Malwa. At the time of his death, Bhillama had sculpted a new kingdom on the debris of the older ones. Its expanse was quite substantial: its northern and southern borders, respectively, spanned the Narmada and the Malaprabha rivers. On the Western coast, it included an impressive swathe of the Konkan and the rest was the whole of today's Maharashtra.

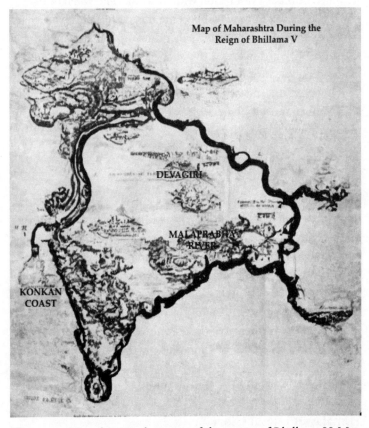

Figure 15: Map showing the extent of the empire of Bhillama V. Map not to scale.

But it was his grandson, Simhana II, who took the Yadava imperial expansion to its greatest extent and made it one of the most formidable empires in Central and Southern India. Such Hindu empires in the region radiated sheer terror in the north, and their fearsome reputation prevented the Turushkas—now, the so-called Delhi Sultanate—from glancing in their direction. Indeed, until the close of the 13th century, the maximum extent of direct territorial control of the Delhi Sultanate did not exceed 120 kilometres in north and northwestern India.

Ascending the throne in 1210,[14] the ambitious Simhana II scrubbed through a vast region with his armies and when he died in 1246, the Sevuna Empire had become the masters of the Narmada in the north and had pushed further down to the Tungabhadra in the south. It had swallowed the Arabian Sea in the west and had made admirable inroads into Telangana in the east.

However, the end of the Sevuna Dynasty had begun 25 years after Simhana's death. Under the active watch of his grandson, the ill-fated Ramachandradeva.

An Epic Greek Tragedy

The history of the Sevuna Dynasty is a gut-wrenching, epic Greek tragedy enacted in the annals of Indian history. It was a magnificent Hindu empire that had soared to an impressive summit during a vital pivot in Indian history. But it had also heedlessly squandered its eminence owing to a fatal flaw of its own creation: a generational myopia born out of a shocking civilizational indifference that caused it to wage relentless and avoidable wars against its own neighbours, all of them Hindus. These neighbours too, wore the same Sevuna spectacles of short-sight and behaved in the same reckless fashion.

The whole Sevuna story is truly stunning in a bizarre style.

Himalayan Hindu Glory

Arguably, few Hindu dynasties in the post-Gupta era can boast of cultural accomplishments rivalling that of the Sevunas, both in quality and abundance. The Guptas had nearly three centuries at their disposal to build and bequeath a grand and enduring Sanatana Cultural Complex. The Yadavas achieved a comparable feat in less than half that time. More crucially, Islam was nowhere in sight in Guptan Bharatavarsha.

A pronounced socio-cultural feature that strikes us is the manner in which the Sevunas sustained the intimate and seamless social and cultural bonds between Karnataka and Maharashtra. They had retained and transmitted the memories of their origins as the feudatories of the *Karnata* Empires of the Rashtrakuta and Kalyana Chalukya. A beautiful evidence for this is found in the very names of rulers, generals, ministers, poets and businessmen hailing from or related to the Sevuna bloodline: Sevunachandra, Dhadiyappa, Bhillama, Vaddiga, Vesugi, Airammadeva, Kaliya-Ballala, Jaitugi, Ammana, Acchanna, Chaudarasa—all common names found in the Karnataka of that period. The large hoard of Sevuna inscriptions, grants and coins found in both Karnataka and Maharashtra are surviving testimonies to this bond. Written primarily in Sanskrit and Kannada, they give us minute and precise details describing this Hindu cultural and social integrity spread over such diverse spheres as agriculture, irrigation, currency, trade, taxation, festivals, temple administration, and local customs and traditions.

On the plane of piety and spirituality, the Yadava era gestated and nurtured several new *Panthas* or Hindu sects. The Mahanubhava sect founded by Chakradhara is perhaps the most notable. While the sect faded out in Maharashtra itself, its reach eventually became pan-Indian, touching as far as Punjab (in undivided India) and Afghanistan. The Bhakti movement was at its most fecund in Maharashtra during the Sevuna regime. A galaxy of exalted spiritual celebrities hailing from all walks of life was birthed: the renowned Namadeva was a tailor by profession, Janabai, a maidservant, Sena, a barber, Narahari, a goldsmith and Gora, a potter. The Sevuna kings lavishly endowed the renowned Pandharpur Vitthala Temple. The Lingayat sect also got a huge fillip and expanded its philosophy in Maharashtra as well.

The regimes of Simhana II, Krishna and Ramachandra are especially distinguished for an explosion in cultural activity and development of new knowledge streams even in the non-religious and non-literary spheres although the distinction is not watertight.

The most noteworthy contribution to the Indian knowledge system occurred in the realm of astronomy. The output was encyclopaedic, learned and prodigious, and most of it emanated from the members of a scholarly family founded by Kavichakravarti Trivikrama, author of the *Damayantikatha*. His son Vidyapati Bhaskarabhatta was a protege of the acclaimed Paramara ruler, Bhoja Raja. Bhaskarabhatta's great-grandson was Kavisvara Mahesvaracharya who composed two works on astrology, *Sekhara* and *Laghutika*. Mahesvaracharya's son was the renowned Bhaskaracharya, who wrote a number of works on Mathematics and Astronomy. His *Lilavati*, *Siddhantasiromani* and *Karanakutuhala* have stood the test of time. Bhaskaracharya's grand-nephew Anantadeva was a protege of Simhana II. He wrote a commentary on the *Brihajjataka* of Varahamihira, and on the seventh chapter of the *Brahmasphutasiddhanta* of the 7th-century mathematician Brahmagupta.

The Sevuna cultural climate gifted to the world the pioneering and genius-standard work on music, *Sangitaratnakara* authored by Sarangradeva. This treatise is the most comprehensive and definitive synthesis of ancient and medieval musical knowledge of India. It has remained an inevitable sourcebook for every single musicology text produced in India—both in the Carnatic and Hindustani tradition—ever since. It is also noteworthy that Sarangradeva was an accountant by profession in Singhana II's court.

In the literary realm, although the output was impressive, it could not match the Gupta standard by any measure. Jalhana, a minister of Krishna compiled the famous anthology of Sanskrit verses, *Suktimuktavali*. Other works of the period include *Vedantakalpataru*, a commentary on the *Bhamati*, which is in turn, a commentary upon Adi Sankaracharya's *Vedantasutra-bhashya*. Marathi language and literature were lovingly nurtured, and flourished under the Yadavas, and the crowning Marathi work of the era is undoubtedly the *Jnaneshwari*.

But the most renowned Sanskrit writer of the Sevuna era is, indisputably, the polymath Hemadri Pandita.[15] His official job title was that of a commander of the Yadava elephant brigade, a title that has been drowned in our historical memory under the ocean of his literary and Dharmic accomplishments. Till date, his prestige rests on the encyclopaedic work of Dharmasastra, the *Chaturvarga-chintamani*. Other minor works in the sub-genre of Dharmasastra include the *Parjanya-prayoga* and the *Tristhali-vidhi*. Hemadri's treatises on astronomy are the *Kala-nirnaya* and the *Tithi-nirnaya*. If this was not enough, he wrote a highly learned dissertation titled *Ayurveda-rasayana* on the seminal work of Ayurveda, *Ashtanga-Hridaya* written by the Sage Vagbhata. Hemadri's minor work on statecraft is the little-known *Danda-vakyavali*. Apart from the *Chaturvarga-chintamani*, Hemadri's crown of knowledge was studded with two more jewels: one was the introduction of the Modi script in Marathi and the other was the establishment of a quasi-independent style[16] of architecture, eponymously named the Hemadpanti Architecture. Most of the renowned medieval temples in Maharashtra[17] follow the Hemadpanti School. Prominent examples include the Gondeshwar Temple at Sinnar, the famous Tulja Bhavani at Dharashiv,[18] the Markanda Mahadev at Chamorshi, Nagnath Temple at Aundh and the Bhimashankar Temple at Khed.

The contemporary socio-cultural consciousness of Maharashtra fondly remembers Hemadri Pandita as Hemadpant.

Phenomenal Wealth Creation

The other glaring element of irony in the Sevuna Greek tragedy is the astonishing security, prosperity and overflowing riches of the empire amidst the ceaseless wars that its monarchs fought.

In the realm of political economy and wealth creation, the Sevunas scrupulously adhered to the time-honoured principles[19] of all Hindu empires: of nurturing and increasing material abundance rather than relying merely on cash. The ubiquitous marker of this abundance was agricultural produce, which included a vast surplus of food grain. The competent, wise and innovative Hemadri Pandita introduced Bajra as a staple crop for the first time in the Sevuna territory. The empire also carried on extensive and vigorous trade, both inland and maritime. Most of the big towns in the kingdom were bustling marketplaces. In some cases, the monarch himself identified some strategic districts[20] and transformed them into lucrative trading centres where business was conducted on a prodigious scale. Commerce also thrived with neighbouring kingdoms such as the Kerala and the Tamil Desams. Maritime and riverine trade routes (known generally as *Jala-Marga*) also constituted a substantial source of revenue for the Sevuna Empire, and tax was exempted on these routes. The Sevuna thrall over Konkan ensured an unending flow of wealth into its treasury via lucrative overseas trade. Gomantaka (Goa), Dabul,[21] and Chaul were transformed into flourishing international seaports. Paithani textiles and silks, made-in-Devagiri clothing items and Deccan textiles were exported on a magnificent scale in exchange for gold. The chronicler Isami lapses into rapture describing the Yadava opulence at Devagiri:

> ....the richly decked ladies of Deogir....Every house possessed heaps of diamonds and was full of silver and gold. Huge stocks of silk were found everywhere and on every side scents were available in abundance. In every street gold could be found in unlimited quantities and there were many treasures.... Very attractive types of clothes were found ; and where else can be had such variety of cloth except at Deogir?[22]

All business activity in the Yadava realm was carried on—as in other Hindu empires—by trade and merchant guilds[23] of varying sizes. They bought and sold and merchandized in an astonishing range of products. The guilds intersected with one another in the professional, social and cultural realms. It was not mandatory that a guild had to be native to the Sevuna dominions. In a broad sense, a guild's headquarters could be located even in enemy territory, but it could still carry out its business unmolested, as long as it followed the laws and customs and traditions of the Sevuna country. The most powerful merchant guild was undoubtedly the *Vira-Banajiga*,[24] an ancient and highly influential business community that eventually developed close trading contacts with Assyria and Babylon among others. During the Sevuna rule, it was headquartered at Aihole, its traditional home. Other guilds included the *Mahajanas*,[25] *Nagaras*[26] *(or Nakharas)*, *Settis*,[27] *Settiguttas*,[28] *Mummuridandas*,[29] *Okkalus*,[30] *Vadda-Vyavaharis*[31] and so on. Specialized professional guilds such as *Telligas*[32] and *Gaatrigas*[33] also wielded considerable influence and commanded respect. Several eye-opening documents published during the reign of the Hoysala King Someshvara, a contemporary of the Sevuna ruler Singhana, reveal a profound insight into the overall climate in the era of medieval Hindu kingdoms in *Dakshinapatha*. The summary of one of these records gives us quite an ennobling portrait of an influential Malayala merchant named Kunjanambi Setti.

> An expert in testing all manner of gems, understanding in a moment the wishes of kings, filled with ability to counsel, skilled in learning, and great in generosity was Kunjanambi, the promoter of the fortunes of the Maleyala [i.e., Malayala] family. *Pleasing both the Hoysala emperor in the south, and Singhana himself in the north, he formed an alliance between the two kings which was universally praised, and obtained credit in negotiating for peace and war as an embodiment of perfect truth (satyavakya) and an ornament of mercy....*
>
> He at once supplied [i.e., goods, business, money, etc], and obtained extensive merit to and from the Chola and Pandya rulers. No Setti was equal to Kunjanambi throughout the Hoysala kingdom. An emperor of justice, honoured in the great Hoysala kingdom, of kind speech, a tree of abundance in natural wisdom, delighting in truth, thus did all the world unceasingly extol Kunjanambi-Setti as a collection of unnumbered good qualities. (Emphasis added)[34]

Most guilds also maintained private armies, a practice[35] dating back to the Vedic era. Apart from paying taxes, they supplied loans to the exchequer in times of emergency, financed and participated in wars, engaged in large-scale philanthropic work and contributed substantially to community-building activities, such as endowing temples, funding community-driven education, sponsoring festivals, and giving patronage to the arts and culture.

The overall picture we get of the Yadava economy is that of a richly studded universe of material abundance including but not limited to a perennial supply of essential needs like food grains, vegetables, betel leaves, fruit, clothes, cattle, jaggery, sugar, oil, camphor, etc. The embellished facet of this prosperity was a similar abundance of valuable goods like precious metals, pearls, rubies and priceless stones, all of which were purchased and sold freely in the bazaars of Devagiri, Aihole, Konkan and elsewhere. A large quantity of these precious items were transported via a dedicated sea-fleet, which the Sevunas had built up after their conquest of Konkan. Other modes included elephants, horses, oxen, bullocks, donkeys and buffaloes.

Indeed, there is no better tribute to the prowess, dexterity and expertize of these business guilds than Singhana's laudatory Kannada inscription etched in their honour:

> Vaiśyakulānvayaprasūtarum kraya vikrayagaḷindarthamaṁ percisi…
> [They were] born of the Vaishya-Kula [business lineage] and increased the wealth of the kingdom by purchase and sale.[36]

The Profuse Yadava Coinage

Perhaps the most telling indicator of the Sevuna economic prosperity is the glittering world of its coinage. Thankfully, some of this coinage has survived into our present, and the first thing that stands out is the use of only gold coins as legal tender. At least 10 inscriptions unearthed from various regions of the Sevuna dominions show that gold coins were issued by the monarch and were extensively used in transactions such as the purchase and sale of land and goods. Specialized mints[37] were established for the purpose and several varieties and designs of coins were issued. Silver coins too, were used to a lesser extent.

Each gold coin weighed 57.25 grams and some were named according to their denomination. The fact that most of these names exactly corresponded with the currency nomenclature and measurements[38] in vogue since the Vedic period is the financial facet that proves the unbroken and perennial stream of Hindu civilization. Coin units such as *Nishka, Suvarna, Pana* and *Tanka,* which were commonplace in the Yadava regime[39] had mostly preserved their ancient usages intact. The generic name for gold coins issued by various Sevuna monarchs is the *Padma-Tanka,* because the image of the *Padma* or lotus is engraved into them. The name of the issuing king is inscribed above the lotus: Singhana, Kanhapa (or Kanhara),[40] Mahadeva and Sri Rama.[41]

Figure 16: Gold Padma tanka issued[42] by Singhana.

Image Source: https://www.marudhararts.com/printed-auction/auction-no-20/lot-no-204/coins-of-india/hindu-medieval-of-india/yadava-dynasty/gold-padma-tanka-coin-of-yadavas-of-devagiri--.html

The Sevuna capital Devagiri naturally reflected the empire's prosperity and its seemingly infinite capacity for generating inexhaustible wealth. A close reading of the sacred work *Jnanesvari* gives us valuable information about the prosperity of *Dakshinapatha* under Yadava rule. In general, this is the portrait of Devagiri that we get after reading the primary sources narrating the history of the Sevunas. The portrait clearly epitomizes Devagiri's name: *mountain of the Gods.*

The main streets of Devagiri and other important towns and cities of the empire were lined with the shops of goldsmiths, silversmiths, and dealers in pearls and fine and costly muslins. There were many wealthy householders and there was therefore a great demand for such articles, since rich men sought eagerly for ornaments with which to adorn themselves, their wives, their children and the images of gods. Ornaments and bullion were often buried underground in the houses of the more opulent. These lived in three-storied houses, with good windows and doors, painted with pictures on the outer sides, and having guards stationed at the entrance. Cooks, umbrella-bearers and betel-carriers were among the servants who usually formed their retinues. The palanquin was the normal fashionable means of conveyance, but when a large number of people were to be transported, as in the case of a marriage party, even the rich used to travel in bullock carts.[43]

—•·•·•·•—

This was the extent of intelligence that Ala-ud-din Khalji had collected about the 'prosperous infidel kingdom in Deogir in the *Dakkan*' during his Bhilsa raid.

The stories made him restless and ravenous to the point of risking his whole future, which had started off so well at Kara. Indeed, the eternal military dictum that your enemy knows more about you than you know about yourself applies eminently to Devagiri's prolific opulence, viewed from Ala-ud-din's perspective. Every Muslim chronicle narrating Ala-ud-din's expedition to Devagiri gives detailed descriptions about its stupendous wealth as we shall soon see.

In a manner of speaking, the Yadavas had invited their own doom through a shocking mixture of complacence, apathy and shortsightedness. But on the larger political stage, the Hindu kingdoms of South and Central India had actually made Ala-ud-din Khalji's job relatively easy.

—•·•·•·•—

Hindu Political Chaos in Madhya Bharata

It was an irredeemable scene.

Of prosperous Hindu empires competing with each other on a mindless voyage towards becoming the 'shipwrecks of history', to borrow Will Durant's memorable phrase.

The geographical theatre of this ensuing political wreckage included the large region comprising parts of southeastern Rajasthan, Gujarat, Malwa, Devagiri, Warangal, Karnataka and Tamil Nadu. This ceaseless multi-cornered contest played out among the Chahamans of Ranastambhapura, the Chalukyas (Vaghelas) of Gujarat, the emaciated Paramaras in Malwa, the Sevunas, now at their peak in Devagiri, the ambitious Kakatiya power in Telangana, the doughty Hoysalas in Karnataka, and the crumbling Pandyas in Madurai. The Sevunas were located at the centre of these senseless Hindu wars, which each of these dynasties had generationally waged. In fact, the Sevunas had fought with *all* these kingdoms except the Pandya and the Chahamana.

Thus, if three imperial Hindu dynasties had cut each others' throats in the 10th century in *Uttarapatha* on the anvil of Mahmud's invasion, *six* did so in central and southern India about three centuries later. With the same ruinous consequences: an irredeemable loss of freedom and in many cases, a permanent destruction of their ancient Dharma.

The Sevunas of Devagiri were the first to lose it due to the accident of their physical location—they were the first in the Vindhya region to encounter the Turushka. The brilliant scholar and historian Dr. Altekar who has written extensively on the Sevunas gives us a summary of this self-inflicted Greek Tragedy:

The Yadava empire reached the zenith of its glory and power in the reign of Simhana. Neither the Hoysalas nor the Kakatiyas, neither the Paramaras nor the Chaulukyas dared to challenge his supremacy in the Deccan....

Simhana followed the traditional policy of the Deccani power, that of continually aggrandising itself at the cost of its neighbours in the south and the north. Events in Northern India do not seem to have perturbed him much. *Even when Malwa and Gujarat were gradually crumbling under the onslaught of the powerful Islamic armies, Simhana could not rise above the narrow dynastic prejudices of his house and go to their assistance. Instead of organising a common front against the northern invaders, he attacked Gujarat and Malwa from the rear and hastened their fall before the armies of Islam. His descendants... had to pay heavily for this political folly within less than fifty years after his death.*[44] (Emphasis added).

That descendant was his great grandson, the jinxed Ramachandradeva, the first Hindu ruler of *Dakshinapatha* to face Ala-ud-din Khalji's Islamic army.

Like his predecessors, Ramachandradeva too, was a distinguished Sevuna monarch who had inherited both military prowess and civilizational myopia from his ancestors. For 25 years, he carried the flaming torch of the Yadava imperial glory and for the next 15, saw his monarchy degraded to an abject vassalage. Until he encountered Ala-ud-din Khalji's barbaric and perfidious army, Ramachandra had spent his career waging avoidable battles against the Gujarat Chalukyas, the Paramaras and the Kakatiyas. While none of these battles had any conclusive outcomes, he still waged them repeatedly. It is said that Ramachandra wrested Varanasi from the Muslims back into Hindu control and retained it for about three years.[45]

By 1292, the Sevuna power was once again at the summit of its glory. However, that summit was actually an iceberg portending the frozen winter under which it would be permanently buried.

CHAPTER 7

The Rising Turushka Vapours in Dakshinapatha

*'In this prosperous country', said Ala-ud-din,
'where the Hindu women do not retreat before us, I do not know what
kind of demons men would prove!'*

Ala-ud-din Khalji's daring expedition to Devagiri was the gravel that would pave his way to the throne of Delhi literally with gold. Unlike Malik Chhajju, Ala-ud-din not only did not give voice to his ambition but consciously stifled it.

From start to finish, Ala-ud-din's Devagiri raid was a campaign of timing, trickery, deceit, misinformation and savagery culminating in triumph. He followed Prophet Muhammad's dictum that 'all war is *al harb khada*, a kind of deception'. Indeed, the sheer brazenness with which he spread lies, propaganda and rumours throughout this expedition qualifies it as the medieval Islamic version of fake news.

This raid would eventually turn into a seminal conquest.

———◆·•·◆———

Ala-ud-din had invested nearly three years in meticulous planning and strategizing before seeking the sultan's permission to ostensibly invade Chanderi. After gratifying Jalal-ud-din with the loot from his savage ransack of Bhilsa in 1293, Ala-ud-din began researching the *Dakkhan* with stealthy earnestness. He sent secret emissaries throughout the region and obtained valuable and accurate information about the routes. He also received multiple confirmations about the wealth that the infidel city of Devagiri was bursting with. Like every Turushka raider, it did not occur to

Ala-ud-din that Devagiri had a booming economy and boasted of the wealth of eons *precisely because no Turushka had ever set his avaricious eye on it.*

Ala-ud-din had also secured the loyalty of the disgruntled amirs at Kara who were itching to betray the sultan. He chose his trusted lieutenant, Malik Ala-ul-Mulk to disclose his true intent of marching to Devagiri. Ala-ul-Mulk was an uncle[1] of the chronicler Zia-ud-din Barani. If the expedition was successful, Ala-ul-Mulk's fortunes would soar to unimaginable heights. But for now, he was appointed the caretaker governor of Kara. His only task was to feed and sustain disinformation on a royal scale.

Only after this groundwork was in place did Ala-ud-din flatter the sultan, and receive the previously mentioned sanction to raid Chanderi.

———— • ·· • ·· • ————

On 26 February 1296, Ala-ud-din Khalji marched from Kara with an 8,000-strong cavalry and 2,000 foot soldiers. His choice of the campaigning season is quite significant, revealing the meticulousness of his preparation. Jadunath Sarkar offers invaluable insights into the spatiotemporal aspects of military campaigns conducted in India from the ancient times:

> A look at the map of India will… explain to us how geography has laid down some inexorable laws for the time and manner of conducting military operations in our country…The physical geography of India has also dictated the campaigning season. *There can be no movement during the three months of rain, 15th June to 15th September.* The rivers are then in high flood, the roads are turned into mud pools, and the fields are submerged….
> [The] Deccan hill ranges, particularly the Sahyadri, are often crowned by lofty forts, towering above the lowlands on some cliff with steep scarped sides and artesian water supply on the flat top or sides. *These forts are Nature's gifts to which the people can*

retire for safety when defeated in a pitched battle in the plain below.[2]
(Emphasis added)

The total duration of Ala-ud-din's campaign encompasses the months from February to June and the nature of his battle at Devagiri also bolsters Jadunath Sarkar's observations.

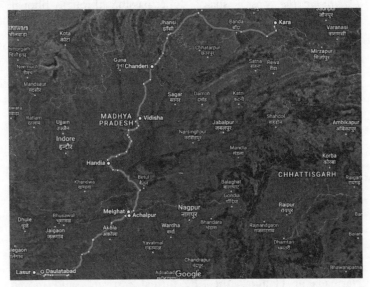

Figure 17: Route taken by Ala-ud-din Khalji on his campaign to Devagiri.

As promised to the sultan, Ala-ud-din headed towards Chanderi, making a great public show of his troops. This was a distance exceeding 400 kilometres. But once Ala-ud-din reached Chanderi, news about movements became shrouded in mist. Unknown to the sultan, Ala-ud-din had not stopped to plunder Chanderi but had directly proceeded southwards, heading first towards the beleaguered Vidisha, once again.

Meanwhile at Kara, Malik Ala-ul-Mulk had put his disinformation machinery in motion. He now began to feed fake news to Jalal-ud-din Khalji, concocting reports of his nephew's glorious march and the successes that he was rapidly notching up along the way. The gullible sultan was happy and the people of Kara were eminently deceived.

—•—•·•·•—•—

The traditional and well-trodden route from Vidisha to *Dakshinapatha* was a snaky slope passing through Bhopal, cutting slightly left before halting, down at Mundi. From there, a straight route southwards led to the historic and strategic fort city of Asirgarh[3] and from there, directly to Devagiri. Ala-ud-din Khalji chose not to molest Vidisha again. Neither did he take the Asirgarh route. Both decisions were the ingredients of his careful planning. Stealth and speed were paramount. Ala-ud-din had staked his entire future on this singular expedition and the slightest leak of the news of his sneaky expedition to Devagiri would invite the sultan's wrath. Accordingly, he had made an estimate of its maximum duration: two months. Taking the familiar Aisrgarh route would instantly invite the sultan's suspicion and simultaneously expose the fabricated reports that Ala-ul-Mulk was sending from Kara.

From Vidisha, Ala-ud-din headed southwest and crossed the Narmada at Handia. Then he turned eastwards and moved towards Melghat, a circuitous and tough route littered with dense jungles, craggy, irregular hills, and swollen rivers situated in the Satpura terrain. Melghat was situated in the Maratha country. His next target was Achalpur (pronounced in Muslim chronicles as Elichpur), the northern frontier of Devagiri under the command of a Sevuna feudatory. Achalpur, according to Barani, was one of the famous and prosperous infidel cities of the Deccan. The distance from Melghat to Achalpur was just 12 kilometres. Ala-ud-din's force covered it in no time.

A measure of Ala-ud-din's behaviour at Achalpur gives another testimony to his unscrupulous nature and his well-honed trickery. Here, he played what is today infamous as the victim card. Knowing that the sudden presence of so many weirdly-dressed trespassers would arouse the suspicion of the officials there, he floated a rumour: he was an estranged noble of the court of the Delhi sultan, now seeking service with the Raja of Telangana, a vassal of the Sevunas. Almost all Muslim chronicles describe the superb success of Ala-ud-din's theatrics in this city.

This is Firishta, giving a summary of the overall tenor of Ala-ud-din's march from Kara to Achalpur.

> Ala-ud-din...left Kara-Manikpur on pretence of hunting, and having passed quietly through the territories of many petty rajas, purposely avoided all hostilities, giving out that he had left his uncle, the King, in disgust, and was going to offer his services to the Raja of Rajmundry, one of the rajas of Telangana.... Accordingly, after a march of two months, he arrived without any remarkable opposition at Elichpur.[4]

The more contemporary historical scholar, Dr. R.M. Joshi paints a miniature of Ala-ud-din's mendacious presence in Achalpur.

> Ala-ud-din had disguised his real intentions so adroitly and so well that *the officials at Elichpur did not find it necessary to send fleet messengers to inform Ramachandra Yadava,* the ruler of Devagiri, of these strange intruders from the North.[5] (Emphasis added)

At Achalpur, Ala-ud-din gave his troops a well-deserved rest of two days to recover from the exhaustion of the long march through an arduous terrain.

It was now time to proceed towards the penultimate target, Lasur,[6] a frontier post lying southwest of Devagiri. Just 25 kilometres from the unprepared Sevuna capital.

The route from Achalpur to Lasur led through a mountain pass known as Ghati Lajaura. Ala-ud-din Khalji revealed his true intent the moment he crossed it. At his signal, his holy Islamic warriors did what they knew best—reckless pillage of the region.

News instantly reached the powerful Sevuna feudatory, Kanha. Unlike the lulled chieftain and officials of Achalpur, the moment Kanha saw the Turushka army interloping his territory, he prepared to launch the offensive. In a parallel move, he dispatched messengers to Devagiri informing Ramachandra of the danger so close to the capital.

Now, Ala-ud-din would not only get a personal taste of Kanha's undaunted valour but would experience his seminal humiliation at the hands of two intrepid Hindu women warriors.

'If a Lion Is Brave in a High Degree, Braver Still Is a Lioness!"

The battle of Lasur should have ideally been celebrated in the annals of Indian history for a variety of reasons, but has been tragically forgotten, like countless such instances of glorious Hindu resistance against alien Muslim invasions. Ironically, the laudatory first hand evidence for the Hindu glory in the Battle of Lasur flows from Islamic sources. The chronicler Isami,[7] who vividly and passionately describes the episode in some detail, wrote the account sitting in Devagiri itself.

> When the Turki army approached Lajaura, Kanha drew out his troops...[and] stood right opposite to the Turks and gave battle in the open. Kanha was seized with war-fever....That day, many were killed; the earth was bestrewed with hands, arms and heads. [8]

Throughout his long and difficult march lasting weeks, Ala-ud-din had skilfully manoeuvred his way, keeping eternal caution in mind. He had intentionally avoided the main routes, concealing his movements from various Hindu chiefs controlling these pathways. He had not fought even a single skirmish so far. But now, the ferocity of Kanha's 'war-fever' stunned Ala-ud-din's force of 'Turks who were astonished at the predominance of his army', and were compelled to retreat under the onslaught.

The intrepid Hindu army had repelled the first Turushka charge in an unprecedented fashion.

Figure 18: Artist's impression of a contingent of female Maratha warriors giving a fierce battle to Ala-ud-din Khalji's troops.

Ala-ud-din recouped his clobbered force and directed a renewed assault the next day. However, a special unit of reinforcements had already joined Kanha. It was led by two battle-hardened Maratha women commanders. Isami describes them.

.... two women in that age [era] were highly skilled in war. When they heard that the Turk had gone beyond the limit (i.e., plundering, etc), both came to the aid of Kanha. Each had a large following of troops and each was rancorous in the day of battle. *Verily, if a lion is brave in a high degree, braver still is a lioness in fight....*

Kanha and those two renowned Hindu women made a stiff resistance and fought with the Turks, shedding much [Muslim] blood in that battlefield. At last, after a great struggle, they fell prisoner....When those two sword-wielding smart women fell into the hands of the Turks, they took them to... Ala-ud-din. He was amazed and said: '*In this prosperous country where Hindu women do not turn back from the presence of lion-vanquishers, I know not what calamity would its men bring on us at the time of fighting.*' Then he summoned his army chiefs and recapitulated the story to them saying: 'We have arrived in the country of mortal enemies.... *When women of this country are vanquishers of men, I do not know what kind of demons would the men prove!*'[9] (Emphasis added)

Unfortunately, no other information about these exceptional women is available.

Ala-ud-din's fiery speech to his army officers commending the bravery of these Hindu women-warriors was in part motivation, in part a battlecry and in part a warning not to underestimate the infidels. Next, he induced the lure of plunder: 'We shall occupy the whole Maratha country, we shall seize their wealth and property...in that raid, whatever one acquires would be his, irrespective of the quantity.'[10]

Kanha too, was taken captive. The last infidel obstacle to Devagiri had been demolished.

Asleep at Devagiri

Ramachandradeva was pushing 70 when Ala-ud-din Khalji stormed into his capital. The last Sevuna monarch had enjoyed a fabulous reign lasting a quarter of a century. Like his eminent predecessors, he too, had greatly enriched the Yadava economy and lavished generous patronage to the Arts and was extolled as a prolific temple-builder. But he had also inherited their self destructive trait of waging indiscriminate and avoidable wars with neighbouring Hindu kingdoms. Little did Ramachandra know in the summer of 1296 that Ala-ud-din's raid was the drumbeat that would herald the eventual end of his independence. Ignorance might be dangerous. Wanton complacence is fatal.

The Battle of Devagiri is the Dakshinapatha equivalent of the Second Battle of Tarain. Barely five years after Ala-ud-din's virgin raid on Devagiri, Hindus located in the deepest corners of southern India would get a firsthand taste of the horrors of a Turushka invasion. Hopelessly disunited Hindu kingdoms would be repeatedly scattered by these recurrent incursions. Long-standing empires would be ground to dust. Southern India would lose its freedom for the next 68 years. And Ramachandra had opened the portals, which allowed this brutal march of Turushka terror.

Sufis as Recce Agents

Ala-ud-din's march into Devagiri reflected the same caution and impeccable planning that had characterized his entire expedition so far. He had already sent spies to gauge the feasibility of directly attacking Devagiri, the Sevuna capital.

But beyond these professional spooks, he also received valuable intel from local help: from Sufis settled in the Sevuna dominions. The role that their furtive intelligence played in fine-tuning the strategy of his surprise raid on Devagiri is a little-known and overlooked element in this chapter of Ala-ud-din's military career. In fact, the Sufi element was not unique or restricted to Ala-ud-din Khalji's Devagiri raid. It is a rather conspicuous fixture preceding or anticipating every Islamic invasion of Hindu kingdom.

About a century prior to Ala-ud-din Khalji, Muin-ud-din Chishti had discharged his pious duty of extending Islam's borders in India by inviting Muhammad Ghori to invade infidel Hindustan and unseat Prithviraja Chahamana. Chishthi's famous *dargah* at Ajmer is a standing testimony to his enduring treachery[11] against the very Hindu king who had allowed him to propagate a predatory faith that ultimately claimed him.

The Sufi presence expanded in Northern and Western India almost in direct proportion to the consolidation of the so-called Delhi Sultanate's power. Ever since Muhammad Ghori's victory, the Chishthiya order had become a force to reckon with. Nizamuddin Auliya, Ala-ud-din's contemporary, was now the reigning Sufi of that order. He had groomed exceptional bigots like Amir Khusrau and Nasiruddin Chiragh Dehlavi as his star disciples.

With all the power, influence and resources that royal patronage brings, the Sufis steadily began trickling into various parts of Hindustan yet unconquered by the sword of Islam. By the first decade of the 13th century, Sufis had a marginal presence in the Sevuna territories as well. They professed piety and advertized themselves as recluses and madmen (*Diwanah*). Their whole attire and behaviour was studiedly modelled on the lines of Hindu Sadhus and *Avadhootas*. Over time, they began proselytizing Islam among the unsuspecting and naive Hindu population. The intrinsic spirit of accommodation, inclusivity and tolerance of the Sevuna rulers[12] made their job easier. It was tolerance, unaccompanied by vigilance.

———•··•··•———

Momin Arif Billah Suhrawardi was the earliest notable Sufi[13] to land in Devagiri. But Jalal-ud-din Ganjrawan is widely credited in the Islamic annals as 'the first holy person of the Suhrawardi Sufi order who arrived in Devagir, Deccan...and due to his good endeavours, there was much progress of Islam in the area of Deccan... he [broke] the darkness of infidelity [Hindu Dharma] in the area'.[14] Both Sufis were allowed to freely proselytize in the Yadava dominion. If this folly was not enough, Kanharadeva, the Mahamandaleshwara (governor) of the monarch Ramachandra, granted permission to build a mosque.[15] The distinguished epigraphist and scholar of Sevuna history, Dr. Ritti provides an ominous assessment of the situation:

> *The policy of religious tolerance*, though in itself a commendable one, *hindered the Hindu kings from anticipating the possible dangers behind it.* Much earlier than the armed forces of the Muslim as rulers traversed the Sevuna border, Islamic elements had already infiltrated into the Sevuna country and were practicing their own religion under the patronage of the ruling [Hindu] kings....This

shows that a considerable number of Muslims had already come and settled in the Sevuna country *and it is not impossible that these people were instrumental in apprising Ala-ud-din of the local conditions.*[16] (Emphasis added)

On the broader plane of the history of the Islamic invasions of India, the writer Ram Avatar Singh is blunt about the role played by the Sufis:

Sufis were the advance party or the sappers and miners of invading Muslim armies. Hundreds of persons, in the garb of Sufi saints, swarmed into India and established their hermitages (?)...They posed as a balm to the insulted, humiliated and plundered Hindus. Look at Medieval History and you find numerous Sufis springing up like mushrooms (*kukurmuttas*) everywhere.[17] (Emphasis added)

The inside information about Devagiri supplied by the Sufis, combined with the reports[18] of the recce done by his spies, infused extraordinary confidence in Ala-ud-din Khalji. The reports also told him that Ramachandra's son, Simhana III,[19] a fearsome military commander, had taken[20] the best of the Yadava contingents on an expedition to the Hoysala country. For Ala-ud-din, the time was ripe. He just could not afford to lose the plot. He had travelled so far down from Kara. He had lied to and misled the old Jalal-ud-din about his expedition. Ala-ud-din's original plan was to finish the *Dakkhan* campaign in about two months, and two months had already expired. If he did not plunder the substantial Sevuna booty *now*, assured death was awaiting his return to north India.

And now, to his joy, Devagiri was exposed and defenceless, and even better, Ramachandra seemed happily asleep. When bad news slapped him awake, it was too late.

———•••••———

Nothing better illustrates the extent of Ramachandra's stupor than the magnificent Devagiri fort itself. At the turn of the 6th century CE, Devagiri had emerged as an important upland town lying along the *Sartha* (Caravan) route that connected Western and Southern India. It took its name from Shiva[21] who was believed to reside in the hills enclosing the formidable Sahyadris. Hence, 'Devagiri', or mountains of the Devas.

Ramachandra's ancestor, the first Sevuna monarch, Bhillama V, had built the impregnable, triangular Devagiri fort in 1187. It stood on a conical hill about 640 feet high. Even after more than a millennium, it is still a breathtaking sight to behold, an ageless monument to the Sevuna genius that fused the raw strength of nature, military strategy, political foresight and architectural prowess into a citadel that exuded invincibility. The brain-spinning steep ascent and its nature-gifted altitude ensured that it required minimal supplementary manmade defences. The Yadavas compounded this toughness by building a narrow bridge on which only two people could walk abreast at a time. This bridge was the only path to reach the summit. A complex maze[22] comprising entrances, curved walls, false doors, bastions, massive palisades, trapdoors and gates were built to confuse the enemy who dared to actually enter the fort from its only entrance and exit. A large moat measuring 50 feet in depth encircled it.

Figure 19: Artist's impression of the medieval Devagiri Fort.

The city that had been built around the Devagiri citadel was known as Kataka,[23] a Sanskrit term that variously means city, cantonment, zone, army camp, royal camp, etc. During the Sevuna era, both the city and the fort were often denoted[24] using a compound word: *Kataka-Devagiri.* The glowing descriptions of Devagiri's splendour, its copious prosperity and its overflowing material abundance that Muslim chroniclers have described are descriptions of the city of Kataka.

For 110 uninterrupted years, no Yadava enemy had come anywhere close to the vicinity of Devagiri, deterred by its impregnability. But towards the blighted end of Ramachandradeva's reign, the impregnability had been taken for granted.

Ramachandra was in Kataka when Ala-ud-din launched his lightning assault. Stunned at the surprise attack and the swiftness of the Turushka army, he assembled a hotchpotch fighting force of 4,000, comprising both soldiers and untrained 'citizens and domestics'[25] and gave an impressive combat at a distance of 2 *Kos* (about 7 kilometres). Both sides knew that he was destined to lose. Choosing discretion over valour, Ramachandra locked himself up inside the fort. Much to Ala-ud-din's delight. The impregnable fort now presented him a delicious opportunity. Its moat[26] was dry. It had only a token garrison. Provisions were dangerously low inside the fort. Before decamping to the citadel, Ramachandra had seized a large number of sacks in a desperate bid and stored them in the fort. Ala-ud-din clearly understood the twin advantages he now possessed. The first was the practical, physical advantage: Kataka was totally defenceless. The second was the psychological advantage: he had Ramachandra boxed inside the fort and his predatory instinct told him that it was just a matter of *when* and not *if* the old infidel king would surrender.

Ala-ud-din decided to exploit both advantages to the hilt. He launched two operations simultaneously.

In the first, he laid siege to the fort and issued an audacious bluff to Ramachandra: you are mistaken if you think that I have come alone. This is just the advance party. A larger troop of

20,000 is closely following me. It should arrive soon. You stand no chance.

The second was the ubiquitous blueprint that characterizes every episode of Islamic aggressions in infidel Hindustan: Ala-ud-din unchained his wolfish troops upon the helpless and undefended Kataka. The ravaging was thorough. Every single home was looted and completely stripped of anything that had value. Merchants, Brahmanas and elites of Kataka were rounded up like beasts and mercilessly tortured to elicit information about their wealth. The fabulous stories of the splendour of Devagiri still spinning inside the looters' brains only enhanced the severity of the torture. What befell the ill-fated Kataka and its cornered infidels is described with violent relish by all Muslim chroniclers. Isami stands at the forefront of this bigoted exultation in the remorseless torment and wanton plunder of these innocent Hindu citizens.

> In every house there were heaps of jewels and enormous quantity of silver and gold. From everywhere, they seized bales of precious clothes and stores of perfumes; from every street they collected enormous gold, many treasures free from dragon guards, numerous attractive vessels and countless valuables—all of these were seized in Deogir.[27] The experienced soldiers laid hands on so much booty that they could hardly count it in their whole lifetime. With such a plunder, the Turks enriched themselves to such an extent that it seemed they were in paradise with houris.

Apart from bagging all this plunder, the recurrent theme of *houris* also forms a powerful motivation in the annals of Islamic Jihad in India and elsewhere. As we have seen in Book 1 of *Invaders and Infidels* and in the earlier chapters of this work, each victorious Jihad was invariably followed by a large-scale ravishing of infidel women. Isami dips his pen in the ink of depraved erotica to describe the raped infidel women of Kataka.

> When Kataka...was conquered and...fell into the hands of the Turks, many girls—angel-enticing in beauty, all tumid and smart,

full of grace and exceedingly charming, each with a well-shaped body and tight loins and bendable silvery legs which eclipsed silver itself, adorned with jewels from head to foot and hunting with enchanting eyes the hearts of men, as deer-like womenfolk— made the lion-like Turks captive; and barring them, I have never seen any deer capturing a lion. *All these charming idols [women and girls], clothed in bejewelled clothes studded with precious pearls, fell booty to the Turks.*[28] (Emphasis added)

Aside from this prodigious loot, Ala-ud-din captured about 40 elephants and 1,000 horses belonging to the infidel king.

Ramachandra withstood the siege for an entire week but ultimately understood that prolonging the stalemate would only hasten the inevitable. The deck was hopelessly stacked against him. Provisions were on the brink. He neither had a sufficient fighting force nor arsenal to boast of, and he had been convinced of Ala-ud-din's crafty bluff of reinforcements coming from Delhi. Two or three days later, he sent messengers to Ala-ud-din seeking truce. His letter was laced with threats for good measure: your invasion of this country was imprudent and reckless. Fortunately for you, you found the city unguarded, and you have been allowed to pillage at large. However, it is possible that the Rajas of the Deccan, who command innumerable armies, may yet encircle you, and not permit even *one* of your people to return from our dominions alive. Even in the improbable event that you're able to safely retreat, remember that you'll have to contend with the princes of Malwa, Khandesh, and Gondwana on your return journey. Each of them have armies of 40,000 or 50,000. Do you really think you can fight them all alone and survive? Also remember that my lion-like son Simhana has already received the news of your impudence and is marching here with a force three times larger than yours. Prudence dictates that you leave my city before he arrives. But I will be generous and offer you favourable terms for a truce. Take a liberal sum from me and keep the loot you have already plundered. That should indemnify your expedition.

The veiled threat-cum-truce worked. Ala-ud-din Khalji opted for prudence yet again. At no point did he forget that he had gambled everything to make this expedition a grand success, and the slightest slip-up could prove fatal. Ramachandra gave him fifty *maunds*[29] of gold and a large quantity of pearls and jewels. He also retained the 40 elephants and 1,000 horses that he had seized. He promised to release all the prisoners of war and depart from Devagiri after a fortnight.

Suddenly, the whole thing fell apart.

Snatching Defeat from the Jaws of Victory

Even as the armistice had been concluded, Singhana had returned at whirlwind speed and was now encamped about three *Kos* outside Devagiri. Ramachandra had not exaggerated the enormity of his son's army. Isami gives a fantastic number: 'That son of [Ramachandra] had with himself strong Hindu forces, all swordsmen and lancers—500,000 infantry and 10,000 cavalry along with 60 ferocious dragon capturers.'

Isami clearly exaggerates the number to glorify the event that followed. However, it is unambiguous that Singhana's force was substantial enough to unnerve Ala-ud-din. Ramachandra sent a message to his son informing him that a truce had been concluded and it would be best to comply with the terms. He was categorical: 'Abstain from molesting the Mahomedans',[30] who are an 'enterprising and war-like race, with whom peace was better than war'.[31] Singhana boiled with rage when he read the letter. His own father was asking him to tread the path of cowards. Accepting Ala-ud-din's terms meant accepting humiliation, accepting defeat. Without pummelling this unclean Turushka interloper who had savaged Kataka and defiled its inhabitants so horribly. Disregarding his father's counsel, Singhana sent his own messengers to Ala-ud-din. His swarthy threat was real: this is your last chance to escape from the whirlpool you've sunk yourself into. Return everything you've looted from us and go back to the north. I will guarantee your safety. The message hit Ala-ud-din like a slap. It was an audacious mockery of the brilliant success he had just wrung out of Ramachandra. He decided that brutal action, and not prudence, was the correct course. Ala-ud-din Khalji seized Singhana's messengers, had their faces blackened with soot and then had them paraded among the ranks of his soldiers. When the humiliation was complete, he literally had them 'booted out of his camp'.[32] With this, Ala-ud-din had set a precedent of dishonour, indecency and crassness, which he repeated on countless occasions later in his career. Until now, it was considered indecent and undignified to insult emissaries either through word or deed.[33] But searing ambition had overpowered even the very notion of dignity in Ala-ud-din.

Next, Ala-udin ordered Malik Nusrat to sustain the siege of the Devagiri fort with a force comprising a 1,000 horse. With the rest of his contingent, he headed the march against the bristling Singhana. The Sevuna army infused deathly terror in the Turushkas and 'overpowered, [they] fell back on all sides'.[34] It was an uneven contest, one which Ala-ud-din was clearly destined to lose. Witnessing these terrible reverses on the battlefield, runners sped to Malik Nusrat and briefed him about the ongoing calamity. Nusrat prioritized on the spot. The fort was no longer important, his own master was, and he raced to his rescue. This momentous decision altered things completely, to the lasting misfortune of the Sevuna Empire. The massive cloud of dust that arose in the wake of the clopping hoofs of a 1,000 horses led by Nusrat misted Singhana's judgement. He thought this was the 20,000 Delhi troops that Ala-ud-din had threatened Ramachandra with. Singhana panicked, and his troops followed suit, scattering and fleeing from the field. However, Ala-ud-din had kept his wits intact throughout. He grasped the futility of pursuing the enemy as well the renewed fortune the retreat presented him with.

Singhana had plucked defeat from the jaws of victory owing to two major factors. Had he accepted his father's original plan to adhere to the settled truce, the course of the history of south India might have been entirely different. But the outcomes of historical events can only be analysed in hindsight because history is not preordained. The Sevuna Empire might have lived to fight another day. But Singhana exhibited a marked trait of most Hindu rulers of early medieval India and onwards: heedlessness. While he was justly confident in the superiority of his forces—both in numbers and valour—he failed to recognize the wisdom in his father's insistence on truce. And then, in the thick of extremely bloody fighting on the battlefield, his nerves had collapsed on sighting an enormous cloud of dust—a commonplace occurrence in wars fought in that era—and believed Ala-ud-din's sly rumour as truth. Dr. Ritti correctly analyses the penultimate Act of the Sevuna Greek tragedy:

> After all, the Muslim forces were in no way superior to the Hindu army and... had proved their superiority of strength when they pushed back the Muslim(s)....In fact, each Hindu king was competent to combat the Muslim army had he a little fore-thought.[35]

The Yadava Empire paid a grave price for this fatal combination of neglect, overconfidence and imprudence.

———— ·· ◆ ·· ◆ ————

Now, Ala-ud-din began rubbing salt and chilli deep into the open wound of the Sevuna empire. The siege this time was more intense. Each day, he brought before the Devagiri fort scores of imprisoned Brahmanas and respectable merchants who were fettered in chains. He then disgraced them even more thoroughly before slaughtering them in full view of the old Yadava monarch. When this didn't work, he paraded Ramachandra's relatives and kin and nobles, customarily bound up in heavy iron chains. A dire warning. It will be their turn next. But he never spoke of a truce. His psychological suzerainty over Ramachandradeva was absolute.

To Ramachandra, a veteran of countless wars, this sort of treatment was not only unfamiliar and unprecedented, it symbolized everything that was abhorrent to *Yuddha-Dharma*, the Hindu ethics of war. Notwithstanding his prior hostilities, he sent anxious feelers to the neighbouring Hindu kings at Gulbarga, Telangana, Malwa and Khandesh but received no response. Their cold apathy was the price of the prolonged sins of waging unnecessary wars against them. Nor were the Yadavas alone in this senselessness, as we have already seen. It was at this point that Ramachandra discovered that the sacks he had seized earlier contained salt, not food grain. That shattered even his last hope: he could no longer wait for the faint prospect of external aid perchance it arrived. Devagiri would starve to death.

More than anybody else, Ala-ud-din Khalji knew it.

And so, when Ramachandra opened his second round of negotiations, Ala-ud-din adamantly refused to even acknowledge it. But the old king persisted and sent his envoys. The Turushka feigned to engage with him, toyed with their messages until they finally confessed the truth he had instinctively known: we are on the verge of starvation, state your terms, our king is ready to accept them. And once more, Ala-ud-din's steely patience had won. He had out-waited the infidel and quagmired him to admit his helplessness. Firishta describes Ramachandra's piteous situation:

> [Ramachandra] with much presence of mind, commanded the circumstance to be kept secret from the troops, and opened a second negotiation with Ala-ud-din. 'It must be known to you,' he said, 'that I had no hand in the late quarrel. If my son, owing to the folly and petulance of youth, has broken the conditions between us, that event ought not to render me responsible for his rashness.' Ramachandra authorized his ambassador privately to accede to any terms rather than protract the siege.[36]

The pound of indemnity that Ala-ud-din extracted in the second round was truly prodigious. Every Islamic chronicler lapses into raptures describing the loot. Here is Firishta again, giving hard numbers.

Ala-ud-din on evacuating the country [received] 600 *maunds* of pearls, 2 *maunds* of diamonds, rubies, emeralds and sapphires,

1,000 mounds of silver, 4,000 pieces of silk, besides a long list of
other precious commodities to which reason forbids us to give
credit.

While Barani gives no numbers, his description of the magnitude
of Ala-ud-din's plunder is similar: 'Ala-ud-din brought so much
wealth from [Devagiri] that despite the squandering of it by his
successors much of it remained till the time[37] of Firoz Tughlaq.'[38]

Here is Nizamuddin Ahmad commenting on the mind
boggling amount of Ala-ud-din's loot: '....so much booty was
obtained, consisting of gold and silver, and gems and pearls, and
various kinds of goods and fabrics, as was beyond the count and
estimation of the intellect.'[39]

The arch-flatterer Amir Khusrau is unstoppable in his lusty
exultation of Ala-ud-din's monumental booty.

> Such was his fortune, that even at the time when he was an *amir,*
> he became a Solomon in the country of Deogir (Demon-land).
> The demon (Deo) became so submissive in the land of Jamshed,
> that Ram Deo's country was ravaged and the Rai himself was first
> captured and then set free. Fate placed in Ala-ud-din's hands...the
> treasure of the whole world—innumerable elephants and more
> precious stones than could be carried by a hundred camels....
>
> Were I to attempt to recount[40] the plunder of jewels and gold
> no measure or balance would suffice, for the treasure had been
> accumulated by the Raid from old. Camels and mules were laden
> with rubies and diamonds, and every kind of precious stone, and
> the most experienced jewellers were unable even to guess their
> value, and who can tell of the heaps of amber and the costly silks?
> He returned victorious with this booty in order to accomplish
> new conquests.[41]

A noble in the Khalji court noted[42] how this loot was sufficient to
lay the foundation for seven kingdoms.

In his ardour to eulogize his master, Isami goes overboard in
mythologizing Ala-ud-din. He invents the fiction wherein 'Ram
Deo' gives his daughter named Jhatiapali in marriage to this
Turushka raider. She was given 'along with a parasol profusely
bejewelled and studded with precious pearls in such abundance

that the clerks could hardly write them out in the course of a 100 years'.[43] In the fevered world of Isami's imagination, 'Ram Deo' actually considered it an honour because, 'O generous chief! My life is a gift of yours. Would that my head, as long as I wear it, be at your feet!' K.S. Lal debunks[44] the fiction by marshalling an impressive wealth of historical evidence.

Material booty apart, Ala-ud-din inflicted another penalty on Ramachandradeva. Henceforth, the Sevuna annual revenue from the Achalpur province had to be deposited into the treasury of Kara. As we shall see, this condition too, characterized Ala-ud-din's insatiable lust for loot and marked his settled policy of splurging money to buy and sustain political power.

————— ·· • · · •—

Ala-ud-din Khalji left Devagiri after 25 days. He released all the prisoners and marched northwards with the sort of wealth that even Sultan Jalal-ud-din Khalji could not dream of. He had marched into Devagiri with trepidation and hope and had exited with triumph and aplomb. Briggs, the translator of Firishta, sums up Ala-ud-din's daring Deccan raid with undisguised admiration:

....in the long volumes of history, there is scarcely any thing to be compared with this exploit, whether we regard the resolution in forming the plan, the boldness of its execution, or the great good fortune which attended its accomplishment.[45]

Ala-ud-din had reduced Ramachandradeva, the proud Sevuna monarch, to the pathetic plight of a tributary. The primary and only goal of the Turushka's maiden raid of Devagiri was plunder, not territorial conquest. Thus, Ramachandradeva had retained a quasi-independent status after Ala-ud-din's departure. But even that status would be short-lived because the old monarch had learned nothing from this humiliating debasement.

Elsewhere, another old monarch seated in Delhi, would soon meet a much worse fate.

————— ·· • · · •—

CHAPTER 8

A Honey-Dipped Invitation to Death

Do not thy enemy as insignificant despise!
For a mountain is made up of stones of small size!

When fate its dark face on a man doth turn
No one can help and succour him

Jalal-ud-din Khalji was in Gwalior on a hunting expedition when news of his nephew's audacious success in Devagiri reached him. He had left for Gwalior roughly around the same time as Ala-ud-din had journeyed towards Devagiri. Until he received this news, the old sultan had gullibly believed the spurious reports that Malik Ala-ul-Mulk had been feeding him from Kara regarding Ala-ud-din's whereabouts. Convinced that all was well in his realm, Jalal-ud-din had spent his time building random mosques and cupolas[1] for securing an honourable place in Allah's unseen realm. At other times, he was partying and composing self-laudatory verses.

I whose footsteps rub the head of heaven,
How can a heap of stone and earth augment my dignity?
Those broken stones with water I have thus arranged,
Some broken heart may find repose there.

Consistent with his highly deluded temperament after becoming sultan, Jalal-ud-din was compelled to seek validation from his flatterers-cum-companions. He summoned Malik Sayid Muntaki and Raja Ali and asked them: 'Is there any defect in this quatrain?' They lost no time replying that it was one of the finest they had ever heard. The sultan smiled and said, 'You say this to humour me

but I will show you its defect by composing two more couplets.'
This is how the *Rubaiayat* read:

> Perchance some traveller may pass this spot
> Whose tattered garment is the satin mantle of the sky;
> Perchance from the felicity of his breath or auspicious footsteps
> One atom may fall to my lot: this will suffice me.

———————————

Jalal-ud-din's first reaction when he heard the news of his nephew's
triumph was one of rapture, 'for, in the simplicity of his heart
he thought that whatsoever his nephew had captured, he would
joyfully bring to him'.[2] Recent experience was the surest proof
of this—just three years ago, Ala-ud-din had dutifully poured
the vast treasures that he had plundered from Bhilsa before the
sultan's luminous feet. It would be no different this time. Jalal-ud-
din immediately organized drinking parties with his courtiers to
celebrate the success of his nephew who had punished the infidels
of the 'Mahratta land' so thoroughly. Till now, 'no Musulman
king or prince had penetrated so far'.

The actual details began tumbling out soon enough.

The booty that Ala-ud-din had captured from Devagiri far
exceeded the wealth that any sultan of Delhi had possessed so
far. Mouth-watering descriptions of pearls, sapphires, emeralds,
rubies, diamonds, gold, precious stones, silk and expensive
garments streamed into Gwalior with frequent urgency.
Exaggeration exceeded itself. As he listened to them, the old
sultan's dreamy greed and salivating anticipation heightened to a
feverish pitch: 'the king, delighted with this news, reckoned upon
the spoil as if already in his own treasury'.[3]

It was at this point that his seasoned confidants, advisers and
genuine well-wishers alerted him to the darker side. Malik Ala-ud-
din Khalji ventured on this reckless and hazardous expedition by
lying to you, the sultan, by acting without your authority. But it has
already gotten even worse, they said: Ala-ud-din is travelling directly
to his safe haven, Kara, instead of coming to see you first. Also

remember, Your Highness, that Ala-ud-din has 'suffered much at the hands of *Malika-i-Jahan,* the consort of the sultan, and also from his own wife…always nursing in his breast sinister intentions. Now…he is in a position perfectly to put his rebellious ideas into execution.'[4]

They were perfectly correct.

——————

Ala-ud-din Khalji's decision to flagrantly bypass the sultan was an integral part of his original plan of capturing the throne of Delhi. Kara was just the penultimate stepping-stone. The flight back to Kara mirrored Ala-ud-din's earlier tactic of studiously avoiding Hindu kingdoms en route to his raid of Devagiri. Some details of his return journey to Kara open several vistas into both the history of Islamic invasions in India and the nature of the Hindu responses to these.

Flushed with the gargantuan loot of Devagiri, Ala-ud-din now opted for a more direct approach. His first port of call was the ill-fated fort of Asirgarh. He had no intention of capturing it. The idea was to send an unambiguous message to the infidels lording over the place. But the path to Asirgarh's assault was oiled by the shocking inaction of Ramachandra. It was one thing to accept a humiliating treaty dictated by this vile Turushka trespasser but entirely a different order of apathy, not to cut off his retreat on a route densely populated by powerful Hindu kingdoms. Indeed, this was the same Ramachandra who had intimidated Ala-ud-din by reminding him of the powerful Hindu kings who each had standing armies of 40,000–50,000 soldiers. A.S. Altekar offers perhaps the best analysis of this suicidal Hindu psyche.

Ala-ud-din's raid [of Devagiri] was no doubt a daring exploit… [but] it reflects little credit on the efficiency of the Yadava administration that it should not have anticipated the danger of a Muslim attack from the north and strongly garrisoned the Vindhyan passes; the capital lay open without any adequate defence. *That Ala-ud-Din's retreat should not have been cut off, and that no effort should have been made to retrieve the disaster at Devagiri by surrounding and destroying the army on its return* through little known passes and forests would seem to prove that *the Yadava leadership was completely demoralized, and its forces confused and discouraged.*[5] (Emphasis added)

Asirgarh's Maiden Molestation at Turushka Hands

As we have noted earlier,[6] the Asirgarh Fort commanded a formidable military gateway to Dakshinapatha, a natural pass linking the Narmada and Tapti Valleys in the Satpura Range. The fort finds a mention in the Mahabharata as the shrine where Ashvatthama offered flowers to Shiva everyday during his Puja. This is the Gupteshwar Mahadev Mandir, which still stands at the site.

The wreckage of the ages has not dented the majestic beauty of the Asirgarh fort, which remains a huge draw for tourists, pilgrims, history buffs and researchers. It consists of three distinct lines of muniments. The uppermost is the Asirgarh proper, its greatest extent measuring 1,005 metres in length and 600 in width running from north to south. The second highest fortification that lies below this is known as Kamargarh and the last is called Malaigarh. The main pathway leading into the fort is located on the southwesterly side, passing through five gateways by a steep climb on stone steps.

Figure 20: View of the Asirgarh Fort from Burhanpur, circa 1856.
Image Source: *Wikimedia Commons.*

Asirgarh was under the control of the Chahamana branch of a Rajput[7] chieftain when Ala-ud-din blasted into it en route to Kara and slaughtered its entire garrison manned by infidels. Its first encounter with the Turushka invader resulted in a 400 year-long loss of independence until it was wrested back by Peshwa Baji Rao in 1760. Akbar's signal victory over Dakshinapatha was, in a way, accomplished after a back-breaking siege of Asirgarh lasting nine months.

⸻ ·•·•· ⸻

Barring Asirgarh, Ala-ud-din did not attack any other infidel kingdom on his return journey, and finally reached Kara on 2 June 1296. He had given himself two months at most, to finish the stealthy adventure but it had actually taken him four. Of these, he had spent almost an entire month encamped in Devagiri. Things could have gone horribly wrong in his fief at Kara at any point in this interim. But now, to his unbelievable luck, Ala-ud-din had returned almost exactly at the dawn of monsoon. Even climatically, the campaign had been a tremendous success: he had left just after the chilly winter had thawed and returned before the tyrannical monsoon began.

But the most critical reason for directly heading to Kara was the confirmed intelligence that news of his Devagiri plunder had already been leaked to Jalal-ud-din Khalji. Ala-ud-din secretly dreaded the cutthroat politics of the sultan's scheming and treacherous courtiers and amirs and maliks, both in Delhi and Kara. After all, Malik Chhajju had sounded the first bugle of revolt right here at Kara. Besides, there had been absolutely no correspondence between Ala-ud-din and the sultan throughout these four months and the nephew was unsure how the old, volatile monarch would react to his success. Staying obstinately in Kara allowed Ala-ud-din to play to his strengths. It was already his stronghold, and the enormous plunder that he had brought from Devagiri would ensure that the loyalty of the old Balbani opportunists would stick like glue. Kara would also give him the time and mental space to outmanoeuvre the sultan by playing a lethal game of cat and mouse. The finely-honed unscrupulous instincts of Ala-ud-din told him that if he faltered even slightly, the roles would be immediately reversed.

As the first step, Ala-ud-din wrote a sugary epistle to Jalal-ud-din Khalji swearing his undying loyalty to the sultan and his unswerving love for his uncle.

At Gwalior, doubt and caution surfaced in the sultan's mind after the hangover of the endless partying had lifted.

Jalal-ud-din's initial delight had slowly transformed into alarm. His nephew's brilliant feat, and the monumental scale of his loot was no doubt impressive but it was also disturbing. What really nagged him was the sheer brazenness of the whole affair. The unsanctioned raid. The lying. The deceit. The concealment. The long disappearance. And now, the direct flight to Kara.

The sultan convened a council of his most intimate maliks in a secret consultation chamber. The assembly included Malik Fakhruddin Kuchi, Malik Kamaluddin Abul Maali, Malik Nasiruddin Kuhrami, and the ever-reliable Malik Ahmad Chhap.

'Advice me', he said, 'what I should do with this new Ala-ud-din? Should I wait here and command him to my august Presence? Should I intercept him somewhere near Kara? Should I go back to Delhi?'

The first and the sincerest advice emanated again, from the *Naib Barbak,* Ahmad Chhap, who was also the sultan's sister's son. Perhaps, his only genuine confidant, 'loyal to the backbone', the one who stood by Jalal-ud-din till the gruesome finale. As on prior occasions, Malik Chhap was brutal in his truth-telling.

Elephants and wealth when held in great abundance are the cause of much strife. Whoever acquires them becomes so intoxicated that he does not know his hands from his feet. Success in one's undertakings and the accomplishment of one's desires become the cause of pride and rebellion; and makes a man, however intelligent and wise, drunk and mad. The cheats and deluders of Karah who carried Malik Chhaju off from the path of loyalty, are now all assembled round Ala-ud-din, and they incited him to go to Deogir without the Sultan's orders. He has gone into a foreign land without permission, has fought battles and won treasure. The wise have said 'Money and strife; strife and money'—the two things are allied to each other. Who knows what he has in his heart? It would be wisest for the Sultan to go with all haste to Chanderi. When Ala-ud-din hears that the Sultan is so near, he will not be able to complete his arrangements, and will be forced to come and pay his homage to the Sultan, and place the booty before the throne, either willingly or otherwise. This will enable the Sultan to discover Ala-ud-din's true designs. Upon the appearance of the imperial army, it is highly probable that the troops of Ala-ud-din, laden with spoil, would not hazard the loss of it by making war, but would rather endeavour to secure their wealth. Thus, by these means, Ala-ud-din, if he meditated revolt, would be deserted by the greatest part of his small army, which would oblige him to abandon whatever plans he might have. After this, the Sultan should take his silver and gold, jewels and pearls, elephants and horses, and leave the other booty to him and his soldiers. His territories also should be increased, and he should be carried in honour to Delhi. If the Sultan considers this an insignificant matter and marches to Delhi without taking the proper measures, the Sultan will have, in a manner, endeavoured to bring about his own destruction, and the ruin and desolation of his house.[8]

The Dhritarashtra within Jalal-ud-din immediately resurfaced at Chhap's sane advice-cum-fatal prophecy. Like the proverbial moth to the seductive flame, the old sultan who was 'in the grasp of his evil angel, heeded not the advice of Ahmad Chhap'.[9] Instead, he chided him, 'what have I done to Ala-ud-din that he should turn away from me, and not present his spoils? For, is he not my protege and my foster child? He can never harbour any evil designs against me.' The intent and sentiment behind the rebuke became clear to the other confidants. The sultan was not seeking advice, but *approval* for his blindness. But who knew?

Perhaps, Ala-ud-din might actually surrender the prolific booty. The oily Malik Fakhruddin Kuchi—the Kotwal of Delhi—toyed with the old man's mind. Every Muslim chronicler heaps outright contempt for Fakhruddin, describing him as untrustworthy, 'a concealer', 'a bad man' and 'cunning'. Fakhruddin knew that Ahmad Chhap had not only uttered the truth but was sincerely concerned for the sultan's safety. Yet, he gave the exact opposite counsel:

> No responsible person on whose word full reliance can be placed has come to the Sultan from Ala-ud-din's camp. It is not certain whether the rumours are false or true. There is a famous maxim that 'socks should not be doffed till water be sighted'. If we march with an army and intercept him, his men would be frightened to hear of the arrival of the Imperial army, and would run away and hide in the jungle and all the treasure that he is bringing would be lost. We should keep a force in readiness, and until we find anybody refractory, it is not justified to march against him. The month of Ramzan is approaching and melons as sweet as sugar-candy have arrived in Delhi. It appears correct to me that Your Majesty should return to Delhi with your army and pass the holy month of Ramzan there.[10]

Music to the sultan's ears.

K.S. Lal correctly observes how the 'last two sentences of Fakhruddin Kuchi specially stand out as a proof of his cunning'.[11] Fakhruddin Kuchi had cynically manipulated Jalal-ud-din's newfound aggressive piety for Islam. But the intrepid Ahmad Chhap would not be silenced. He lambasted Fakhruddin's insincere advice in harsh language.

> The time passes even as we sit here. Oh, Shame! Men like you, Fakhruddin, who know better should not have the courage to give honest counsel when required to do so. If Malik Ala-ud-din departs from Karah with his numerous elephants and vast treasure, and crossing the Sarayu goes toward Lakhnauti, no one will then be able to do anything against him.[12]

Chhap's fury also elicited a couplet from him:

> Do not thy enemy as insignificant despise!
> For a mountain is made up of stones of small size!

And once more, the outburst had the opposite outcome. Jalal-ud-din was furious with this lone and dogged dissenter.

> Malik Ahmad Chhap has always had an evil opinion of Malik Alauddin. But such private rancour shall have no weight with us. I have cradled Ala-ud-din in my arms and have made him my son. It is possible that one of my own sons should turn against me but that Ala-ud-din should turn away his face from me, that is absolutely impossible.[13]

Avarice had blinded the old sultan by cloaking itself as filial emotion. And Malik Chhap had had enough. Matching fury with fury, he stood up and recited another couplet.

> When fate its dark face on a man doth turn,
> No one can help and succour him at all.[14]

And before he stormed out of the council, Chhap clapped his palms loudly and directly challenged the sultan: 'If the Sultan returns alive to Delhi from Kara, he may slay us with his own hands!'[15]

Nizamuddin Ahmad, author of the *Tabaqat-i-Akbari* pens an emotional verse extolling the unflinching loyalty of Malik Ahmad Chhap.

> He bringeth joy, and gladness, to the hearts of his foes,
> Who listeneth not to the words of his true and loyal friends.[16]

Jalal-ud-din Khalji commended Fakhruddin's 'wisdom' and returned to Delhi. A few days later, Ala-ud-din's epistle reached him. It was a honeyed invitation to his own death.

--- · ·· · ·· · ---

CHAPTER 9

Jalal-ud-din Khalji's Fatal Ramzan

The destroying angel was close behind the Sultan,
he had no apprehension, and would listen to no advice.

When one to whom advice of a friend will not attend,
The gods above will penalty award.

Ala-ud-din's epistle read as follows:

I have brought the magnificent booty obtained in my recent expedition: 31 elephants, a number of horses, and quantities of gold and gems and pearls, and all kinds of goods and fabrics, and I wish to bring it all before your Presence. But I am scared. I went on the expedition without your orders and I have been absent for a long time. The march has been long and tedious and I needed repose at Kara.

Now, a frightening fancy has seized my brain and the brains of all your servants who are with me. I am nothing but the Benevolent Emperor's humble slave and son. I had intended to present myself at His Majesty's august court, but you know as well as I do of the vile enemies I have there. In my absence, those villains might have defamed my character and poisoned your ears with the intent of depriving me of His Majesty's abiding favour. If His Majesty issues a *Farman* which will give me and my companions some assurance of our safety, we would present ourselves at your gate without any anxiety about ourselves and this slave will happily present the full booty of elephants and horses and treasures at your feet and bestow upon myself the honour of kissing the foot of Thy imperial throne.[1]

The message unerringly found its target as he had known it would. Trounced by avarice and slobbering at the prospect of Ala-ud-din's arrival with the plunder, the sultan was only glad to grant the *Farman*.

At Kara, Ala-ud-din had already dispatched his trusted aide, Zafar Khan eastwards to initiate an invasion of Lakhnauti, the capital of Gaur. Zafar Khan's task was to arrange a well-armed and fully-equipped flotilla, which would cross the Sarayu river at Avadh, and then enter Bengal. This was Ala-ud-din's Plan B in case Jalal-ud-din didn't trust his deceit-laden letter and decided to march against him. If that happened, Ala-ud-din would immediately decamp with his entire booty and establish his own sultanate at Lakhnauti. He was confident that Jalal-ud-din would be powerless to follow him there.

Given the tense political climate, it didn't take long for his Plan B to leak and flow all the way to Delhi. Incredibly, except Jalal-ud-din, almost every courtier and malik and amir was fully aware of the deadly game Ala-ud-din was playing. And so, when they read the syrupy letter that he had sent, it was clear that he was luring the sultan to his doom. But none could summon the guts to caution the 'foolish sultan for fear of receiving an unjust treatment at his hands'.[2]

By writing the *Farman* in his own handwriting, Sultan Jalal-ud-din had essentially signed his death warrant. Two confidential messengers named Imadu-l-Mulk and Zia-ud-din took it to Ala-ud-din. But the reception they received at his hands in Kara confirmed the worst truths about the palace gossip in Delhi. Zia-ud-din Barani writes how 'they saw that all was in vain, for Ala-ud-din and all his army were alienated from the Sultan'.[3] Ala-ud-din had already prepared the 'dish of death for the Sultan'[4] and was merely waiting for an opportune moment to serve it. Jalal-ud-din's messengers were not allowed to return. Ala-ud-din put them under house arrest and posted intimidating sentries to guard them so closely that 'not even a bird should be able to flap its wings near them'.[5] As he had done during his renewed siege of the Devagiri fort, Ala-ud-din deliberately kept the sultan in a state of agonizing suspense. For days, he didn't send a reply. Finally, when he did send it, it was addressed to Almas Beg, his younger brother, and another son-in-law of Jalal-ud-din.

Almas Beg was a co-conspirator who would lead Jalal-ud-din to his peril with his kindly tongue.

This letter was a more intense version of the previous epistle of perfidy. Ala-ud-din wrote that he had received His Majesty's kind correspondence but,

'I am still fearful. I have earned great notoriety at Kara for being a traitor. Men of experience in worldly affairs tell me that His Majesty has decided to take my life for undertaking the Devagiri raid without his authorisation. This loyal slave sincerely repents for his rash action thereby earning the Sultan's displeasure, which to him is worse than death. My sorrow grows daily, and there is only one way to overcome it. I carry a poisoned handkerchief with me at all times, and when I can no longer bear my grief, I will sniff it and end the whole accursed affair. Or maybe I will quietly renounce everything and become a wanderer and lose myself forever. But the Sultan, if he is really forgiving, can allay this loyal slave's fear. If his magnanimous heart permits it, he should favour this slave by coming to Kara, take my hand and comfort me and lead this sinner to Delhi.'[6]

When Almas Beg showed the letter to Jalal-ud-din, the sultan was overcome with intense feeling. Jalal-ud-din completely trusted Almas Beg, who further enticed the sultan: 'People frighten my brother, and I am afraid that in his shame and fear of your majesty, he will poison or drown himself. If the Sultan would travel *Jarida*—with only a small retinue—and meet Ala-ud-din, he would feel reassured.'[6] And then, Beg rubbed it in, 'if not, Ala-ud-din would take poison or maybe he would march forth with his elephants and treasures to seek his fortune elsewhere in this wide world'. The last bait did the trick. As Firishta writes, the sultan, 'infatuated by greed, conceived that the final possession of the treasure depended on the preservation of his nephew's life',[7] and gave his ultimate order to Almas Beg: go to Kara now. Stop your brother from undertaking any reckless action. Comfort him. I will follow you as soon as possible.

Almas Beg climbed into a boat, and in the pouring monsoon that had just set in, travelled 'as swiftly as wind on water',[8] and reached Kara after seven days.

Ala-ud-din welcomed his brother warmly and ordered drums of joy to be beaten throughout the city. After much feasting and partying, Ala-ud-din declared that it was time to invade Lakhnauti. But the coterie of power-hungry opportunists and schemers told him that that would be unnecessary now. The fact that Sultan Jalal-ud-din has sent Almas Beg here was the clear indication of his irresistible desire for his nephew's elephants and treasures. They predicted that the sultan would brave the terrible rains to meet him.

Ala-ud-din endorsed the sound advice.

'Death Was Dragging Jalal-ud-din by the Hair!'

Sultan Jalal-ud-din Khalji's passage to death began the moment he stepped into the boat, a few days after Almas Beg had departed. Jalal-ud-din left Delhi on horseback with some trusted nobles and maliks and an armed entourage of 1,000 cavalry. He reached a place named Damhai[9] and took boats for himself and his closest companions. The trusted Malik Ahmad Chhap marched at the head of the army by road.

The sacred Ganga, already in spate, was swelling each second, fed by the unrelenting rain. Roads were washed away and familiar routes were blocked. Jalal-ud-din's overwhelming greed drove him on, undeterred.

Barani describes how the sultan, willingly headed towards a brutal execution: 'Death was dragging Jalal-ud-din by the hair and taking him to his assassin.'[10]

Nizamuddin Ahmad composes a couplet on the occasion.

When one to advice of friend will not attend,
The gods above will penalty award.[11]

Badauni is blunter.

> Since the cup of the life of Sultan Jala-ud-din was full and his
> heart was brim-full of lust and greed for that fancied and ill-omened
> treasure, and Fate too, had rendered him deaf and blind, not one
> of [Ala-ud-din's] evil designs was perceived by him.[12]

Like Nizamuddin, Badauni too, composes verses befitting the
occasion:

> If the listener will not turn his ear to counsel,
> He will reap retribution from the high heaven.

> When Fate lets fall from the sky a feather,
> All the wise men became blind and deaf.

— · + · + · —

The moment Ala-ud-din heard the news that the sultan had departed
from Delhi, he left Kara, crossing the Ganga and pitched his camp
at Manikpur on the opposite bank. He had taken all his elephants
and booty with him. It was characteristic of the same foresight. His
strategy was to evade the sultan's troops which were marching by land
to reach Kara. With the river in spate, it would not be easy for the
army to cross over to Manikpur, if at all a battle ensued.

17th Day of Ramzan, 695 A.H.[13]

Ala-ud-din Khalji sighted the imperial boats at Kara. Badauni
describes the event with some literary flourish: 'The Sultan, whose
life's boat had been wrecked by a contrary wind, and had been
cast on the shore of destruction, arrived at Kara on the 17th of the
blessed month of Ramzan.'[14] As Jalal-ud-din's royal canopy came
into view, Ala-ud-din sent for Almas Beg with terse but specific
instructions. Flatter the greedy old man. Be submissive. Splurge
these jewels on him, and 'try every deception [you] can think of
to effect a separation between the Sultan and his army'.

Bring him to me alone.

Accordingly, Almas Beg crossed the river, presented himself before the sultan, kissed the dust at his feet, handed over an enormous quantity of wealth and began beguiling him. While the sultan was suitably flattered, he also asked the obvious question: 'Why didn't Ala-ud-din come?' The 'artful traitor', Almas Beg's well-rehearsed reply was an extension of the same disarming flattery.

> I came to Kara upon the wise orders of His Majesty, the lord of the world. If I had not comforted my brother, by this time, he would have disappeared to some unknown place. In spite of my repeated assurances, there is still some fear in his heart. And now, if he sees Your Majesty with so many armed horsemen, it is highly likely that he would once more become a prey to fresh hallucinations, and would again attempt to run away.[15]

When he heard this, Jalal-ud-din Khalji opened the curtains to the penultimate Act of a self-scripted play of doom. He ordered his stunned cavalry escort to stay behind. Then he stepped into a boat with Almas Beg. Only two other boats[16] followed him. Both boats carried his closest aides including Khurram, the *Vakildar*, Malik Fakhruddin Kuchi, Malik Amaji Akhurbeg, Malik Jamaluddin,[17] Abul Maali, Malik Nasiruddin Kuhrami, Malik Ikhtiyaruddin, and Turmati, the *Tashtdar*. As the boats approached the opposite bank, the 'arch-deceiver', Almas Beg 'loosened his lying tongue' and uttered these 'bloodthirsty words':

> My brother is now near at hand. If he sees these men, who are with your majesty, armed and ready for any emergency, it is quite likely that, owing to the fancy and fear which have overwhelmed his mind, he may become despondent about your mercy and love. I entreat His Majesty to order them to cast off their weapons.[18]

Almas Beg's outrageous 'request' was only surpassed by Jalal-ud-din's deluded assent to it. According to Firishta, only Malik Khurram raised an alarm of protest, opposing 'this step with great vehemence, for he now began to suspect treachery; but the traitor Almas Beg, had such a winning and plausible tongue, that he, too, at last yielded, though with great reluctance'.[19]

'He Who Cometh against thee Shall Lose His Head in the Boat!'

Jalal-ud-din Khalji's amirs and maliks felt a chill coursing down their spine the moment they spotted the riverbank at Manikpur. Ala-ud-din's vast army was drawn up in a perfect order, a fully equipped and battle-ready array. The *Vakildar* Malik Khurram exploded when he saw this. He said to Almas Beg, 'We left our army behind, duped by your words. We laid down our arms at your instigation. And *your* army is ready for battle?' Almas Beg was nonplussed. He ignored Khurram and directly addressed the sultan, 'This show is for His Majesty's benefit. My brother, your loyal slave and affectionate son, wishes you to review his army. He has made a well-ordered display of his strength before the Sultan with an eye to future advantage.' The sultan was overpowered by affection. Badauni allegorically describes Jalal-ud-din's pathetic condition. 'When fate comes, the plain becomes narrow. Up to that moment, he did not even discover the deceit of his enemy but of his own free will, walked deliberately into the jaws of the dragon.'[20]

And then, the sultan asked Almas Beg: 'In spite of my old age…after braving the rains and floods, I have come so far just to meet Ala-ud-din. I am experiencing weakness due to fasting during this holy Ramzan. Yet, your cruel brother's heart melts not. Can't he come at least now and meet me?' Thoroughly enjoying the game and the psychological thrall he held the sultan in, Almas Beg replied, 'His Majesty must not grieve. My brother is unwilling to receive the Sultan empty-handed. He is busy selecting elephants and valuables and fabrics to present to the Sultan, befitting his royal dignity. He has been personally supervising the kitchen to prepare the best delicacies for His Majesty to break his sacred fast and wishes that your Majesty should break it in his house, so that he may be raised above his comrades and equals by that honour.'[20] Almas Beg then quoted a couplet to further nail in the flattery:

> If thou goest empty-handed to visit a Sheikh,
> Thou will get no profit, nor will thou even see him.

Throughout the journey peppered by such conversations, Jalal-ud-din was busy reading the Quran.

——•—··—•—··—•——

Just a day or three before Jalal-ud-din's fateful journey, Ala-ud-din had visited the *Khanqah* of Hazrat Sheikh Karak, a renowned Sufi in Kara, and paid him obeisance like a supplicant. Sheikh Karak, 'the absorbed', raised his head from his pillow and sounded a prophecy in extempore verse:

> He who cometh against you shall lose his head in the boat,
> And his body shall be thrown into Ganga.[21]

Both Firistha and Nizamuddin Ahmad narrate this episode claiming that it had come down from trustworthy tradition. Karak's *dargah* is still visited by Muslims who attach great reverence to it.

Notwithstanding the historical truth of the prophecy, it is clear that Jalal-ud-din had come in the way of Ala-ud-din's limitless ambition.

——•—··—•—··—•——

The boats reached the other side just as it was time for the afternoon *Namaaz*. As Sultan Jalal-ud-din Khalji disembarked it, he held the Quran in his hand and reading it, proceeded onward, 'fearless and [confident] as a father to his sons'.[22]

Likewise, all the companions who had accompanied him were also reading the Quran.

But they were reading a different chapter.

The *Sura-i-Yasin*. The 36th chapter.

It was extolled as the heart of the Quran[23].

Among other occasions, it was also recited at death because 'its recitation begets the forgiveness of Allah and helps the dying person to peacefully pass to the other side'.

Jalal-ud-din saw elephants and treasures and the profuse affection of Ala-ud-din waiting for him.

His companions saw death staring at them.[24]

'Ah! You Wretched Villain, Ala-ud-din!'

Ala-ud-din greeted his uncle just as the boat was docked. Feigning great joy, he rushed forward with his nobles and fell at the sultan's feet and kissed it. Jalal-ud-din lifted him up, and exuding immense warmth, kissed his eyes and cheeks and stroked his beard and gave two affectionate taps on his cheeks and spoke with great emotion, 'I have brought you up from infancy…. I've always promoted you to ever higher ranks… look how great you've grown now! You have always been to me dearer than my own sons. Did you really think I came here to assassinate you?' Then he took Ala-ud-din's hand in his and began leading him towards the barge.

At that exact moment, Nusrat Khan, the malik who had rushed to Ala-ud-din's aid in the battle against Singhana III, gave the fatal signal.

Figure 21: Artist's sketch of Jalal-ud-din Khalji's assassination.

Like lighting, the designated assassin, a *Silahdar* named Muhammad Salim, struck the sultan from the rear with his sword. Every Muslim chronicler heaps the choicest of invectives against Muhammad Salim. He is described as the 'very scum of Samana', 'the basest of Muslims from Samana', and a 'bad fellow from a bad family'. Muhammad Salim missed the blow and injured his own hand but quickly struck a second blow, harder than the previous one. Before Jalal-ud-din could fathom what was happening. This time, the blade found its mark on his shoulder, ripping it open. His gushing blood was the acid which finally washed away the sultan's delusion. Grievously wounded, and screaming in pain, he rushed towards his boat, cursing loudly, 'Ah! You wretched villain, Ala-ud-din! What have you done!' It was futile. Another assassin, Ikhtiyaruddin Hud, intercepted him. He 'seized the feeble old man, and throwing him on the ground, chopped off his head'.[25] Ikhtiyaruddin, another protege, a prime beneficiary of countless favours from the sultan, and a person he had implicitly trusted, had ultimately turned into a mephitic traitor.

Next, Jalal-ud-din's companions were ruthlessly hunted down. Some were slaughtered outright while others were drowned in the river. Only Malik Fakhruddin Kuchi was captured alive, imprisoned and then murdered.

Familiar scenes followed in the aftermath of all such assassinations in the annals of the Muslim history of India. Ikhtiyaruddin lifted the dead sultan's severed head in his hand and brought it before Ala-ud-din Khalji. It was skewered to a spear and paraded throughout Kara and Manikpur, and then sent to Avadh for public display: a grisly exhibition of the fate and the blood-drenched face of the head of the sultanate. An ominous message and a cruel harbinger of things to come.

The royal canopy of the murdered sultan was raised over Ala-ud-din's head by the members of his cabal. They proclaimed him the new sultan. But on his part, Ala-ud-din was sharply aware that real sultan-hood was still faraway. No doubt, the biggest obstacle had been crushed but what needed to be done after this was equally, if not more crucial.

Sultan Jalal-ud-din Khalji's grisly assassination expectedly radiated shockwaves far and wide. While treachery, betrayal, fratricide and patricide were accepted norms of succession in Muslim politics, Ala-ud-din's backstabbing was particularly loathed for its cold nonchalance and the unapologetic brazenness with which it was executed. Ala-ud-din Khalji had violated a fundamental tenet held sacred by Islamic scripture: murdering his own uncle in the holy month of Ramzan. A period in which the Prophet himself had forbidden war.

Barani condemns Ala-ud-din's treachery in extremely venomous language. He had held Jalal-ud-din in special esteem, regarding him as a 'guileless monarch', as one who was truly magnanimous and kind even to those who had revolted against him. His piety towards Islam during the last days of his life had also captured Barani's affection. As the author of the *Fatwa-i-Jahandari*, a book on Islamic statecraft, Barani was one of the most pious bigots in the gallery of Muslim chroniclers of the history of Islam's victories in infidel Hindustan. He was a literalist in the sense that his *Fatwa-i-Jahandari* advocates the physical re-creation of Prophet Muhammad's glorious Arabia in Hindustan. Till the very end, Barani had unconcealed contempt for Ala-ud-din's betrayal.

> The murder was perpetrated on the 17th Ramzan, and the venerable head of the Sultan was placed on a spear and paraded about. When the rebels returned to Kara-Manikpur, it was also paraded there, and was afterwards sent to be exhibited in Oudh. While the head of the murdered sovereign was yet dripping with blood, the ferocious conspirators brought the royal canopy and elevated it over the head of Ala-ud-din. Casting aside all shame, the perfidious and graceless wretches caused him to be proclaimed king by men who rode about on elephants... *Ala-ud-din...shed more innocent blood than any Pharaoh was guilty of.*[26]
> (Emphasis added)

All chroniclers except Isami and the artful Amir Khusrau share Barani's outrage. Like him, even they take enormous relish in giving macabre descriptions of the horrible fate that befell the conspirators and assassins of Jalal-ud-din Khalji.

Even here, Barani leads the charge.

He brands Almas Beg as a vile traitor and deceiver.

Nusrat Khan is condemned as the fatal signal-giver.

Zafar Khan is similarly reviled.

Barani's own uncle, Ala-ul-Mulk is guilty of being the original breeder of the mischief.

Muhammad Salim, who struck the first blow, is called a hell-hound.

Ikhtiyaruddin who cut off the sultan's head gets an even harsher treatment.

The following is a gist of what each conspirator and murderer underwent.

Almas Beg, Ala-ud-din's own brother, fell into terrible misfortune and misery and died.

Nusrat Khan too, died a similar death as did Zafar Khan.

Muhammad Salim was infected by leprosy, which dissolved his flesh piece by piece from his bones and died after a full year of agonizing suffering.

Ikhtiyaruddin went insane and could be seen incessantly screaming in public that Jalal-ud-din was cutting off his head. Firishta pronounces the final verdict: 'Thus, this wretch also suffered a 1,000 deaths in his imagination before he expired.'[27]

But Ala-ud-din not only remained unaffected, unmoved and guiltless, he also ascended to the summit of power and prosperity on a scale and extent that no prior sultan in infidel Hindustan had enjoyed. Indeed, the whole torrid saga of Ala-ud-din's betrayal of his own uncle and father-in-law reads like a user manual of no-holds-barred treachery.

Ala-ud-din's agony would come much later and would last longer.

—◆·◆··◆—

CHAPTER 10

A Career of Bigotry and Bloodletting Eclipsed by an Unlikely Martyrdom

Everyday, the Hindus, the deadliest enemies of Islam, pass by my palace beating drums and trumpets and go to the Jamuna and practice idolatory openly.

Jalal-ud-din Khalji's ghastly assassination made him a martyr who was almost revered in the annals of the Islamic chronicles of India. Both the circumstance and the manner of his murder successfully eclipsed the gory record of his long career of bloodletting, brutality, betrayal and bigotry. He was a devout Muslim, a hardcore tribal warlord from the badlands of Afghanistan and he exhibited the same savage manners. His pre-sultan career clearly brings out these facets.

Jalal-ud-din's genuine and incurable awe towards Balban was rooted in his capacity for instilling terror and unleashing casual barbarism against his own aristocracy, bureaucrats and citizens. Jalal-ud-din aspired to be Balban and did imitate him when he was a military officer and later, a *Naib*, and finally, a sultan. His ruthless conduct in the battle against the infidel Mongols in Punjab was one of the earliest instances of his Balbanesque brutality. This battle earned him the coveted title of 'Warrior of Allah', in which he took immense pride. Jalal-ud-din's administration of his *iqta*[1] comprising Kaithal, Samana and Bulandshahr shows the same heartlessness. He launched an unprovoked assault against the Mundahar[2] Rajputs in Kaithal[3] and pillaged and burnt several villages. Despite being vastly outnumbered, the heroic Rajputs fought back with exemplary valour, and one of the soldiers slashed Jalal-ud-din's face with such ferocity that it left a permanent scar.

Following the lead of their master, Jalal-ud-din's officers and revenue collectors mercilessly extorted revenue from the already impoverished villagers. In Samana, his officers bled a certain village dry. As retaliation, Sirajuddin Sawi, a Maulana of the village composed a long versified satire titled *Khalji-Nama*[4] violently lampooning Jalal-ud-din Khalji.

Like all his predecessors, Jalal-ud-din too, climbed to the imperial throne via bloodshedding. He had the wasted Kaiqubad, murdered by a commoner thirsting for retribution. Treacherous murder was how Jalal-ud-din had repaid Kaiqubad who had elevated him as War Minister. A Kaiqubad who was physically rotting away and helpless to resist. Jalal-ud-din followed this up with the ugliest blot on his blood-soaked career: the cold-blooded butchery of a child, the last 'obstacle' from the house of Balban. Next, he stripped off the property and wealth of scores of Balbani amirs, nobles and loyalists and literally flung them on the streets. All of them were forced to live off the dole of Sidi Maula.

Jalal-ud-din's mass deportation of the *Thags* (Thugs) to Bengal had another side to it. He had spared their lives only because they were Muslims. However, he had declared his firm belief in the Islamic dictum laid down by Prophet Muhammad himself. 'How shall I kill those who repeat the Kalma because in the religion of the prophet, the murder of none else except the murderer, apostate and adulterer is ordained.'[5]

But the actual reason behind the deportation was both political and sinister. The scholar N.B. Ray, in his wonderful paper on Jalal-ud-din Khalji fleshes it out:

> Jalaluddin had no aversion to shedding the blood of the apostate, murderer and adulterer. Moreover, in course of his campaign in the east, he destroyed the nest of the robbers, and hanged them by batches. The transplantation of the thousand thugs to Lakhnauti...was not an entirely impolitic step, for Ruknuddin Kaikas, grandson of Ghiyasuddin Balban was still holding sway in Lakhnauti and Bihar and this enemy of the Khaljis could be

kept better occupied at home by letting loose in his territory a band of dangerous criminals. Jalaluddin's policy towards the rebels and criminals was dictated by political and certainly not by humanitarian considerations. He kept the mailed fist concealed within the velvet glove. *Jalaluddin's claim to the throne rested not on right but on might.* An upstart usurper, he came to the throne by shedding blood; he had to win over hostile elements and broadbase the rule of the Khaljis on popular support and goodwill which had been strongly wedded to the Balbani cause. A policy of terror and violence ill-suited this task; it was necessity that drove the Sultan to a mild policy but mildness should not be confounded with weakness.[6] (Emphasis added)

An extension of these policies included stuffing the administration and the military with people drawn from the Khalji stock. Like the Turkic-Muslims had done to the Arab Muslims about three centuries earlier, Jalal-ud-din Khalji extinguished the Turkic political power in infidel Hindustan.

Pious Bigotry against Infidels as State Policy

As an orthodox Sunni Muslim, Jalal-ud-din zealously observed all the mandatory Islamic practices: offering the *Namaz* five times everyday, fasting on *Ramzan*, giving the *Zakat,* etc. He also read one chapter of the Quran everyday before going to bed. Mandatory oppression of and hatred against the *Kaffir* Hindus also formed part of this zealotry. This is best evidenced by his own anguished and angry invectives on numerous occasions.

> What is our defence of the Faith, cried Sultan Jalal-ud-din Khalji, that we suffer these Hindus, who are the greatest enemies of Allah and of the religion of Mustafa, to live in comfort and do not flow streams of their blood?

While Jalal-ud-din's trail of temple destructions is not as prolific as the sultans who preceded and succeeded him, it was certainly not for the lack of intent or shortage of Islamic piety. The feral demolition of the temples in Jhain, which he exultingly describes, is an eminent representative of his iconoclastic enthusiasm. His bigotry against Hindus also revealed itself in several other ways. In the wake of a victorious battle, he separated the Muslim and Hindu prisoners of war and had the Hindus trampled[7] under the feet of elephants but spared the Muslims. In this connection, K.S. Lal offers an interesting insight:

> Jalal-ud-din, like an old septuagenarian, used to fume and bluster against the Hindus, but he had neither the time nor the means... to deal with them sternly. His many problems—the Ilbari malcontents, the Mongol invaders...would not let him rest in peace. In these circumstances, he could not, even if he had so desired, deal with the non-Muslims severely. *Neither the sultan was so strong nor the Hindus so weak that the large-scale persecution of the Hindus could have been possible.*[8] (Emphasis added)

And so, Jalal-ud-din consoled himself through regular outbursts of anti-Hindu bigotry. In a particularly violent ejection of rage, the sultan tells his trusted aide, Ahmad Chhap:

> *The infidel Hindus chew paan unmindful of anything, dressed in white and move among the Musalmans with comfort and case. Everyday, the Hindus, the deadliest enemies of Islam, pass by my palace beating drums and trumpets and go to the Jamuna and practice idolatory openly...and we call ourselves Muslims! Shame on us!* Shame on our *Padshahi* and on our championship and protection of our holy religion that we allow our name to be read every Friday from the mosque's pulpit and the enemies of Allah and the religion of the Prophet to pass their lives in a thousand comforts, enjoy wealth and other blessings and live honourably amongst Muslims with all pride and glory and practices of *Kufr* and *Shirk* in our capital under our rule and before our very eyes. May dust fall on our heads and our *Padshahi!*[9] (Emphasis added)

Following the familiar proverb that celibacy is lack of opportunity, Jalal-ud-din inflicted indignities upon Hindus within the aforementioned constraints. A good method was to exclude the infidels from government service. And in wartime,

Jalal-ud-din was especially merciless against the accursed 'Rawats and Paiks', whom he hunted down like beasts while quelling Malik Chhajju's revolt and cut down jungles and 'terrorized the recalcitrant infidel villages of Tarsiya, Kahsun and Khatrak'.[10]

——•——•—•—•——

In the overall assessment, Jalal-ud-din Khalji stands as a transitional figure who permanently eliminated the Turkic-Muslim Sultanate in infidel Hindustan. But his death inaugurated a darker Khalji regime, which was crueller, bloodier and more rapacious and oppressive than any previous Muslim rule. It was also the period when the fire and sword of Islam reached its peak of expansionism into the farthest reaches of infidel Hindustan under Ala-ud-din Khalji's savagery, fuelled by fanaticism and thirst for plunder. Ala-ud-din practically implemented what his uncle could only satisfy through ranting and blustering—an all-encompassing oppression of the infidels.

The feathered treatment that Jalal-ud-din gets in Muslim chronicles owes almost exclusively to the sainthood which Barani has conferred upon him. Barani was indebted to him for life for a straightforward reason. He was the son of Muyyid-ul-mulk, an aide of Jalal-ud-din's eldest son, Arkali Khan. Muyyid was one of the grandees of Jalal-ud-din's court and thoroughly indulged in every vice and depravity that his position got him. He had an opulent mansion in Kilugarhi living in quasi regal extravagance. Barani spent his boyhood and adolescence in this environment, and when the political climate changed in a demonic fashion, he found himself suddenly in the abyss of penury, rejection, shame and humiliation. His narrative about his denuded condition drips with self-pity.

> When I write an account of [Jalal-ud-din's] court, I wish I blacken my face, paint my accursed forehead with the 'tika' mark of Brahmans, in calling to mind the images of those lovely persons having moon-like appearance, their blandishments and amorous glances, their songs and dancing which I witnessed; I wish also

that I move among the lanes and bazars in lamenting for them....
I have been afflicted by infirmity and poverty at this time and the
suitors turn away disappointed; So, I being the son of a nobleman,
prefer death a thousand times to this (miserable) day. I possess
nothing nor can I borrow from others.[11]

And so, when he began writing the *Tarikh-i-Firuz Shahi* 60 years
after Jalal-ud-din's death, he was drowned in emotion at the fond
memories of his growing up years. Years which were paradisical
and made lush by the grapes and wine of Jalal-ud-din Khalji's
munificent sultanate.

However, the cold verdict of history[12] tells the real truth.

Vincent Smith candidly says that 'Jalal-ud-din, although he
did not deserve his cruel fate, was unfit to rule'.[13] The British
scholar and civil servant, Haig is blunter: 'Such culpable weakness,
would have thrown the kingdom into complete disorder had his
reign been prolonged.'[14]

Jalal-ud-din Khalji's rickety sultanate and volatile regime had
lasted seven years and some months.

CHAPTER 11

Ala-ud-din Khalji's Throne Soaked in Blood and Gravelled by Glitter

Hast thou seen the acts of the tyrant-heaven and its star,
How it has cast the sun of the kingdom into dust!

M alik Ahmad Chhap bolted towards Delhi with his troops
the moment he heard that the arch-ingrate Ala-ud-din had
murdered his master, his own uncle, Sultan Jalal-ud-din Khalji.
His conniving flatterers had already raised the royal canopy and
declared him the new sultan. K.S. Lal provides a brilliant insight
on a critical question hiding in plain sight: Why did Ala-ud-din
find it necessary not only to betray his uncle but do it in such a
conscience-free manner?

> When did the idea of murdering the sultan enter Ala-ud-din's
> mind? It is certain that after his return from Devagiri, he never
> thought of making an attempt on the king's life, although his
> instructions to Ram Chandra to send tribute to Kara instead of
> Delhi hint at a contemplated revolt. But his letters to the sultan
> do betray his fears from an inimical section of the nobility at
> court. He had, therefore, made full preparations to fly to Bengal
> in case men like Ahmad Chap could impress upon the king the
> need for firm action. But when he saw the Sultan coming to Kara
> "unattended," he decided to murder him [and told Almas Beg in
> so many words]....Thus the resolve of murder was an eleventh
> hour decision. *But once the crime was committed, Ala-ud-din never
> regretted having done it.*[1] (Emphasis added)

At Delhi, Malik Chhap sternly told the *Malika-i-Jahan* that there was no time to waste mourning Jalal-ud-din if she was serious about preventing the throne from slipping into the hands of her husband's wretched murderer. Not that she needed convincing. Crafty, scheming and ambitious, she immediately placed her youngest son, Qadr Khan on the throne and styled him as Sultan Ruknuddin Ibrahim Shah. Qadr Khan had been born in the dead sultan's old age and the parents doted on him. With garish ostentation, the *Malika-i-Jahan* marched from Kilugarhi to the *Kaushak-i-Sabz* (the Green Palace) with a procession of amirs and maliks and other nobles and made it the new sultan's official residence. The coronation had been done without calling a council, without consulting the nobles, without proper formality. And yet, she began to randomly distribute fiefs and offices among the maliks. The temptation to wield despotic power by operating behind the throne had proven irresistible to her. She began ruling in Qadr's name and heard petitions and issued *Farmans* all the while being behind the *Purdah*. Barani displays special aversion to her, calling her the 'silliest of silly', 'weak-minded', 'foolish', 'imprudent', 'hasty' and 'rash'.[2]

Hostilities and dissensions erupted within days. The first discordant note was sounded by her elder son, Arkali Khan, the Governor of Multan. But it was simply the crescendo of a lifelong orchestra of tense relations between mother and son. Arkali Khan, now bitter and furious at the naked injustice that she had meted out to him, sulked and stayed back in Multan. He was the rightful heir to the throne. His battle-hardened and ruthless military career was the ultimate proof of his fitness for the crown. He had proven his bloodlust during the hunt of the accursed rebel Malik Chhaju. He had pitilessly ordered several rebels to be trampled under the feet of elephants. Even Ala-ud-din feared and respected him as the 'Rustum of the age'. But unknown to Arkali, this *Rustum* had just made Ala-ud-din's life much easier.

The new 'sultan' Ruknuddin barely lasted a month.

Betrayal and bloodletting apart, the road to Ala-ud-din's triumphal ascent was also paved by his unshakeable conviction in the dictum that all that glitters leads to the throne.

He decided to strike first. Before Arkali Khan changed his mind and staked his claim for the throne.

If greed had compelled Jalal-ud-din to brave the torrential monsoon and riverine spate, ambition for sultanhood urged Ala-ud-din to do the same. This time, in the reverse direction—from Kara to Delhi. Barani describes the rain which was

> ....more heavy than any one could remember....from the excess of rain that year, the Ganga and Jamuna had become vast rivers, and every paltry stream was as a Ganges or a Jamuna, and from the depth of mud and mire, the road remained impassable.[3]

Ala-ud-din gave explicit instructions to his fellow-traitors. Splurge all the money you want but raise a fabulous army. If people demand high salaries, exceed their demand. Scatter all the gold you want so that 'vast hordes might be collected by such bountiful largesse'. And Ala-ud-din led by example. He constructed lightweight and highly mobile *Manjaniks*. At every halting place en route to Delhi, the *Manjaniks* would be placed on the portico outside his tent and five *maunds* of gold coins were fired, 'whereupon the soldiery and the neighbouring population used to congregate all round and carry off the coins'.[4] By the end of two weeks, the crowds swelled and the message spread like wildfire: Ala-ud-din is on his way to occupy Delhi.

Ala-ud-din's aforementioned dictum had worked like magic. Greed was indeed good. Vast multitudes of people, 'military and non-military' joined him in large numbers, and when he arrived at Badaun, his army had ballooned into 56,000 cavalry and 60,000 infantry.

At Badaun, Ala-ud-din detached a unit and ordered Zafar Khan to march to Delhi via Aligarh. He would personally head the larger force via Bulandshahar. Both contingents would march in parallel and he timed both marches so that they converged in Delhi at the same time.

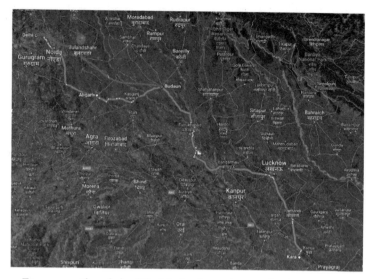

*Figure 22: Ala-ud-din Khalji's final march to Delhi from Badaun.
Red line from Badaun shows Ala-ud-din's route to Delhi. Blue line
shows Zafar Khan's route to Delhi.*

At Bulandshahar, his trusted aide Nusrat Khan quickly began to enlist almost every man in the place irrespective of rank or station. Ala-ud-din himself addressed a large gathering at the grounds outside the city's mosque:

> If Delhi falls into our hands, I will be able to acquire in the first year a hundred times as much wealth as what I will now disburse. Should the kingdom not come into my possession, it is better that the wealth which I have brought from Deogir with such infinite trouble, should fall into the hands of you, the people, instead of those of my foes and adversaries.[5]

While this naked temptation did its trick, copious support suddenly flowed in from rather unexpected quarters: Jalal-uddin's confidants. His intimate circle of maliks and amirs who had been dispatched from Delhi to stop the vile traitor Ala-ud-din in his tracks. Tajuddin Kuchi, Abaji Akhurbeg, Amir Ali Diwanah, Usman Amir Akhur, Amir Kalan, Umar Sarkhah, and Hiranmar unscrupulously switched over to Ala-ud-din's camp.

Their purchase price varied from 20 to 50 maunds of gold, which Ala-ud-din gladly gave. Then there was the prospect of even more substantial goodies in the future. The troops that had accompanied these maliks and amirs were given 100 *tankas*[6] each. Ala-ud-din's boundless generosity left this fresh batch of qualms-free renegades spellbound in awe, and they publicly justified their betrayal.

....the people of the City [Delhi] certainly find fault with us and declare that we have been guilty of base ingratitude...but these inconsiderate persons do not perceive that in reality, the kingdom of Jalal-ud-din came to an end the day he set out from the palace of Kilughari and of his own free will went in hot haste to Kara, and there put his neck and those of his intimate associates in jeopardy. What can we do but join Ala-ud-din?[7]

News of this latest wave of desertion shattered whatever confidence the *Malika-i-Jahan* had. But the worse was yet to come.

——◆—◆—◆——

The first death blow landed in the form of open factionalism. The reasoning among the remaining Jalali loyalists in Delhi was simple: if Jalal-ud-din's closest nobles could renege so casually, Ruknuddin's 'sultanate' was not worth saving.

The faction loyal to Arkali Khan now began to candidly voice its displeasure over the Queen's injustice of denying him the throne. Others wavered in their loyalty to the house of Jalal-ud-din, now represented by his wife and sons. Still others spotted the golden opportunity that Ala-ud-din presented.

Even as the *Malika-i-Jahan* saw the warning signs, she launched a last-ditch effort. She wrote to Arkali Khan: I was wrong in elevating your younger brother to the throne. None of the maliks and amirs fear him, and now they are openly deserting him in large numbers to seek Ala-ud-din's favour. It is a mistake which I have now realized. The throne is slipping out of our hands. Come, occupy it before it's too late.

INVADERS AND INFIDELS

However, Arkali Khan proved shrewder. This was a dying cause which he did not wish to risk supporting. He sent a dodgy response: by your own admission, most of the nobles have abandoned you. Whether or not I come, what outcome will be served, ultimately? News of Arkali Khan's reply reached Ala-ud-din a few days later. It was Allah-sent luck. He immediately ordered drums of celebration to be beaten and quickly proceeded towards the fort, wildly flinging and scattering gold and jewellery along the way. He gathered more followers and nobles and officers of different ranks. Still more gold was distributed. He finally stood on the banks of the Jamuna and was forced to halt due to excessive flooding. A couple of days later, he crossed the river at the ford of Baghpat and pitched his tent on its banks.

The Final Triumph of Treachery

'Sultan' Ruknuddin decided to fight Ala-ud-din.

Accoutred in full royal insignia, he emerged from Delhi with a dinky contingent and pitched his camp on the opposite bank. He would begin the offensive the next morning. A morning which never came because the night proved fatal. The entire left wing of his army simply mounted their horses 'about midnight and a tremendous uproar arose and they all went bodily over to Ala-ud-din'.[8] Thoroughly demoralized and scared witless, Ruknuddin managed to reach the Badaun Gate the same night with some of his diehard loyalists. He scooped out as much treasure as he could manage. Then he got out some horses from the stable, placed his mother and other women members of his family on them and sent them ahead. Finally, he 'issued forth under cover of the darkness from the Ghazni gate and took the road to Multan'.

Only two maliks remained loyal to the house of Jalal-ud-din Khalji till the pathetic end. Qutub-ud-din Alawi and Ahmad Chhap.

Both abandoned their homes and followed the jinxed Ruknuddin and his fatuous mother.

Ala-ud-din Khalji had finally extracted his burning revenge against his mother-in-law.

*Figure 23: Artist's sketch showing the escape of Ruknuddin and his
loyalists from Delhi.*

The Coronation of Betrayal

The next morning, Ala-ud-din Khalji rode into Delhi with royal
splendour and pomp and finally reached the vast plain at Siri
where he dismounted. In a magnificent pavilion erected to
celebrate the occasion, 'sovereignty was delivered to him'.[9]

He bestowed upon himself the pompous title of *Abul Muzaffar
Sultan Alaud-duniya-va-din Muhammad Shah Khalji.*

Everybody who was somebody in Delhi queued up to honour
him and swore their undying allegiance. The nobles of Delhi, the
Kotwal, Qazis, masters of elephant and horse stables, custodians
of the fort gates and other dignitaries supplicated themselves
before him. According to Barani, the earth itself 'assumed a totally
different aspect'.

Following the time-honoured Islamic tradition, the *Khutba* was read and coins were minted in Sultan Ala-ud-din Khalji's name. Barani records a bitter observation. 'By the immensity of his wealth, and the vast number of his adherents, no matter whether an individual took the oath of allegiance to him or not, the public prayers were offered on his behalf.'[10]

Sovereignty was delivered indeed. All that remained was coronation.

On 20 October 1296, Sultan Ala-ud-din Khalji 'entered the city with a most wonderful retinue and countless multitude, and took his seat on the throne of Delhi in the *Daulat Khanah'*. His personal residence was the *Koshak-i-Lal*, the crimson palace that Balban had built and before which Jalal-ud-din Khalji had gaped and wept with wonder and awe. Ala-ud-din suffered no such compunctions.

And then the rewards flowed like rivers.

For weeks, the new sultan rained money and gifts on the citizens of Delhi. The army was given six months' salary, *gratis*. The shaikhs and the ulema were given even more generous grants. The countless 'hoard of wealth accumulated in his treasury'[11] swelled the purses of the people with *Tankahs* and *Jitals*, and they gave themselves up to 'gaiety and pleasure, and indulged in wine and all kinds of revelry'. If this was not enough, Ala-ud-din erected large pavilions and pleasure houses where wine, sherbet and *paan* was sumptuously distributed, and 'in almost every house, an entertainment was held'.

If this was the party scene of the ordinary citizens, the landscape of debauchery of the nobles was on an entirely different scale. They invited each other to their vast Mahals and feasted and drank wine and gorged on a heady diet of music, dance and unrestrained licentiousness. This celebration owed to a reason far more fundamental than money: Ala-ud-din had distributed the spoils of office to them.

Khwaja Khatir was appointed as the *Vazir*.

Qazi Sadruddin Arif was elevated as the chief Qazi of the empire. He was awarded the grandiloquent titles of *Sayyad Ajall* (the most glorious Sayyad) and *Sheikh-ul-islam* (the chief priest).

Umdat-ul-Mulk Hamiduddin was promoted to the office of *insha* (correspondence).

Izzuddin was allowed to become the new sultan's confidant.

Nusrat Khan was promoted to the post of *Kotwal* (superintendent of security).

Fakhruddin Kuchi was appointed as the *darogha* (inspector) of the capital.

Zafar Khan got the coveted post of the Commander-in-Chief of the Forces.

Abaji Jalali was raised to the post of the *Tajirbegi* (Minister of Commerce).

Huran became the *Naib Barbegi* (Deputy Master of Ceremonies).

Barani's uncle Ala-ul-mulk, the faithful scribe of deceptive reports to Jalal-ud-din Khalji, was entrusted with the lucrative fiefs of Kara and Avadh.

Other eminent traitors also received *iqtas* and *Paraganas* and generous cash stipends and trust funds, to borrow a contemporary term.

It was precisely this immensity of Ala-ud-din's wealth that bedazzled and benumbed everyone into effortlessly forgetting[12] the ghastly assassination of Jalal-ud-din Khalji and erasing Ala-ud-din's villainy from 'their black hearts',[13] because:

> Liberality is the alchemy of the copper of faults;
> Liberality is the remedy for all pain.

Firishta is entirely justified in his brutal assessment.

> [Ala-ud-din] commenced his reign by splendid shows, and grand festivals, and encouraged every description of gaiety, which so pleased the unthinking rabble, that they soon lost all memory of their former King, and of the horrid scene which had placed the present one on the throne. *He who ought to have been viewed with detestation, became the object of admiration to those who could not see the blackness of his deeds through the splendour of his munificence.*[14]
> (Emphasis added)

The munificence, the splendour, the showers of money, and in fact, the entire journey that had culminated in the sultanate of Ala-ud-din Khalji was entirely financed by his reprobate plunder of the generational wealth earned by the infidels of Devagiri. They would not only get a renewed taste of the same barbarism much later, but on that occasion, the barbarism would be more extensive and their independence obliterated forever.

Ala-ud-din Khalji would also demolish the gates of Dakshinapatha and give the slumbering infidels out there a first-hand taste of what 'being honoured by Islam' really meant.

END OF BOOK 2

Notes

Preface

1   Goel, Sita Ram. *The Story of Islamic Imperialism in India*. Voice of India, 1982.

2   Jackson, Peter. *The Delhi Sultanate: A Political and Military History*. Cambridge: (Cambridge University Press), 2003, 1.

Prologue

1   Qalat is known by the following names: Kalat, Qalat-i Tokhi, Qalati Ghilji, Qalati Ghilzay and Qalati Zabul.

2   The term 'Khalji' will be used henceforth throughout this work.

3   Some chroniclers like Khwaja Nizamuddin Ahmad have spun fantastic theories that the Khaljis descended from Chengiz Khan. However, almost all early-medieval and later Islamic chroniclers like Ibn Haukal, Fakhruddin, Firishta and Badaoni confirm the Turkish origins of the Khaljis. The classic work on the subject is V. Minorsky's *The Turkish Dialect of the Khalaj*.

4   See: *Invaders and Infidels: Book 1*.

5   Bowsworth, C.E., ed. *The Encyclopedia of Islam*, 4, Vol. 4. (Leiden: E.J. Brill, 1995), 917.

6   al-Kashgari. *Dīwan Lughat Al-Turk*, trans., Besim Atalay, Vol. 3 (Ankara: TDK Press, 1992), 523.

7   For a fuller discussion, see: Minorsky, V. 'The Turkish Dialect of the Khalaj.' *Bulletin of the School of Oriental Studies* Vol. 10, No. 2 (August 29, 2005), 417–37.

8   Image courtesy: Classical Numismatic Group, Inc. http://www.cngcoins.com, CC BY-SA 3.0, https://commons.wikimedia.org/w/index.php?curid=97457748

9   For the full account of Alptigin, see: *Invaders and Infidels: Book 1*.

10 al-Mulk, Nizam. *Siyasat-Nama: The Book of Government or Rules for Kings*, trans., Darke, Hubert, (London: Routledge, 2002), 105–06.

11 See: *Invaders and Infidels: Book 1*.

12   The contemporary name is Guzgan in Northern Afghanistan. Other historical names include Quzghan, Juzjan and Juzjanan. Its name is derived from walnut, a fruit that exists in abundance even today in the region.

13   Minorsky, V. 'The Turkish Dialect of the Khalaj.' *Bulletin of the School of Oriental Studies* 10, No. 2 (August 29, 2005), 417–37.

14   Ibid.

15   For the full story of Anandapala's resistance, see: *Invaders and Infidels: Book 1.*

16   For a superb account and historical analysis of this epochal war, see Majumdar, R.C. 'Hindu Reaction to Muslim Invasions,' *Professor D.V. Potdar Commemoration Volume,* (1950), 341–51.

17   Contemporary Bundelkhand.

18   Dowson, H.M., Eliot and John. *The History of India as Told by Its Own Historians* Vol. 2, (London: Trubner & Co, 1869), 447.

19   The Gakkhars were an ancient Hindu tribe spread over the general region of the Salt Range, who traced their origins to Arjuna. Over time, they became experts at building hill forts and fortified cities. Today, they have become completely Islamized. See for example: *Gakkhar,* A.S. Bazmee Ansari, in *Encyclopedia of Islam,* (2nd edition), ed. J.H.Kramers et al., E.J Brill, (Leiden) 972–74.

20   Quoted in: Majumdar, R.C. *Hindu Reaction to Muslim Invasions,* above.

21   Known as the Battle of Parwan.

22   Mangbarni's story has been narrated in *Invaders and Infidels: Book 1.*

23   In this backdrop, the historian V. Minorsky in his classic work *The Turkish Dialect of the Khalaj,* provides the following assessment of the rise of the Khalji tribe by the early 13th century: 'This historical sketch very clearly shows the gradual expansion of the southern branch of the Khalaj from the lower course of the Helmand to the environs of Ghazna and later to the neighbourhood of Peshawar; on the other hand, it indicates how the Khalaj were utilized by the lords of the time and how gradually they found their way to power.'

24   The place takes its name from its climate: 'hot.'

25   Minhaj-i-Siraj. *Tabakat-i-Nasiri,* trans., H.G. Raverty, (London: Asiatic Society of Bengal, 1873), 548–49.

26   Jackson, Peter. *The Delhi Sultanate: A Political and Military History,* (Cambridge: Cambridge University Press, 2003), 25.

27 Budaun, in Western Uttar Pradesh. A historic city, its original name was Vodamayuta, one of the important cities of the Kanauj Empire. It was founded by the Rashtrakutas in 905 and remained an important seat of the Rathore Dynasty until Qutub-ud-din Aibak wrested it. For fuller details, see, Majumdar, Ramesh Chandra *Ancient India*. (Motilal Banarsidass, 1977), 315.

28 Also known as Charanadri or Chandrakanta Chunargarh, its legacy is rich and chequered. The Chunar Fort was built by the Pala Kings of Bengal sometime in the 9th century and was considered as one of the most impregnable forts in India. A profound history says that the great saint, grammarian and poet, Bhartuhari lived in one of the caves of this mountain spending his life in meditation. This portion of the fort is still called Bhartuhari's palace and a small shrine named 'Bhatinath' has been built in his honour. See: Dey, Nundo Lal. *The Geographical Dictionary of Ancient and Medieval India*, (Calcutta: W. Newman & Co, 1899).

29 For a brief history of the Gahadawalas, see *Invaders and Infidels: Book 1*.

30 Now, Munger.

31 Sarkar, Jadunath. *The History of Bengal Volume II: Muslim Period*, (Delhi: B.R. Publishing Corporation, 2003), 2.

32 Minhaj-i-Siraj. *Tabakat-i-Nasiri*, 1873, 551.

33 For more information on what is known as the Karnata Dynasty of Mithila, see: (a) Sinha, C.P.N. 'Origin of the Karnatas of Mithila— A Fresh Appraisal.' *Proceedings of the Indian History Congress*, 31, (1969) 66–72; (b) Majumdar, R.C. *The Struggle for Empire*, (Bharatiya Vidya Bhavan, 1957), 47.

34 Pronounced as 'Naa-landa'.

35 The famous Chinese Buddhist pilgrim Xuanzang (or Hiuen-Tsang) derives the word as *Na al, lllam dā* meaning 'no end in gifts or charity without intermission'. A substantial body of scholarship exists on Nalanda. See for examples: (a) Ghosh, Amalananda. *A Guide to Nalanda*, (Delhi: Archaeological Survey of India, 1939); (b) Nilakanta Sastri, K.A. ed., *Age of the Nandas and Mauryas*. (India: Motilal Banarsidass, 1988); (c) Sastri, Hiranand. *Nalanda and Its Epigraphic Material*, (India: Sri Satguru Publications, 1986); (d) Chandra, Moti. *Trade and trade routes in ancient India* (Sārthavāha, engl. 1. Publ., South Asia Books, 1977); (e) Sankalia, Hasmukh Dhirajlal. *The Nalanda University* (Madras: B.G. Paul &, 1934).

36 *Darshana,* loosely speaking, means 'school of philosophy'. *Sampradaya* is a philosophical tradition.

37 It was not a coincidence that when the project to revive this ancient Nalanda University was mooted in 2006 by the then Indian President Abdul Kalam, it met with enthusiastic response and generous funding from countries as diverse as South Korea, China, Japan, Singapore, Malaysia and Australia. For the full story of the fate of this project, see: Balakrishna, Sandeep. 2020. *Blinded by Communism: The Story of How Amartya Sen Ruined the Nalanda Revival,* 30 December. Accessed 4 August 2021. https://www. dharmadispatch.in/commentary/blinded-by-communism-the-story-of-how-amartya-sen-ruined-the-nalanda-revival

38 Dutt, Sukumar. *Buddhist Monks and Monasteries of India: Their History and Contribution to Indian Culture.* (London: George Allen and Unwin Ltd, 1988). (Reprint).

39 For a vividly detailed panorama of this profound and extensive atmosphere of high scholarship, and the culture of learning of this era, see Dr. S.L. Bhyrappa's Kannada novel, *Saartha.* (*Caravan* in English).

40 Brave. Daring. Generally, a person who is willing to do dangerous things, and does not show fear in difficult or perilous situations.

41 Minhaj-i-Siraj. *Tabakat-i-Nasiri,* 1873. 552.

42 Image source: By unknown author. See, https://archive.org/details/ hutchinsonsstory00londuoft, Public Domain, https://commons. wikimedia.org/w/index.php?curid=39273227

43 Goel, Sita Ram. *Hindu Temples: What Happened to Them: The Islamic Evidence.* (Delhi: Voice of India, 1993), 272.

44 Ambedkar, B.R. *Dr. Babasaheb Ambedkar Writings and Speeches,* Vol. III, (Delhi: Dr. Ambedkar Foundation, 2014), 232–33.

45 See for example: (a) Shourie, Arun. *Eminent Historians: Their Technology, Their Line, Their Fraud.* Revised edition. (Delhi:. HarperCollins, 2014); (b) Shourie, Arun. (28 June 2014). 'How history was made up at Nalanda.' *The Indian Express.* https://indianexpress. com/article/opinion/columns/how-history-was-made-up-at-nalanda/

46 Generally speaking, the contemporary Bihar region.

47 See, for example: Taranatha. *Tāranātha's History of Buddhism in India,* ed. Chattopadhyaya, Debiprasad, (Delhi: Motilal Banarsidass, 1990), 272.

48 A good work is: Dharmasvamin. *Biography of Dharmasvamin: Chag lo tsa-ba Chos-rje-dpal*, trans., Roerich, Dr. George, (Patna: K.P. Jayaswal Research Institute, 1959).

49 Quoted in the aforementioned, *Biography of Dharmasvamin: Chag lo tsa-ba Chos-rje-dpal*, xix.

50 For another scholarly exposition of this, see: K.T.S. Sarao. 'On the Question of Animosity of the Brāhmaṇas and Persecution by Brāhmaṇical Kings Leading to the Decline of Buddhism in India.' *The Chung-Hwa Buddhist Studies*, No. 10, (2006).

51 Smith, Vincent A. *The Oxford History of India*, (Oxford: Clarendon Press, 1919), 221.

52 Eliot, H.M., and John Dowson. *The History of India as Told by Its Own Historians*, Vol. 2, (London: Trubner & Co, 1869), 232.

53 Minhaj-i-Siraj. *Tabakat-i-Nasiri*, 1873. 554.

54 Ibid, 557.

55 Ibid, 558.

56 See: Historical Places.

57 See: Historical Places.

58 Hunter, W.W. *A Statistical Account of Bengal*, (London: Trubner & Co, 1876), 51–52.

59 For additional reading on Gaur, see: (a) Dey, N. *The Geographical Dictionary of Ancient and Mediaeval India*, (Calcutta: W. Newman & Co, 1899), 21, 26, 36, 47, 68; (b) Layard, F.P. *The Journal of the Asiatic Society of Bengal* 22 (1853), 51–52.

60 Also spelled as 'Gauriya'.

61 They were also known as Varendra Brahmanas, named after the Varendra Tract, now known as the Barind Tract. See: 'Barind.' Encyclopedia Britannica, 27 August 2009. https://www.britannica.com/place/Barind. Last accessed: 4 August 2021.

62 Sarkar, Jadunath. *The History of Bengal Volume II: Muslim Period*, (Delhi: B.R. Publishing Corporation, 2003), 8.

63 Minhaj-i-Siraj. *Tabakat-i-Nasiri*, trans., H.G. Raverty, (London: Asiatic Society of Bengal, 1873), 559–60.

64 Bada'uni, Abd al-Qadir. *Muntakhab-ut-Tawarikh*, Vol. 1, 1990. 83.

65 From Lakhnauti, the name reverted to Gaur. Under Humayun, it became Bakhtabad, evidently named in Bakhtiyar's honour. For some time, it was renamed as Jannatabad.

66 Minhaj-i-Siraj. *Tabakat-i-Nasiri*, 1873, 556–57.

67 Or Burdhan-Kot in Muslim chronicles.

68 Minhaj-i-Siraj. *Tabakat-i-Nasiri*, 1873, 561.

69 Tibet.

70 For a good discussion of these weapons, see 1873. In *Tabakat-I-Nasiri*, by Minhaj-i-Siraj, trans. by H.G. Raverty, 548–49, 566.

71 Minhaj-i-Siraj. *Tabakat-i-Nasiri*, 1873. Translated by H.G. Raverty, London. Asiatic Society of Bengal, 568–69.

72 For a good discussion on this and for a general history of Kamarupa, see: Bahadur, Rai K.L. Barua. *Early History of Kamarupa*, (Rai K.L. Barua Bahadur, 1933).

73 Minhaj-i-Siraj. *Tabakat-i-Nasiri*, 1873, 572.

74 See *Invaders and Infidels: Book 1*.

75 Sarkar, Jadunath. *The History of Bengal Volume II: Muslim Period*, (Delhi: B.R. Publishing Corporation, 2003), 12–13.

76 Bada'uni, Abd al-Qadir. *Muntakhab-ut-Tawarikh*, Vol. 1, 1990, 86.

77 Also spelled Husam-ud-Ewaz. For a detailed account of the early life and rise of Iwaz, see: Minhaj-i-Siraj. *Tabakat-i-Nasiri*, 1873, 581–82. Even in his case, Minhaj adopts the same pattern of divine-prophecy-in-hindsight. Accordingly, Iwaz's future greatness was already foretold by some Muslim Dervishes in the Ghur region.

78 The place remains unidentifiable.

79 Minhaj-i-Siraj. *Tabakat-i-Nasiri*, 1873, 583.

80 He also called himself Ghiyas-ud-din Khalji.

81 Ibid, 586–87.

82 (a) Legend of the coin: Obverse—'Al-Sultan Al-Muazzam Ghiyath Al-Dunya Wa'l Din Abul FathIwad Bin al-Hussain Nasir Amir Al-Muminin.' Reverse—La ilala illaillah Muhammadun rasulullah. For a pictorial depiction of the coin, see 'Coins of Bengal Sultanate Part 1.' Mintage World. Team Mintage World, 27 September 2019. Last accessed: 10 August 2021. https://www.mintageworld.com/blog/coins-bengal-sultanate-part-1/; (b) For a detailed discussion on the coinage of Iwaz, see Sarkar, Jadunath. *The History of Bengal Volume II: Muslim Period*, (Delhi: B.R. Publishing Corporation, 2003), 39–40.

83 For the full story, see: Sarkar, Jadunath. *The History of Bengal Volume II: Muslim Period*, 2003, 26 onwards.

84 See: *Invaders and Infidels: Book 1*.

85 Some accounts narrate that Iltutmish personally marched against Iwaz, while others record that his son Nasir-ud-din defeated and killed Iwaz.

86 Sarkar, Jadunath. *The History of Bengal Volume II: Muslim Period*, 2003, 28.

87 The Islamic faith.

Chapter 1: Turkic-Muslin Tribal Chaos in Delhi

1   Uris, Leon. *The Hajj*, (United States: RHUS (Reprint), 1985).

2   Generally speaking, Lord Chamberlain. The official who superintended all court ceremonies, regulated protocol, and controlled contacts between the ruler and his subjects.

3   Generally, Abyssinians.

4   Paiks were Hindus forcibly converted to Islam, typically serving as infantrymen. They formed the lowest rung in the new Delhi Sultanate irrespective of loyalty or meritorious service. Under Balban, 1,000 Paiks formed his personal retinue when he went on hunting expeditions. For a brief discussion on Paiks, see later in this book.

5   For an exhaustive history, see: Ayalon, David. *Studies on the Mamluks of Egypt: 1250–1517*, (London: Variorum Reprints, 1977).

6   For a detailed account, see *Invaders and Infidels: Book 1*.

7   For the full account, see *Invaders and Infidels: Book 1*.

8   Also called Firoz Baghrash Khalji.

9   Chief of the royal bodyguards.

10 Now part of the Patiala district, Punjab.

11 For a detailed discussion see: Day, U.N. 'North-West Frontier of the Sultanate during the 13th Century.' *Indian Historical Quarterly*, Vol. XV, No. II, (1941), 59.

12 Sirhindi, Yahya bin Ahmad bin Abdullah. *Tarikh-i-Mubarakshahi*, 53.

13 The chronicler Barani gives the title as Siyasat Khan.

14 Master of Ceremonies.

15 In charge of the management of the royal household.

16 Eliot, H.M., and John Dowson. *The History of India as Told by Its Own Historians*, Vol. 3, (London: Trubner & Co, 1871), 133.

17 Not clearly identifiable today. It is traced to the vicinity of the Jamuna river six or seven miles east of old Delhi and south west of Kilughari.

18 Sirhindi, Yahya bin Ahmad bin Abdullah. *Tarikh-i-Mubarakshahi*, 1932, 53.

19 Ibid, 54.

20 Lal, K.S. *History of the Khaljis*, 1950. Allahabad, The Indian Press, Ltd, 9.

21 Eliot, H.M., and John Dowson. *The History of India as Told by Its Own Historians*, Vol. 3, 1871, 135.

22 Sirhindi, Yahya bin Ahmad bin Abdullah. *Tarikh-i-Mubarakshahi*, 1932, 55–56.

23 According to a time-honoured practice of the pagan Mongols, it was considered a sin to spill royal blood on the ground. The practice was later adopted and followed by Muslims as well. For a good discussion on this, see John Andrew Boyle. 'The Death Of The Last Abbasid Caliph: A Contemporary Muslim Account.' *Journal of Semitic Studies*, Vol. 6, Is. 2, (Autumn 1961), 145–161.

24 Firishta offers a variation of this murder: 'Malik Firoz...sent assassins to cut off Kaiqubad, who lay sick at Kilughari. The ruffians found him lying on his bed, in a dying state, entirely deserted by all his attendants. They beat out his brains with bludgeons, and then, rolling him up in the bed-clothes, threw him out of the window into the river. The chief assassin was a Tartar of some family, whose father had been unjustly put to death by Kaiqubad, and who willingly undertook the office out of revenge.' Firishta. *Tarikh-i Firishta*, trans., John Briggs. (Calcutta: R. Cambray & Co, 1908), 282–83.

Chapter 2: The Senile Sultan's Grotesque Sultanate

1 Niyogi, Roma. 'A Note on Turuska-Danda.' *The Indian Historical Quarterly*, Vol. XXV, No. I, (Mar. 1949), 135–38.

2 For a good discussion, see: Lal, K. S. 'Chapter 4: Muslim Rule in India.' *The Legacy of Muslim Rule in India*. (Voice of India, 1992).

3 Or *Dhimmis*.

4 Razia.

5 Ibid, 16.

6 Bada'uni, Abd al-Qadir. *Muntakhab-ut-Tawarikh*, Vol. 1, trans., Ranking, George, (Delhi: Atlantic Publishers & Distributors, 1990), 230.

7 For a slight disagreement on the name of the town, see: Lal, K.S. *History of the Khaljis*, (Allahabad: The Indian Press, Ltd, 1950), 9, footnote 3.

8 Sirhindi, Yahya bin Ahmad bin Abdullah. *Tarikh-i-Mubarakshahi*, trans., K.K.Basu, (Baroda: Baroda Oriental Institute, 1932), 58.

For an even more detailed list, see: Lal, K.S. *History of the Khaljis*, 1950, 19–20.

9   Lal, K.S. *History of the Khaljis*, 1950, 10–11.

10 Eliot, H.M., and John Dowson. *The History of India as Told by Its Own Historians,* Vol. 3, (London: Trubner & Co, 1871), 135.

11 Ibid.

12 Ibid.

13 Firishta. *Tarikh-i Firishta*. 1908, 290–91.

14 Lal, K.S. *History of the Khaljis*, 1950, 21.

15 Firishta. *Tarikh-i Firishta*, 1908, 289–90.

16 Here, we find one of the earliest mentions in medieval Muslim histories of India of the term now familiar to us as 'thug'. In contemporary parlance, it means 'knave', 'thief', 'cheat', 'rogue', 'swindler' and 'rowdy'. In its original sense, it had a specific denomination: 'a peculiar class of highway robbers and murderers'. For more information, see: (a) Hodivala, S. H. *Studies in Indo-Muslim History.* (Original Publisher name unavailable), (1939), 266–67; (b) Sahai, Ishwar. 'The Crime of the Thagi and Its Suppression under Lord W.C. Bentinck.' *Indian Culture*, Vol. VIII, No. 1–4, (July 1936), 148.

17 For additional details see: Sarkar, Jadunath. *The History of Bengal Volume II: Muslim Period.* (Delhi: B.R. Publishing Corporation, 2003), 69–76.

18 Smith, Vincent A. *The Oxford History of India*, (Oxford: Clarendon Press, 1919), 231.

19 Blochmann, H. 'Contributions to the Geography and History of Bengal (Muhammedan Period).' (Calcutta: Asiatic Society, 1968), 115.

20 Malik Ali was the son of a slave of Balban. The chronicler Barani addresses him by his title, *Maula Zada-i Sultan-i Balban,* literally meaning, 'Freedman of Sultan Balban'. Kaiqubad had elevated him to the post of the *Sarjandar* of Awadh. Jalal-ud-din Khalji's capture of Delhi had grievously shattered Malik Ali's prestige and like other Balbani loyalists, he was also biding his time.

21 *Dhanuk* is derived from the Sanskrit word, *dhanu* meaning 'bow'.

22 In fact, Ziauddin Barani, Khusrau's contemporary, admirer and friend, makes no secret of his distaste for this sycophant. He writes in his *Tarikh'i-Firoz-Shahi*: 'as [Khusrau] wrote the history of Ala-ud-din [Khalji] during that Sultan's reign and every volume

of it was presented to the Sultan, it was impossible for him, to refrain from praising that terrible king or to speak of anything but his greatness.' Quoted in: Amir Khusrau. *Khaza'inul Futuh*, trans., Muhammad Habib, (Bombay: B. Taraporewala, Sons & Co., 1931), xi.

23   Eliot, H.M., and John Dowson. *The History of India as Told by Its Own Historians*, Vol. 3, 1871, 536–37.

24   Eliot, H.M., and John Dowson. *The History of India as Told by Its Own Historians*, Vol. 3, 1871, 137.

25   Ibid, 138.

26   Ibid, 536–38.

27   Ibid, 538.

28   Yahya Sirhindi gives the name, Pira Deo Kotla. Other chroniclers call him Bairam Deo.

29   Eliot, H.M., and John Dowson. *The History of India as Told by Its Own Historians*, Vol. 3, 1871, 138.

30   Ibid, 139.

31   Firishta. *Tarikh-i Firishta*, 1908, 295.

32   Eliot, H.M., and John Dowson. *The History of India as Told by Its Own Historians,* Vol. 3, 1871, 139–40.

33   See: Mohammad Habib, K.A. Nizami, et al. *A Comprehensive History of India: The Delhi Sultanat*, Vol. 5, (Delhi: People's Publishing House, 1970), 315–16.

34   Eliot, H.M., and John Dowson. *The History of India as Told by Its Own Historians*, Vol. 3, 1871, 538–39.

35   The Islamic faith.

36   For a highly interesting discussion on Rihan, see: Saran, P. 'Sultan Nasir-Uddin Mahmud and his two Ministers: General Survey And Estimate.' *Proceedings of the Indian History Congress*, 5 (1941), 290–95.

37   For Rihan's full story, see: *Invaders and Infidels: Book 1*.

38   Firishta gives the following list of members in Jalal-ud-din Khalji's close circle:

Amirs and Nobles:

(a) Tajuddin Katchi; (b) Fakhruddin Katchi; (c) Izzuddin Ghori; (d) Karra Beg; (e) Nusrat Sabah; (f) Ahmad Habib; (g) Kamaaluddin Abdul Mali; (h) Nasiruddin Kohrami; (i) Saad'ud din Mantakhi.

Scholars and Poets:

(a) Tajuddin Irakki; (b) Amir Khusrau; (c) Khwaja Hussain; (d) Mauid Diwana; (e) Amir Arslan; (f) Ikhtiyaruddin Yahgi; (g) Baaki Khutir.

Singers and Instrumentalists:

(a) Mohammed Shah Hatki; (b) Fattoo Shah; (c) Naseer Khan; (d) Behroz.

39 Eliot, H.M., and John Dowson. *The History of India as Told by Its Own Historians*, Vol. 3, 1871, p 142 onwards.

40 The more recalcitrant conspirators were banished from Delhi and forbidden from returning to the city for a full year.

41 Also known as Shaikh Fariduddin Shakarganj.

42 Present-day Pakpattan in the Punjab province of Pakistan. Its original Hindu name was derived from the ancient Yaudheya Dynasty, whose empire occupied the territory between the Sindhu and the Ganga rivers. The Yaudheyas are perhaps as old as Bharatavarsha itself. They are mentioned in the Mahabharata and by Panini, and were recognized as a Mahajanapada (roughly speaking, a Republic) by Chandragupta Maurya. Their capital was the modern-day Rohtak. At various points in their rule, that lasted from the 5th century BCE to the 4th century CE, they controlled all of Punjab up to the border of Gandhara (Kandahar) on the northwest, all of Haryana, and much later, Northern Rajasthan, Western Uttar Pradesh, Garhwal and Kumaon, and parts of Himachal Pradesh. Among other things, a substantial hoard of the Yaudheya coins were discovered in these regions and they continue to be a fascinating topic for scholars of ancient Indian history, in itself a huge testimony to their enduring impact. For good material on this topic, see: (a) Saklani, Dinesh Prasad. *Ancient Communities of the Himalaya*, (Delhi: Indus Publishing Company, 1998); (b) Sharma, Arvind. 'Did the Hindus Lack a Sense of History?' *Numen* 50, No. 2 (2003): 190–227; (c) Thakur, Upendra. 'Early Indian Mints.' *Journal of the Economic and Social History of the Orient*, 16, No. 2/3 (1973): 265–97; (d) Sahni, B. 'Yaudheya Coin Moulds from Sunet, near Ludhiana in the Sutlej Valley.' *Current Science*, 10, No. 2 (1941): 65–67. Another good summary is provided in: Cunningham, Alexander. *Report of a Tour in the Punjab in 1878–79*, (Office of the Superintendent of Government Printing, 1882), 153–57.

The original Hindu character of Ajodhan/Pakpattan was completely wiped out over the centuries beginning with Sabuktigin's capture in 977–78. Its current renown as the seat of the Chisti order of Sufi Islam owes to the aforementioned Shaikh Fariduddin. For good historical discussions, see: (a) Zilli, I.A. 'Successors of Shaikh Nasiruddin Mahmud and the Disintegration of the Chishti Central Organisation.' *Proceedings of the Indian History Congress*, 44 (1983), 320–26; (b) Kamran, Tahir, and Amir Khan Shahid. 'Shari'a, Shi'as and Chishtiya Revivalism: Contextualising the Growth of Sectarianism in the Tradition of the Sialvi Saints of the Punjab.' *Journal of the Royal Asiatic Society*, Third Series, 24, No. 3 (2014): 477–92.

43 Direct disciple of Shaikh Moinuddin Chisti.

44 See the discussion in Rizvi, Saiyid Athar Abbas. *Muslim Revivalist Movements in Northern India in the Sixteenth and Seventeenth Centuries*, (Munshiram Manoharlal Publishers, 1965), 17–19.

45 Eliot, H.M., and John Dowson. *The History of India as Told by Its Own Historians*, Vol. 3, (London: Trubner & Co, 1871), 144.

46 Firishta. *Tarikh-i Firishta*, 298.

47 For roughly similar estimates, see: Bada'uni, Abd al-Qadir. *Muntakhab-ut-Tawarikh*, Vol. 1, 1990, 233–4.

48 Quoted in: Lal, K.S. *History of the Khaljis*, 1950, 28.

49 Firishta. *Tarikh-i Firishta*, 298.

50 Briggs, who has translated Firishta's work, makes a blunt but eminently realistic observation regarding titles used by Muslim invaders: 'It is instructive and interesting to trace throughout this work the various distinctions which marked the several races of conquerors in the appellations belonging to their chiefs. Thus, among the early Arabians, we find the simple title of "Sheikh"'.... The caliphs first brought into use those high-sounding titles, the cheap but valued reward of military merit; such as, 'The Commander of those to be saved', 'The Lion of God', 'The Sword of the Lord', 'The Defender of the Faith', 'The Splendour of Islam', 'The Glory of the Faithful', 'The Strength of the Government', 'The Right Arm of the State', with numerous others.

51 Bada'uni, Abd al-Qadir. *Muntakhab-ut-Tawarikh*, Vol. 1, 1990, 234.

52 Sirhindi, Yahya bin Ahmad bin Abdullah. *Tarikh-i-Mubarakshahi*. trans., K.K.Basu, (Baroda: Baroda Oriental Institute, 1932), 62.

53 Bada'uni, Abd al-Qadir. *Muntakhab-ut-Tawarikh*, Vol. 1, 1990, 235.

54 Technically called *Agni-Divya,* where 'Divya' means 'ordeal'. Here, it means 'trial by the ordeal of fire'. Typically, in a dispute, the guilt or otherwise of the accused was proven by making the person place his hands or feet or the entire body in a pit of fire. If the fire did not harm the person, the non-guilty verdict was pronounced. The system of *Divya*-s formed one of the main pillars of Hindu jurisprudence from unknown antiquity. The ancient lawgiver Brihaspati enumerates nine *Divyas:* (a) *Tula* or balance/scales; (b) *Agni* or fire; (c) *Jala* or water; (d) *Visha* or poison; (e) *Dharma-Adharma:* where two metal or clay Murtis are made, one signifying the deity of Dharma and the other, Adharma. They are thrown inside a large earthen jar and if the accused takes out the Murti of Dharma, he or she is regarded as innocent; (f) *Tandula* or rice; (g) *Tapta-masaka* or hot gold coin; (h) *Phaala* or spearhead and (i) *Kosha*: literally, 'Murti-washed water'. The accused person is made to drink water with which the Murtis of the deities of Surya, Devi, etc., have been washed. If the accused falls sick within 14 days of drinking it, a guilty verdict is pronounced.

For a scholarly paper on *Divyas,* see: Sircar, Dines Chandra. 'The Divyas.' *Journal of the Andhra Historical Research Society* VII (April 1933), 195–206.

For an exhaustive discussion on Hindu jurisprudence, see: 'Vyavahara' in Kane, Pandurang Vaman. *History of Dharmasastra.* II. Vol. III. (Pune: Bhandarkar Oriental Research Institute, 1973), 242–824.

Without judging the merit of these ordeals using yardsticks of our own time, history conclusively shows that they had proven to be extraordinary deterrents. One measure of this is the fact of their remarkable longevity. As recent as 1958, one or more of these ordeals were in vogue in the East Godavari district, (undivided) Andhra Pradesh. For a good discussion, see: Sircar, Dines Chandra. 'Successors of the Satavahanas in the Eastern Deccan.' *Journal of the Department of Letters* XXVI (1935), 1–126.

55 For a historical context, see: 'The Religion of the Arabs.' *The Indian Antiquary,* XV (Bombay: 1886). 312–16.

56 Some chroniclers write that he was imprisoned at Badaun.

57   The Sufi order of Haidari Qalandars, founded by Shaikh Najmuddin Tusi follows a rather intriguing practice. The Qalandars completely shave their head, facial hair and eyebrows. It was customary to carry a razor with them all the time. For a good study, see: (a) Rizvi, Saiyid Athar Abbas. *Muslim Revivalist Movements in Northern India in the Sixteenth and Seventeenth Centuries*, (Munshiram Manoharlal Publishers, 1965); (b) B. Lawrence. 'Abū Bakr Ṭūsī Ḥaydarī.' *Encyclopaedia Iranica*, I/3, p. 265; an updated version is available online at http://www.iranicaonline.org/articles/abu-bakr-tusi-haydari-7th-13th-century-indo-muslim-saint (accessed on 31 August 2021).

58   Firishta. *Tarikh-i Firishta*, 300.

59   Shourie, Arun. *The World of Fatwas*. Revised edition-, (Noida: Harper Collins, 2012), 60–62.

60   Quoted in: Lal, K.S. *History of the Khaljis*, 1950, 32.

61   Eliot, H.M., and John Dowson. *The History of India as Told by Its Own Historians*, Vol. 3, 1871, 146.

62   Firishta. *Tarikh-i Firishta* 300–01.

63   Bada'uni, Abd al-Qadir. *Muntakhab-ut-Tawarikh*, Vol. 1, 1990. 235.

64   In the assessment of the scholar Ishwari Prasad, 'The superstition of the age ranged itself on the side of the Maula and the chronicler records that on the day of his death there arose a terrible storm which darkened the world.' For the full discussion, see: Prasad, Ishwari. *History of Medieval India*, (Allahabad: The Indian Press Ltd, 1933), 233.

65   Sirhindi, Yahya bin Ahmad bin Abdullah. *Tarikh-i-Mubarakshahi*, trans., K.K.Basu, (Baroda: Baroda Oriental Institute, 1933), 62–65.

66   The term 'Shaikh' is used in the sense of a Sufi.

Chapter 3: The Indomitable Defiance of Hammiradeva

1   Ranthambore. Literally, 'City of the Battle Tower'.

2   Most Muslim chronicles are either tight-lipped or gloss over the death of Ikhtiyaruddin, characterizing it politely as 'illness'. It remains a mystery and a topic for further exploration given two non-coincidental facts: (a) that he was the chief patron of Sidi Maula; (b) that he was one of the chief contenders for Jalal-ud-din's throne, and a dogged rival of his younger brother, Arkali Khan.

3   Bada'uni, Abd al-Qadir. *Muntakhab-ut-Tawarikh*, Vol. 1, 1990. Translated by Ranking, George, Delhi. Atlantic Publishers & Distributors, 232–33.

4   Firishta. *Tarikh-i Firishta*, 301.

5   Or Guhilot. The contemporary spelling is 'Gehlot'.

6   Srivastava, A.K. *Khalji Sultans in Rajasthan*, (Gorakhpur: Purvanchal Prakashan, 1981) 21.

7   Suri, Nayachandra. *Hammira Mahakavya*, trans., Kirtane, N.J., (Bombay: Education Society's Press, 1879) 21.

8   This story of this campaign has been narrated more fully in *Invaders and Infidels: Book 1*.

9   Aligarh.

10 Eliot, H.M., and John Dowson. *The History of India as Told by Its Own Historians*, Vol. 2, 225.

11 Ibid, 220–21.

12 Hasan Nizami calls the kettledrums as 'golden melons'. Ibid, 220.

13 Known locally as Masjid-i Jāmi'-i Herāt. It was originally a Zoroastrian temple converted into a mosque in the 7th century. The structure underwent several upheavals over time until Muhammad Ghori acquired substantial land around it and laid the foundation for constructing an imposing mosque. His slave, Qutub-ud-din Aibak, gave it its current form and imposing size. As narrated above, the money came from the sale of just one golden kettledrum given by Prithviraja Chahamana's own son.
    For further reading on the history of this mosque, see: (a) Verfasser, Hansen, Erik. *The Ghurid Portal of the Friday Mosque of Herat, Afghanistan: Conservation of a Historic Monument*, (Aarhus University Press, 2015); (b) Patel, Alka, 'Architectural Cultures and Empire: The Ghurids in Northern India (ca. 1192–1210).' *Bulletin of the Asia Institute*, (2007).

14 Sharma, Dasharatha. *Early Chauhan Dynasties*, (Delhi: S. Chand & Co, 1959), 101.

15 For a good discussion on this topic, see: Sharma, Dasharatha. 'Chapters IX and X,' *Early Chauhan Dynasties*, (Delhi, S. Chand & Co, 1959).

16 Kautilya. *Arthasastra*, Books 2.10, 6–7, 10.

17 For a detailed discussion on the origins and history of the Sapadalaksha dynasty, see: Sharma, Dasharatha. Chapter III, *Early Chauhan Dynasties*, (Delhi: S. Chand & Co, 1959).

18 For a brilliant assessment of this phenomenon, see, R.C. Majumdar. *The History and Culture of the Indian People*, Vol. 5, (Bombay: Bharatiya Vidya Bhavan, 1960), 145–47.

19 The popular surname 'Dahiya', found even today in and around Rajasthan, Haryana and Gujarat, is a corruption of 'Dadicha'. The Dahiya Kshatriyas till date worship Dadhmat Devi as their *Kula Devata* or family deity. An inscription of the Dahiya Kshatriyas was discovered in the famous Kevaya-Mata Temple in Kinsariya, Rajasthan. For a truly illuminating history on this subject, see: Ramakarna, Pandit. 'Kinsariya Inscription of Dadhichika (Dahiya).' *Epigraphia Indica,* Vol. 12, (Archeological Survey of India, 1913–14), 56–61.

20 Derived from Sanskrit: *Maru* = Barren or Desert; *Wad* = area or region.

21 The most authoritative study of this inscription is the following: Ramakarna, Pandit. 'Manglana Stone Inscription of Jayatrasimha.' *Indian Antiquary,* Vol. 41, (Bombay: British India Press, 1912), 85–88. Of special note in this inscription are the details related to the nuances of local administration, and management of charitable activities by the community.

22 Shipra.

23 Betwa.

24 Minhaj-i-Siraj. *Tabakat-i-Nasiri*, trans., H.G. Raverty, (London: Asiatic Society of Bengal, 1873), 610–11.

25 Nayachandra Suri. *Hammira Mahakavya*, trans., N.J. Kirtane, (Bombay: Education Society's Press, 1879) 24–25.

26 Ibid, 25.

27 Ibid, 25–26.

28 The scholar and historian Dasharatha Sharma, identifies this king as Devapala but his real identity remains a mystery. See: Dasharatha Sharma. *Early Chauhan Dynasties*, (Delhi: S. Chand & Co, 1959), 103.

29 For good discussions on this episode, see: (a) Jackson, Peter. *The Delhi Sultanate: A Political and Military History* (Cambridge: Cambridge University Press, 2003: 132); (b) Karna, Pandit Rama. 'Indian Antiquary.' *Mangalna Stone Inscription of Jayatrasimha*, 41, (Bombay: The British India Press, 1912), 85–88.

30 Raverty, the translator of *Tabakat-i-Nasiri* comments on the Hindu reconquest of Rantambhor in a rather interesting language: 'It was

soon restored, however, by the Hindus. What a flourish might have been made of this affair in the Rajput annals!' Quoted in: Minhaj-i-Siraj. *Tabakat-i-Nasiri*, trans., H.G. Raverty, (London: Asiatic Society of Bengal, 1873), 642, footnote 1.

31 Nayachandra Suri, *Hammira Mahakavya*, trans. N.J. Kirtane, (Bombay: Education Society Press, 1879), 26.

32 For a good assessment, see: Srivastav, A.K. *Khalji Sultans in Rajasthan*. (Gorakhpur: Purvanchal Prakashan, 1981), 10–11.

33 Eliot, H.M., and John Dowson. *The History of India as Told by Its Own Historians,* Vol. 2, 370–71.

34 This Jaitra Simha should not be confused with his namesake who had built the Mangalana stepwell.

35 For a brief discussion on Jaitra Simha's career, see, Majumdar, R.C. *History and Culture of the Indian People*, Vol. 5, (Bombay: Bharatiya Vidya Bhavan, 1957), 84–86.

36 Srivastav, A.K. *Khalji Sultans in Rajasthan*. 1981. 12.

37 In general, such a protagonist is known as a *Dhirodātta,* who is naturally brave, gentle, forgiving, merciful, determined, humble, highly qualified, scholarly, chivalrous, is in possession of an attractive personality and pleasing to look at.

38 For an exposition of the psyche of the medieval Muslim chronicler, see:

  i Balakrishna, Sandeep. 'The Far-Reaching Implications of the Medieval Muslim Chronicler's Psyche on the History of the Future: A Deep-Dive into the Mindset of Medieval Muslim Chroniclers: Preface.' *The Dharma Dispatch*. Accessed 17 April 2022. https://www.dharmadispatch.in/history/a-deep-dive-into-the-mindset-of-medieval-muslim-chroniclers-preface

  ii Balakrishna, Sandeep. 'The Qualifications of a Medieval Muslim Chronicler and the Nature of Muslim Histories.' *The Dharma Dispatch*. Accessed 17 April 2022. https://www.dharmadispatch.in/history/the-qualifications-of-a-medieval-muslim-chronicler-and-the-nature-of-muslim-histories

  iii Balakrishna, Sandeep. 'The Far-Reaching Implications of the Medieval Muslim Chronicler's Psyche on the History of the Future.' *The Dharma Dispatch*. Accessed 17 April 2022. https://www.dharmadispatch.in/history/the-far-reaching-implications-of-the-medieval-muslim-chroniclers-psyche-on-the-history-of-the-future

39 Suri, Nayachandra. *Hammira Mahakavya*, 26.

40 For an interesting discussion regarding Sanskrit literary sources that mention Hammiradeva, see Gopala-Giri, Radhakrishna Choudhary, and Surendra Nath Sastri. 'The Prabodhacandrikā of Baijaladeva along with the Incomplete Commentary, Subodhinī.' *Annals of the Bhandarkar Oriental Research Institute*, 44, No. 1/4 (1963): 75–146.

41 For a detailed account of this campaign, see N.J. Kirtane. 'The Hammira Mahakavya of Nayachandra Suri.' *The Indian Antiquary* Vol. 8, (1879), 55–73.

42 Mandalgarh.

43 Mount Abu.

44 Badnor.

45 Suri, Nayachandra. *Hammira Mahakavya*, 28.

46 A village lying to the west of Siri. Now untraceable.

47 Another untraceable village that was located south-west of Delhi.

48 Narnaul is now renowned mostly for the historic battle fought on 16 November 1857 between the East India Company and Indians during the first war of Indian Independence.

49 Eliot, H.M., and John Dowson. *The History of India as Told by Its Own Historians*, Vol. 2, 540.

50 The location is untraceable.

51 For enriching discussions on Jhain, see: (a) Lal, K.S. *History of the Khaljis*, (Allahabad: The Indian Press, Ltd, 1950), 101; (b) Gupta, Satya Prakash. 'Jhain of the Delhi Sultanate: Summary.' *Proceedings of the Indian History Congress* 34 (1973), 202.

52 Srivastav, A.K. *Khalji Sultans in Rajasthan*, (Gorakhpur: Purvanchal Prakashan, 1981), 34.

53 Eliot, H.M., and John Dowson. *The History of India as Told by Its Own Historians*, Vol. 3, 542.

54 Ibid.

55 One *maan* in the period of the Delhi Sultanate measured 15 kilograms.

56 Isami, Abdul. *Futuhu's Salatin*, Vol. 2, trans., Husain, Agha Mahdi, (New York: Asia Publishing House, 1969) 389.

57 Eliot, H.M., and John Dowson. *The History of India as Told by Its Own Historians*, Vol. 3, 542.

58 Lal, K.S. *History of the Khaljis*, (Allahabad: The Indian Press, Ltd, 1950) 35.

59 In this case, Purohitas, etc.

60 For a brilliant account of war technologies used in the medieval Muslim world, see Crowley, Roger. *Accursed Tower: The Crusaders' Last Battle for the Holy Land*, (New Haven & London: Yale University Press, 2019), 133 onwards.

61 For details, see *Invaders and Infidels: Book 1*.

62 For this conversation between Jalal-ud-din Khalji and Ahmad Chhap, see: (a) Eliot, H.M., and John Dowson. *The History of India as Told by Its Own Historians*, Vol. 3, 147; (b) Firishta. *Tarikh-i Firishta*, 302.

63 Nizamuddin Ahmad. *Tabaqat-i-Akbari*. 1927, 143.

64 Eliot, H.M., and John Dowson. *The History of India as Told by Its Own Historians*, Vol. 3, 542–43.

65 Sixth month in the Islamic calendar.

66 Eliot, H.M., and John Dowson. *The History of India as Told by Its Own Historians*, Vol. 3, 543.

67 It is now known as Sunam, about two hours from Sirhind.

68 Lal, K.S. *History of the Khaljis*, 38.

69 Eliot, H.M., and John Dowson. *The History of India as Told by Its Own Historians*, Vol. 3, 147.

70 The place remains unidentified.

71 Isami, Abdul. *Futuhu's Salatin*, Vol. 2, trans., Husain, Agha Mahdi (New York: Asia Publishing House, 1969), 379.

72 The exact Mandor which Jalal-ud-din Khalji destroyed is unclear. For good discussions on the topic, see: (a) Thomas, Edward. *The Pathan Kings of Dehli*, (London: Trubner & Co, 1871), 78; (b) Hodivala, S.H. *Studies in Indo-Muslim History*, (Bombay: 1939), 393–94; (c) Reu, V.N. *Marwar Ka Itihas* Vols 1 & 2 (Jodhpur: Rajasthani Granthagar, 2019); (d) Jain, Kailash Chand. 'History of Mandor.' *Proceedings of the Indian History Congress* 22 (1959): 228–33.

73 Srivastav, A.K. *Khalji Sultans in Rajasthan* (Gorakhpur: Purvanchal Prakashan, 1981) 39.

74 Sirhindi, Yahya bin Ahmad bin Abdullah. *Tarikh-i-Mubarakshahi*, trans., K.K.Basu, (Baroda: Baroda Oriental Institute, 1932), 61.

Chapter 4: The Embers of Treachery at Kara

1   Now a town panchayat in the Barabanki district.

2   Wealthy merchants, businessmen, prominent townsfolk, etc.

3 Eliot, H.M., and John Dowson. *The History of India as Told by Its Own Historians*, Vol. 2, 536.

4 Ibid, 537.

5 Ibid, 537.

6 Ibid, 538, 541–544.

7 For details of identification, see: Cunningham, Alexander. *Archaeological Survey of India. Four Reports: 1862-1865*, (Simla: Government Central Press, 1871), 328–330.

8 Eliot, H.M., and John Dowson. *The History of India as Told by Its Own Historians*, Vol. 2, 545–47.

9 Ibid, 547.

10 Ibid, 548.

11 Chisti is narrating the story set during the period of Mahmud of Ghazni.

12 Literally, 'that which cannot be slain'.

13 For an exhaustive history of Manikpur, see, *Gazetteer of the Province of Oudh*, Vol. 2, Allahabad: Government Press 1877), 458–483.

14 Eliot, H.M., and John Dowson. *The History of India as Told by Its Own Historians*, Vol. 3, 36.

15 Ibid, 140–41.

16 i   For a brilliant historical sketch of Vidisha from the dawn of Indian civilization, see:
      Law, B.C. 'Vidisa in Ancient India.' *Journal of the Ganganatha Jha Research Institute*, Vol. 9, (November 1951), 1–10.
    ii   For the pivotal role played by Vidisha in Indian history, see: Moti Chandra. *Trade and Trade Routes in Ancient India*. (Delhi: Abhinav Publications, 1977).

17 Now known as Betwa.

18 Kalidasa: *Meghaduta*.

19 Also known as Besnagar. Since 1956, the whole region was administratively merged in the district Vidisha.

20 For truly brilliant and detailed studies of Bhilsa, see: Sircar, D.C. *Studies in the Religious Life of Ancient and Medieval India*, (Delhi: Motilal Banarasidass, 1971), 115–132. Other sources include: (a) *Journal of the Asiatic Society of* Bombay Vol. 31 (1862) III; (b) M. Venkataramayya. 'Maser Inscription of a Sulki Chief.' *Epigraphia Indica* 29 (April 1951), 18–28; (c) Sircar, DC. 'Two Inscriptions from Bhilsa.' *Epigraphia Indica* 30 (1953), 210–219; (d) Sircar, Dineschandra. *Select Inscriptions Bearing on*

Indian History and Civilization, Vol. 1. (Calcutta: University of Calcutta, 1942).

21 Other names include Bhaillasvamin, Bhailasvamin, Bhayila or Bhailla.

22 The Sanskrit root *Bha* means 'light', 'Sun', 'resplendence', etc.

23 Sachau, Edward. *Alberuni's India*, Vol. 1, (London: Kegan Paul, Trench, Trubner & Co. Ltd, 1910), 202.

24 For a detailed description, see: Sircar, DC. 'Two Inscriptions from Bhilsa.' *Epigraphia Indica* 30 (1953): 210–219.

25 A real-life story of delivering justice based on this model is narrated in: Sircar, D.C. *Studies in the Religious Life of Ancient and Medieval India*, (Delhi: Motilal Banarasidass, 1971), 128–132.

26 See also: *Invaders and Infidels: Book 1*.

27 The chronicler Minhaj Siraj was an eyewitness, participant and a beneficiary of this siege. The name 'Milak Deo' has been the subject of some discussions among historians. Some scholars like Hodivala identify his real name as 'Melag'. Others call him 'Mangal'.
'Basil, the accursed' was the Parihara ruler, 'Vishala Deva'.
For Minhaj's account, see: Minhaj-i-Siraj. *Tabakat-i-Nasiri*, 1873, 620.
For discussions about Milak's identity, see: Hodivala, S.H. *Studies in Indo-Muslim History*, (Bombay: 1971), 216–17.

28 Vishaladeva.

29 Minhaj-i-Siraj. *Tabakat-i-Nasiri*, 1873, 622.
The dating of 300 years given by Minhaj differs from the traditional account of the Bhayillaswamin Temple. D.C. Sircar states that the earliest record mentioning it is dated 842 CE but that it was in continuous existence for centuries before it. See: Sircar, D.C. *Studies in the Religious Life of Ancient and Medieval India*, (Delhi: Motilal Banarasidass, 1971), 115–132.

30 Ganguly, D.C. *History of the Paramara Dynasty* (Dacca: University of Dacca, 1933), 218–19.

31 Eliot, H.M., and John Dowson. *The History of India as Told by Its Own Historians*, Vol. 3, 1871, 31.
The trajectory of this Hindu political suicide in Malwa is also described in tragic detail by the scholar of history, D.C. Ganguly in his fine work. See: Ganguly, D.C. 'Fall of the Paramaras of Malwa' in *History of the Paramara Dynasty*, (Dacca: University of Dacca, 1933).

32 Eliot, H.M., and John Dowson. *The History of India as Told by Its Own Historians,* Vol. 3, 1871, 543.

33 Nizamuddin Ahmad. *Tabaqat-i-Akbari,* 1927, 144.

34 Mohammad Habib, K.A. Nizami, et al. *A Comprehensive History of India: The Delhi Sultanat,* Vol. 5, (Delhi: People's Publishing House, 1970), 321–22.

35 Ganguly, D.C. *History of the Paramara Dynasty,* 1933, 234.

Chapter 5: A Fatal Bait

1 Quoted in: Lal, K.S. *History of the Khaljis,* 1950, 45.

2 Eliot, H.M., and John Dowson. *The History of India as Told by Its Own Historians,* Vol. 3, 1871, 148–49.

3 Lal, K.S. *History of the Khaljis,* 1950, 43.

4 Eliot, H.M., and John Dowson. *The History of India as Told by Its Own Historians,* Vol. 3, 1871, 149.

5 This has been more fully discussed in Book 1 of *Invaders and Infidels.*

6 See: 'Khajuraho Inscription.' *Epigraphia Indica,* Vol. 1, (Archeological Survey of India, 1892), 146.

7 The legend of this portrait reads as follows: 'THE END OF A LONG AND PROSPEROUS REIGN (Capitalized in the original). In the centuries immediately preceding the Muhammadan conquest, the Chandellas of Mahoba and Khajuraho were one of the most powerful Rajput ruling Families. The name that has come down most prominently to modern times is that of Raja Dhanga, who ascended the throne at fifty-five and reigned with success forty-six years. In 999, when over 100 years old, he drowned himself at the confluence of the Ganges and Jamna at Prag (Allahabad). To the Hindu this was a fitting end for a very old man after a life of prosperity, as it brought him entire salvation.'
Quoted in: *Hutchinson's Story of the Nations,* (London: Hutchinson & Co. Publishers, Ltd., 1915), 149.

8 See: 'Jabalpur Inscription.' *Epigraphia Indica,* Vol. 2, (Archeological Survey of India, 1892), 1.

9 Near Ujjain.

10 Quoted in: Hari Ram Gupta, ed., *Life and Letters of Sir Jadunath Sarkar,* (Hoshiarpur: Punjab University, 1957), 59.

11 She was the sister of Malik Sanjar who eventually prospered under Ala-ud-din Khalji and was titled Alp Khan.

12 Lal, K.S. *History of the Khaljis,* 1950, 43.

13 Mohammad Habib K.A. Nizami ed, *A Comprehensive History of India*, Vol. 5, (Delhi: People's Publishing House, 1970), 321.

Chapter 6: Dakshinapatha in Disarray

1 Sarkar, Jadunath. *Military History of India*, (Calcutta: M.C. Sarkar & Sons, 1960), 2.

2 The doyen of Indian history, Dr. Jadunath Sarkar provides a superb observation about this extraordinary geography: 'From Calcutta to Lahore the distance is 1,300 miles and yet the difference in height above sea-level between these two cities is only a 1,000 feet, or in other words the ground rises only 9 inches in 1 mile of road.... This would not be surprising in the Bengal Delta, but a 1,000 miles upcountry from Calcutta, the ground formation is the same in the Delhi district; The River Jamuna enters the district at a height of some 710 feet (at the north end) and leaves it at about 630 feet above sea level, with a course within the Delhi limits of rather over 90 miles and the average fall of between 10 and 11 inches to the mile.' See: Sarkar, Jadunath. *Military History of India*, (Calcutta: M.C. Sarkar & Sons, 1960), 2.
   For Sarkar's quote, see: *Delhi Gazetteer of 1883–84*, 3.

3 More generally known as the Gangetic Plain.

4 Punjab.

5 Vindhya is also known as *Vindhyachala*, where 'achala' means mountain. The Mahabharata also calls it the *Vindhyaparvata*. The Kaushitaki Upanishad calls it the *Dakshinaparvata*. Ptolemy, the Greek geographer called it Vindius or Ouindion.

6 Muslim chronicles pronounce it as *Dakhin* and *Dakkhan*. 'Deccan' is the anglicized form of this Islamic linguistic corruption.

7 For a good discussion, see: Ritti, Shrinivas. *The Seunas: The Yadavas of Devagiri*, (Dharwad: Karnatak University, 1973).

8 Sarkar, Jadunath. *Military History of India*, 2–4.

9 The correct historical name is 'Sevuna', the dynasty named after one of its initial founders. However, because the dynasty itself traces its bloodline to the ancient Yadava clan sanctified by Sri Krishna, the terms have been used interchangeably in this book.

10 Original name: Chandradityapura.

11 In northern Karnataka.

12 Contemporary Halebid.

13 Now Basava Kalyana in Bidar district.

14 Some historians ascribe the year to 1200.

15 For valuable information about Hemadri, see: (a) Kate, P.V. *Marathwada under the Nizams, 1724–1948*, (Delhi, India: Mittal Publications, 1987); (b) Nilakanta Sastri, Kallidaikurichi Aiyah. *A History of South India: From Prehistoric Times to the Fall of Vijayanagar*, 4th ed. Oxford India Paperbacks. (Delhi: Oxford University Press, 2005); (c) Ritti, Shrinivas. *The Seunas: The Yadavas of Devagiri*, (Dharwad: Karnatak University, 1973).

16 This style involves incorporating black stone and lime without using any mortar. It uses the technique of tenon and mortise joints.

17 See: Deo, Prabhakar. *Temples of Marathwada*, (Jaipur: Publication Scheme, 1993).

18 Later renamed as Osmanabad.

19 For a brilliant exposition of this system, see Ghoshal, U.N. *Contributions to the History of the Hindu Revenue System*, (Calcutta: Saraswat Library, 1972).

20 Kandagal, now a forgotten village southwest of the Hungund taluk in Bijapur was one such thriving business district. It is specifically described as a *Penthe-Daana* and *maligeya mane*. This clearly implies that it was a trade centre that housed godowns (or *malige*) for storing various goods. See: *Annual Report of South Indian Epigraphy*, 1929–30.

21 Now Dabhol in the Ratnagiri district, Maharashtra. It is the site of the infamous Dabhol LNG Power Plant that Enron had set up. Dabul had retained its commercial dominance over several centuries. The Russian traveller Athanasius Nikitin who visited the town in the 15th century describes it as a large city with an extensive port, which had direct links to all major ports in India and connected Ethiopia as well. It was also a hub of horse trade with breeds coming in from Mysore, Khorasan, Arabia and Nighostan. See: *Maharashtra State Gazetteer: Ratnagiri District*.

22 Isami, Abdul. *Futuhu's Salatin*, Vol. 2, trans., Husain, Agha Mahdi, (New York: Asia Publishing House, 1976), 234.

23 For a brilliant study of guilds in ancient India, see, Majumdar, R.C. *Corporate Life in Ancient India*, (Calcutta: Firma K.L. Mukhopadhyay, 1969).

24 The *Vira-Banajiga*, also known as *Vira-Balanja*, had branches throughout all major cities and towns in South India. Its executive council comprised a whopping *500* members. An excellent

monograph on this community is available in, Saletore B.A. *Karnataka's Trans-Oceanic Contacts*, (Dharwad: Karnatak University, 1956).

25 The familiar surname, 'Mahajan' is derived from this. In the colonial British era, Mahajans were moneylenders, giving substantial loans to serving British officials.

26 Generally meaning, 'prominent men of the city'.

27 A corruption of the Sanskrit term, *Shreshti*, or a merchant.

28 Generally, a 'guild of Settis or Shreshtis'.

29 A Kannada word generally meaning, 'association of merchants'.

30 A Kannada word meaning 'agriculturist or farmer who sells produce'. This is the familiar community name, 'Vokkaliga' in Karnataka.

31 *Vadda* is derived from the Sanskrit root, *Vrddhi*, meaning 'interest', in the financial sense. In Kannada, this becomes *Baddi*. Thus, *Vadda-Vyavahari* means 'one who transacts the business of interest'—i.e., a moneylender, financier, etc.

32 Guilds involved in making and selling oils. From the Sanskrit word, 'Taila', corrupted in Hindi and other languages as 'Tel'.

33 Guilds selling betel leaves.

34 Rice, Lewis Benjamin (ed). *Epigraphia Carnatica: Inscriptions in Hassan District*, Vol.5 Part 1, (Bangalore: XXVI, 1920), 157–59.

35 See: (a) Majumdar, R.C. *Corporate Life in Ancient India*, (Calcutta: Firma K.L. Mukhopadhyay, 1969); (b) Chandra, Moti. *Trade and Trade Routes In Ancient India*, (Delhi: Abhinav Publications, 1977).

36 Ritti, Shrinivas. *The Seunas: The Yadavas of Devagiri*, (Dharwad: Karnatak University, 1973), 339.

37 Called as *Kammata*, in Kannada.

38 For an informative study on this topic, see: Sarkar, A.K. 'Coins and Weights of Ancient India.' The *Indian Historical Quarterly VII* (1931), 689.

39 i For a brief list of the important coinage used in the Sevuna Empire, see: Ritti, Shrinivas. *The Seunas: The Yadavas of Devagiri*, 335–36.

ii For a history of the long-lasting currency *Dramma*, see: Balakrishna, Sandeep. 'The Brief and Delightful History of the Dramma in India.' The Dharma Dispatch. Accessed 1 May 2022. https://www.dharmadispatch.in/history/the-brief-and-delightful-history-of-the-dramma-in-india

iii For pictures of the extant coinage of the Yadavas, see:
   (a) http://www.worldofcoins.eu/forum/index.php?topic=
        40167.0. Accessed on 1 May 2022
   (b) https://www.vcoins.com/en/stores/ganga_numismatics/
        216/product/india_yadavas_singhana_silver_dramma_
        scarce/1246229/Default.aspx. Accessed 1 May 2022
40 The Yadava ruler, Krishna.
41 Ramachandradeva.
42 Legend of the coin: Obverse: five punches, central punch of a lotus
    flower and punches around the text 'Sri-Singhana', twice 'Sri' and
    conch shell, Reverse: uniface.
43 Altekar, A.S. *The Early History of the Deccan*, Parts VII–XI, ed,
    G. Yazdani, (London: Oxford University Press, 1960), 573–74.
44 Ibid, 542–43.
45 This campaign is narrated by Dr. Altekar as follows:
    '[Ramachandra] marched northwards to Tripuri near Jabalpur,
    which had once been the capital of the defunct Kalachuri
    kingdom, and occupied it without any difficulty. With this city
    as his base of operations, he resolved on a bold invasion of the
    Muslim empire. He was anxious to restore Banaras to Hindu
    rule, marched straight upon that city, and occupied it. Since
    Purushottamapuri plates state that he built a temple at Banaras
    after its conquest, which was dedicated to the god Sarangdhara,
    we may well presume that Ramachandra not only took possession
    of Banaras but also occupied it for at least two or three years. This
    must have been after the death of Balban in AD 1286 and before
    the accession of Jalal-ud-Din Khalji'.
    See also: Mirashi, V.V. 'Purushottamapuri Plates of Ramachandra.'
    Epigraphia Indica, Vol. 25 (1939), 199.

Chapter 7: The Rising Turushka Vapours in Dakshinapatha

1 Barani describes Ala-ul-Mulk as 'one of the favoured followers of
   Ala-ud-din'. Eliot, H.M., and John Dowson. *The History of India as
   Told by Its Own Historians*, Vol. 3, (London: Trubner & Co, 1871),
   149.
2 Sarkar, Jadunath. *Military History of India*, 2–4.
3 Asirgarh commanded preeminence in the political and military
   history of India for more than a millennium, all the way up to its
   capture by the British in the Third Anglo-Maratha War, 1819. Its

strategic importance owes to it acting as a natural pass connecting
the Narmada and Tapti Valleys in the Satpura Range. At various
points, Asirgarh was also considered as the key to the Deccan.

4   Firishta. *Tarikh-i Firishta*, trans., John Briggs, (Calcutta: R.
     Cambray & Co, 1908), 305.

5   Joshi, R.M. 'Ala-ud-din Khalji's First Campaign against Devagiri.'
     Dr. Ghulam Yazdani Commemoration Volume, (Hyderabad: Maulana
     Abul Kalam Azad Oriental Research Institute, 1966), 204–11.

6   Now in the Aurangabad District.

7   For a discussion on Isami, see: Lal, K.S. *History of the Khaljis*, 51,
     395.

8   Isami, Abdul. *Futuhu's Salatin*, Vol. 2, trans., by Husain, Agha
     Mahdi, (New York: Asia Publishing House, 1976), 398–400.

9   Ibid.

10   Ibid, 400.

11   The chapters titled 'Khwaja Muinuddin's Arrival in Ajmer' and
     'Shahabuddin Ghauri carries the day at Tarain with the blessings
     of Khwaja Muinuddin' in 'The Holy Biography of Hazrat Khwaja
     Muinuddin Hasan Chishti' provide a firsthand, detailed glimpse
     into the psyche of Muinuddin Chishti.
     See: Begg, Mirza Wahiduddin. *The Holy Biography of Hazrath
     Khwaja Muinuddin Hasan Chishti*, (Ajmer: W. D. Begg, 1960).

12   i The Rashtrakuta Kings initiated the policy of allowing Arab and
        other Muslim merchants and preachers to build mosques in their
        dominions and enabled the free propagation and conversion
        activities, especially along the western coast in Gujarat and in
        some southern coastal towns. See: Altekar, A.S. *The Rashtrakutas
        And Their Times: Being a Political, Administrative, Religious, Social,
        Economic and Literary History of the Deccan during C. 750 AD to
        c. 1000 AD* (Poona: Oriental Book Agency, 1934).

     ii For a creative depiction of the disastrous consequences of the
        Rashtrakuta patronage to Muslims, see S.L. Bhyrappa. *Sartha—
        The Caravan*, (Bangalore: OUP, 2005).

13   Momin = Believer of Islam. Arif = Knower of the Islamic tenets.
     Not much is known about his life except for a vague reference that
     he was eighth in descent from the Shia Imam Ali Reza, and had
     migrated to India from Iran. Momin Arif's *dargah* is located east
     at the foothills of the Devagiri fort, and the Muslim faithful visit it
     every Thursday. See: Aal-e-Qutub Aal-e-Syed Abdullah Shah Ghazi.

'Sufis of Daulatabad Region.' https://aalequtub.com/sufis-of-daulatabad-region/. Last accessed: 12 June 2022.

14   Ganjrawan, literally meaning, 'moving treasure', was born in Bukhara and migrated to India with his order. Typically, all sorts of fantastic miracles are attributed to Jalal-ud-din Ganjrawan. One fable passionately narrates his miraculous powers, which bestowed pregnancy upon infertile women. However, a skeptic, who was also a *Hijra* (transgender) once mocked this supposedly divine power of Ganjrawan. Lo and behold! The transgender became pregnant. Ganjrawan's *Dargah* is located near Devagiri (Daulatabad) and is a popular place for Muslim women who believe that taking a vow there will help them conceive. See: 'A Brief Biography of Hazrat Jalauddin Ganj Rawan Khuldabad'. https://www.calameo.com/read/000309382233bf349473e. Accessed 14 March 2022.

15   Sircar, D.C. (editor).
      Inscription No. B 170. 'Annual Report on Indian Epigraphy for 1958–59.' *Archeological Survey of India*, 44.

16   Ritti, Shrinivas. *The Seunas : The Yadavas of Devagiri*, (Dharwar: The Karnatak University, 1973), 275–76.
      K.M. Munshi too, echoes the same assessment of this misplaced and uncritical policy of toleration of Hindu kings: 'The Indian kings, steeped in their tradition of tolerance, could scarcely envisage the danger to which their policies towards Islam exposed them. In spite of what was happening in North India, Indian kings permitted foreigners to settle freely in their kingdoms and granted them free exercise of their religious practices. Even before the Turkish invasion, some sects of Islam had drifted into the country and their religious and proselytizing activities had not heen interfered with. Jayasimha Siddharaja of Gujarat (AD 1094-1143) punished some of his Hindu subjects for interfering with the worship of Muslims. Proselytising activities were freely carried out in the days of the Yadavas by a Sufi teacher, Mumin 'Arif, who settled near Devagiri in the South, and by Jalal-uddin Ganjrawan… another Sufi from Iran. Sarangadeva (AD 1294-1297) of Gujarat gave a grant for a masjid to the local Muslim community of Prabhasa Pattana with the blcssings of the high-priest of Somnatha, when, for decades, the Turks had been destroying thousands of temples in Varanasi and other sacred places.' See: Majumdar, R.C., *History*

and Culture of the Indian People, Vol. 5, 1957. Bombay. Bharatiya
Vidya Bhavan, xvi.

17   See: '39. Ram Avatar Singh' in Goel, Sita Ram ed. *Time for Stock
Taking: Whither Sangh Parivar*, (Delhi: Voice of India, 1996).

18   Islamic chroniclers such as Barani write that prior to Ala-ud-din's
raid, Islam had no presence in Devagiri. This is untrue. Barani was
clearly misinformed or had little knowledge of Devagiri. For a good
discussion on this point, see: Joshi, R.M. 'Ala-Ud-Din Khalji's First
Campaign Against Devagiri.' *Dr. Ghulam Yazdani Commemoration
Volume*, (Hyderabad: Maulana Abul Kalam Azad Oriental Research
Institute, 1966), 206.

19   Muslim chroniclers call him variously as Sankul-Dev and Sankardev.

20   *Annual Reports Archaeological Survey of India 1930-34: Part I*,
(Government of India, 1936), 236.

21   'Devgiri Fort Story - m.Divyamarathi.Bhaskar.Com,' 4 March
2016.
https://web.archive.org/web/20160304103931/http://m.
divyamarathi.bhaskar.com/news/Aurangabad/5528/MAH-MAR-
AUR-devgiri-fort-story-2853466.html. Last accessed 28 July
2022

22   i   For a vivid description of the Devagiri fort, see: Piggott, Stuart.
Some Ancient Cities of India, (Bombay: Oxford University Press,
1945), 79.

     ii   The Wikipedia entry has an elaborate and rich description of the
Devagiri fort. See: 'Daulatabad Fort.' In Wikipedia,
https://en.wikipedia.org/w/index.php?title=Daulatabad_
Fort&oldid=1100755238. Last accessed 27 July 2022.

23   The well-known city in Odisha, Cuttack takes its name from this
term.

24   For example, see: Sri Govindaprabhu-Charitra, verse 99. For other
references, see: Joshi, R.M. 'Ala-Ud-Din Khalji's First Campaign
Against Devagiri.' Maulana Abul Kalam Azad Oriental Research
Institute, Hyderabad Dr. Ghulam Yazdani Commemoration
Volume (1966), 207, footnote 15.

25   Firishta. *Tarikh-i Firishta*, 306.

26   John Briggs, the translator of Firishta, gives an eyewitness
description of the Devagiri fort at the beginning of the 20th
century: 'The ditch [i.e., moat] of [Devagiri], the scarp of which is,
in many places, 100 feet, excavated out of the solid rock, is now one

of the most remarkable objects of curiosity in the Deccan.' Firishta. *Tarikh-i Firishta*, 306.

27 Isami, Abdul. *Futuhu's Salatin*, Vol. 2, trans., Husain, Agha Mahdi, (New York: Asia Publishing House, 1976), 402.

28 Ibid. 401–02.

29 As a measure, the maund varied from region to region and from place to place. One Deccan maund was 30 pounds. One Goan maund was 24 pounds.

30 Firishta. *Tarikh-i Firishta*. 308.

31 i This was a pretty shameful admission of powerlessness on the part of Ramachandradeva. Several inscriptions he had commissioned describe him as the *Maha-Varaha*, 'The Great Boar who succoured the earth from the oppression of the Turukas.' See: 'Uddari Stone Inscription.' *Annual Report of the Mysore Archaeological Department*, (1929) 142–143.

ii An interesting narrative poem titled *Rukmini-Svayamvara* composed around 1291 by Ramachandra's court poet, Narendra hints at the prowess and ruthlessness of the Mlechchas or Muslims. By implication, it shows that Ramachandra had indeed vanquished some Muslim governors and chieftains earlier in his reign. For a brief discussion on this point, see Joshi, R.M. 'Ala-Ud-Din Khalji's First Campaign Against Devagiri.' *Dr. Ghulam Yazdani Commemoration Volume*, (Hyderabad: Maulana Abul Kalam Azad Oriental Research Institute, 1966), 206–07.

32 Ibid. 308.

33 Much later, Ala-ud-din would deliver a similar humiliation to the emissary of the Persian king Ilkhan Sultan Aljaitu. The chronicler Vassaf condemned this treatment saying that by this action, Ala-ud-din had thrown 'the pearl of his good name into the river of Nile'.

34 Firishta. *Tarikh-i Firishta*, 309.

35 Ritti, Shrinivas. *The Seunas (The Yadavas of Devagiri)*, (Dharwar: The Karnatak University, 1973), 275.

36 Firishta. *Tarikh-i Firishta*, 309–10.

37 Quoted in: Lal, K.S. *History of the Khaljis*, (Allahabad: The Indian Press, Ltd, 1950), 56.

38 Firoz Shah Tughlaq's reign lasted from 1351–1388.

39 Nizamuddin Ahmad. *Tabaqat-i-Akbari* trans., B. De. (Calcutta: Asiatic Society of Bengal, 1927) 145.

40   See: Khusrau, Amir. *Khazainul Futuh* (Treasures of Victory), trans., Muhammad Habib, (Bombay: D.B. Taraporewala, sons & Co, 1931), 112.

41   Joshi, R.M. 'Ala-ud-din Khalji's First Campaign against Devagiri.' *Ghulam Yazdani Commemoration Volume*, (Hyderabad: Maulana Abul Kalam Azad Oriental Research Institute, Dr. 1966), 209.

42   Ibid. 209.

43   Isami, Abdul. *Futuhu's Salatin*, Vol. 2, 1976. Translated by Husain, Agha Mahdi. New York, Asia Publishing House, 403–04.

44   See: Lal, K.S. *History of the Khaljis*, 56–57.

45   Firishta. *Tarikh-i Firishta*, 311.

Chapter 8: A Honey-Dipped Invitation to Death

1   Sirhindi, Yahya bin Ahmad bin Abdullah. *Tarikh-i-Mubarakshahi*, trans., K.K. Basu, (Baroda: Baroda Oriental Institute, 1932) 64–65.

2   Eliot, H.M., and John Dowson. *The History of India as Told by Its Own Historians*, Vol. 3, (London: Trubner & Co, 1871), 150.

3   Firishta. *Tarikh-i Firishta*, 311–12.

4   Bada'uni, Abd al-Qadir. *Muntakhab-ut-Tawarikh*, Vol. 1, trans., Ranking, George, (Delhi: Atlantic Publishers & Distributors, 1990) 237.

5   Altekar, A.S. *The Early History of the Deccan*, VII–XI, ed, G. Yazdani, (London: Oxford University Press, 1960), 553.

6   See the previous chapter.

7   'Central Provinces. Asirgarh.' *Archaeological Survey of India Annual Report: 1922–23*, (Archaeological Survey of India: 1923). 45–47. The name of the Rajput chieftain has not been traced.

8   Summarized from various chroniclers including Barani, Yahya, Firishta and Badauni.

9   Barani. Quoted in: Eliot, H.M., and John Dowson. *The History of India as Told by Its Own Historians*, Vol. 3, 1871. London, Trubner & Co, 151.

10   Barani. Quoted in: Lal, K.S. *History of the Khaljis*, 60.

11   Ibid. Footnote 6, p 60.

12   Summarized from various chroniclers including Barani, Yahya, Firishta and Badauni.

13   Summarized from various chroniclers including Barani, Yahya, Firishta and Badauni.

14 Nizamuddin Ahmad. *Tabaqat-i-Akbari,* trans., B.De, (Calcutta: Asiatic Society of Bengal, 1927), 147.

Firishta gives another version of this couplet:
'When the sun of prosperity is eclipsed,
Advice ceases to enlighten the mind.'

15 Haig, Wolesley. *The Cambridge History of India,* Vol. 3. (London: Cambridge University Press, 1928), 97.

16 Ahmad, Nizamuddin. *Tabaqat-i-Akbari,* trans., B.De, (Calcutta: Asiatic Society of Bengal, 1927), 146.

Chapter 9: Jalal-ud-din Khalji's Fatal Ramazan

1   Summarized from various chroniclers including Barani, Yahya, Firishta and Badauni.

2   Lal, K.S. *History of the Khaljis,* (Allahabad: The Indian Press, Ltd, 1950), 63.

3   Eliot, H.M., and John Dowson. *The History of India as Told by Its Own Historians,* Vol. 3, (London: Trubner & Co, 1871), 152.

4   Bada'uni, Abd al-Qadir. *Muntakhab-ut-Tawarikh,* Vol. 1, trans., Ranking, George, (Delhi: Atlantic Publishers & Distributors, 1990), 239.

5   Ibid. 239.

6   Barani. Quoted in: Eliot, H.M., and John Dowson. *The History of India as Told by Its Own Historians,* Vol. 3, 1871, 152–53.

7   Firishta. *Tarikh-i Firishta,* trans., John Briggs. (Calcutta: R. Cambray & Co., 1908), 316.

8   Ahmad, Nizamuddin. *Tabaqat-i-Akbari,* trans., B.De, (Calcutta: Asiatic Society of Bengal, 1927), 148.

9   Now, Dibai, about 21 kilometres from the Anupshahr town, Bulandshahar District.

10 Quoted in: Lal, K.S. *History of the Khaljis,* (Allahabad: The Indian Press, Ltd, 1950), 64.

11 Ahmad, Nizamuddin. *Tabaqat-i-Akbari,* trans., B.De, (Calcutta: Asiatic Society of Bengal, 1927), 149.

12 Bada'uni, Abd al-Qadir. *Muntakhab-ut-Tawarikh,* Vol. 1, trans., Ranking, George, (Delhi: Atlantic Publishers & Distributors, 1990), 240–1.

13 26 July 1296.

14 Bada'uni, Abd al-Qadir. *Muntakhab-ut-Tawarikh,* Vol. 1, 1990, 241.

15 Firishta. *Tarikh-i Firishta*, trans., John Briggs, (Calcutta: R. Cambray & Co., 1908) 316.

16 Some chroniclers write that there were only two boats.

17 Or Kamaluddin.

18 Summarized from various chroniclers including Barani, Yahya, Firishta and Badauni.

19 Firishta. *Tarikh-i Firishta*, 1908, 317.

20 Bada'uni, Abd al-Qadir. *Muntakhab-ut-Tawarikh*, Vol. 1, 1990, 242.

21 For a discussion, see: Lal, K.S. *History of the Khaljis*, (Allahabad: The Indian Press, Ltd, 1950), 67.

22 Barani. Quoted in: Eliot, H.M., and John Dowson. *The History of India as Told by Its Own Historians*, Vol. 3, 1871, 154.

23 For detailed information about this chapter, see: 'Qur'an Wiki - Surah 36: Ya Sin.' Accessed 19 August 2022. http://www.quran-wiki.com/Surah-Overview-36-0-YaSin

24 Barani writes, 'All the people who were in the boat with him saw death plainly before them, and began to repeat the chapter appropriate to men in sight of death.'
See: Eliot, H.M., and John Dowson. *The History of India as Told by Its Own Historians*, Vol. 3, 1871, 154.

25 Vassaf, author of the *Taziyat-ul-Amsar*, narrates the incident as follows: 'As [Jalal-ud-din] placed one foot on the boat and was about to lift the other upon it, Ikhtiyaruddin struck at him with a sword and wounded his hand. [Jalal-ud-din] in alarm, tried to throw himself into the boat, but Muhammad Salim came up and dealt him such a blow that his head fell into the water and his trunk into the boat.' Quoted in: Eliot, H.M., and John Dowson. *The History of India as Told by Its Own Historians*, Vol. 3, 41. This description apparently satisfies the prophecy of Sheikh Karrak.

26 Quoted in: Eliot, H.M., and John Dowson. *The History of India as Told by Its Own Historians*, Vol. 3, (London: Trubner & Co, 1871), 155–6.

27 Firishta. *Tarikh-i Firishta*, trans., John Briggs, (Calcutta: R. Cambray & Co., 1908), 318.

Chapter 10: A Career of Bigotry and Bloodletting Eclipsed by an Unlikely Martyrdom

1 Fiefdom.

2 Also spelled, 'Mundahir'.

3   For several interesting accounts of the region, see: Elliot, H.M. *Memoirs on the History, Folk-Lore and Distribution of the Races of the North Western Provinces of India*. 2 vols. Delhi: Asian Educational Services, 1859.

4   The work is hard to locate.

5   Quoted in: Ray, N.B. 'Career of Jalaluddin Firuz Khalji.' *New Indian Antiquary*, No. 2, November (1939). 548.

6   Ibid. 548.

7   Srivastava, Kanhaiya Lal. *The Position of Hindus under the Delhi Sultanate, 1206–1526*, (Delhi: Munshiram Manoharlal, 1980), 174.

8   Lal, Kishori Sharan. *Studies in Medieval Indian History*, (Delhi: Ranjit Printers and Publishers, 1966), 203.

9   Srivastava, Kanhaiya Lal. *The Position of Hindus under the Delhi Sultanate, 1206–1526*, (Delhi: Munshiram Manoharlal, 1980), 129.

10 Singh, Surinder. 'Political Culture in the Delhi Sultanate: Compulsions of a Transitional Phase.' *Proceedings of the Indian History Congress*, Vol. 63, (2002), 251–62.

11 Quoted in: Ray, N.B. 'Career of Jalaluddin Firuz Khalji.' *New Indian Antiquary*, No. 2, November (1939). 547.

12 For interesting assessments of Jalal-ud-din Khalji's career, see:

    i   Ray, N.B. 'Career of Jalaluddin Firuz Khalji.' *New Indian Antiquary*, No. 2, November (1939).

    ii Rashid, S.A. 'Jalaluddin Firoz Shah Khalji.' *Muslim University Journal*, Vol. 1, No. 1, (1931).

    iii Lal, K.S. *History of the Khaljis*, (Allahabad: The Indian Press, Ltd., 1950)

    iv Srivastava, Ashirbadi Lal. *The Sultanate of Delhi*, (Agra: The Educational Press, 1950), 146–47.

13 Smith, Vincent A. *The Oxford History of India*, (Oxford: Clarendon Press, 1919), 231.

14 Haig, Wolesley. *The Cambridge History of India*, Vol. 3. (London: Cambridge University Press, 1928), 93.

Chapter 11: Ala-ud-din Khalji's Throne Soaked in Blood and Gravelled by Glitter

1   Lal, K.S. *History of the Khaljis*, (Allahabad: The Indian Press, Ltd, 1950), 68.

2   Eliot, H.M., and John Dowson. *The History of India as Told by Its Own Historians*, Vol. 3, (London: Trubner & Co, 1871), 156.

3 Barani, Ziauddin. *Tarikh-i-Firuz Shahi*, trans., A.R. Fuller & A. Khallauqe, (Calcutta: Pilgrim Publishers, 1960), 10.

4 Ibid. 11.

5 Ibid. 11–12.

6 Gold coin.

7 Lal, K.S. *History of the Khaljis*, 1950. Allahabad: The Indian Press, Ltd, 72.

8 Barani, Ziauddin. *Tarikh-i-Firuz Shahi*, trans., A.R. Fuller & A. Khallauqe, (Calcutta: Pilgrim Publishers, 1960), 14–15.

9 Ibid. 15.

10 Ibid. 15.

11 Ibid. 16.

12 Almost all chroniclers severely condemn this mass psychology. Barani is harsh when he says, '[Ala-ud-din] scattered so much gold that the faithless people easily forgot the murder of the late Sultan, and rejoiced over his accession.' Eliot, H.M., and John Dowson. *The History of India as Told by Its Own Historians*, Vol. 3, (London: Trubner & Co, 1871), 157.

13 Bada'uni, Abd al-Qadir. *Muntakhab-ut-Tawarikh*, Vol. 1, trans., Ranking, George, (Delhi: Atlantic Publishers & Distributors, 1990), 244.

14 Firishta. *Tarikh-i Firishta*, trans., John Briggs, (Calcutta: R. Cambray & Co., 1908), 324.

Bibliography

Aal-e-Qutub Aal-e-Syed Abdullah Shah Ghazi. 'Sufis of Daulatabad Region.' https://aalequtub.com/sufis-of-daulatabad-region/. Accessed 12 June 2022.

'A Brief Biography Of Hazrat Jalauddin Ganj Rawan Khuldabad.' https://www.calameo.com/read/000309382233bf349473e. Accessed 14 March 2022.

al-Kashgari. *Diwan Lughat al-Turk*, Vol. 3. Translated by Besim, Atalay, Ankara. TDK Press, 1992.

al-Mulk, Nizam. *Siyasat-Nama: The Book of Government or Rules for Kings*, 2002. Translated by Darke, Hubert, London. Routledge.

Altekar, A.S. *The Early History of the Deccan, Parts VII - XI*. (ed. G. Yazdani). London: Oxford University Press, 1960.

Altekar, A.S. *The Rashtrakutas and Their Times: Being a Political, Administrative, Religious, Social, Economic and Literary History of the Deccan during c. 750 AD to c. 1000 AD*. Poona: Oriental Book Agency, 1934.

Ambedkar, B.R. *Dr. Babasaheb Ambedkar Writings and Speeches*, Vol. III, Delhi: Dr. Ambedkar Foundation, 2014.

Amir Khusrau. *Khaza'inul Futuh*. Translated by Muhammad Habib. Bombay. I). B. Taraporewala, Sons & Co., 1931.

Amīr Khusraw Dihlavī., Ahmed, Habibuddin. *The Writings of Amir Khusrau: 700 Years after the Prophet: a 13th-14th Century Legend of Indian-sub-continent*. India: Islamic Thought and Science Institute, 2007.

Annual Report of South Indian Epigraphy, 1929-30.

Annual Report of the Mysore Archaeological Department, 1929.

Annual Report on Indian Epigraphy for 1958-59. Archeological Survey of India.

Annual Reports Archaeological Survey Of India 1930–34: Part I. Government of India, 1936.

Ashraf, Kunwar Muhammad. *Life and conditions of the people of Hindustan (1200-1550 AD): Mainly Based on Islamic sources*. India: Gyan Publishing House, 2000.

Ayalon, David. *Studies on the Mamluks of Egypt: 1250-1517*. London: Variorum Reprints, 1977.

Bada'uni, Abd al-Qadir. *Muntakhab-ut-Tawarikh*, Vol. 1. Translated by Ranking, George, Delhi. Atlantic Publishers & Distributors, 1990.

Bahadur, Rai K.L. Barua. *Early History of Kamarupa*. Rai K.L. Barua Bahadur, 1933.

Balakrishna, Sandeep. *Invaders and Infidels: From Sindh to Delhi: the 500-year Journey of Islamic Invasions*. India: Bloomsbury, 2021.

Balakrishna, Sandeep. 'The Brief and Delightful History of the Dramma in India.' The Dharma Dispatch. Accessed 1 May 2022. https://www.dharmadispatch.in/history/the-brief-and-delightful-history-of-the-dramma-in-india

Balakrishna, Sandeep. 'The Far Reaching Implications of the Medieval Muslim Chronicler's Psyche on the History of the Future A Deep-Dive into the Mindset of Medieval Muslim Chroniclers: Preface.' The Dharma Dispatch. Accessed 17 April 2022. https://www.dharmadispatch.in/history/a-deep-dive-into-the-mindset-of-medieval-muslim-chroniclers-preface

Balakrishna, Sandeep. 'The Far Reaching Implications of the Medieval Muslim Chronicler's Psyche on the History of the Future.' The Dharma Dispatch. Accessed 17 April 2022. https://www.dharmadispatch.in/history/the-far-reaching-implications-of-the-medieval-muslim-chroniclers-psyche-on-the-history-of-the-future

Balakrishna, Sandeep. 'The Qualifications of a Medieval Muslim Chronicler and the Nature of Muslim Histories.' The Dharma Dispatch. Accessed 17 April 2022. https://www.dharmadispatch.in/history/the-qualifications-of-a-medieval-muslim-chronicler-and-the-nature-of-muslim-histories

Barani, Ziauddin. *Tarikh-i-Firuz Shahi*. Translated by A.R. Fuller & A. Khallauqe. Calcutta: Pilgrim Publishers, 1960.

Begg, Mirza Wahiduddin. *The Holy Biography of Hazrath Khwaja Muinuddin Hasan Chishti*. Ajmer: W. D. Begg, 1960.

Bendrey, Vasudeo Sitaram. *A Study of Muslim Inscriptions: With Special Reference to the Inscriptions Published in the Epigraphia Indo-Moslemica, 1907–1938: Together with Summaries of Inscriptions Chronologically Arranged*. India: Indus Publications, 1981.

Bhyrappa, S. L. *Sartha*. India: Oxford University Press, 2006.

Blochmann, H. *Contributions to the Geography and History of Bengal (Muhammedan Period)*. Calcutta: Asiatic Society, 1968.

Bosworth, C.E., et al. *The Encyclopedia of Islam*, Vol. IV. Leiden. E.J. Brill, 1997.

'Central Provinces. Asirgarh.' *Archaeological Survey Of India Annual Report: 1922-23.* Archaeological Survey Of India, 1923.

Chandra, Moti. *Trade and Trade Routes in Ancient India.* South Asia Books, 1977.

Crowley, Roger. *Accursed Tower: The Crusaders' Last Battle for the Holy Land.* New Haven & London: Yale University Press, 2019.

Cunningham, Alexander. *Archaeological Survey of India. Four Reports: 1862–1865.* Simla: Government Central Press, 1871.

Cunningham, Alexander. *Report of a Tour in the Punjab in 1878–79.* Office of the Superintendent of Government Printing, 1882.

Day, U.N. 'North-West Frontier of the Sultanate during the 13th Century.' *Indian Historical Quarterly*, Vol. XV, No. II, 1941.

Deo, Prabhakar. Te*mples of Marathwada.* Jaipur: Publication Scheme, 1993.

Dey, Nundo Lal. *The Geographical Dictionary of Ancient and Medieval India.* Calcutta, W. Newman & Co, 1899.

Dharmasvamin. *Biography of Dharmasvamin: Chag lo tsa-ba Chos-rje-dpal.* Translated by Roerich, Dr. George, Patna: K.P. Jayaswal Research Institute, 1959.

Dutt, Sukumar. *Buddhist Monks and Monasteries of India: Their History and Contribution to Indian Culture.* London: George Allen and Unwin Ltd, 1988 (Reprint).

Eliot, H.M., and John Dowson. *The History of India as Told by Its Own Historians,* Vol. 2. London, Trubner & Co, 1869.

Eliot, H.M. and John Dawson. *The History of India as Told by Its Own Historians,* Vol. 3. London, Trubner & Co, 1871.

Elliot, H.M. *Memoirs on the History, Folk-Lore and Distribution of the Races of the North Western Provinces of India* (in 2 vols). Delhi: Asian Educational Services, 1859.

Encyclopaedia Iranica.

Encyclopedia Britannica.

Epigraphia Indica, Vol. 1. Archeological Survey of India, 1892.

Epigraphia Indica, Vol. 2. Archeological Survey of India, 1892.

Eraly, Abraham. *The Age of Wrath: A History of the Delhi Sultanate.* India: Penguin Books Limited, 2015.

Firishta. *Tarikh-i Firishta.* Translated by John Briggs. Calcutta: R. Cambray & Co, 1908.

Ganguly, D.C. *History of the Paramara Dynasty.* Dacca: University of Dacca, 1933.

Gazetteer of the Province of Oudh, Vol. 2, Allahabad: North Western Provinces and Oudh. Government Press, 1877.

Ghosh, Amalananda. *A Guide to Nalanda,* Archaeological Survey of India, 1939.

Ghoshal, U.N. *Contributions to the History of the Hindu Revenue System.* Calcutta: Saraswat Library, 1972.

Goel, Sita Ram (ed). *Time for Stock Taking: Whither Sangh Parivar.* Delhi: Voice of India, 1996.

Goel, Sita Ram. *Heroic Hindu Resistance to Muslim Invaders, 636 AD to 1206 AD.* Delhi: Voice of India, 1994.

Goel, Sita Ram. *Hindu Temples: What Happened to Them: The Islamic Evidence.* Delhi: Voice of India, 1993.

Gopala-Giri, Radhakrishna Choudhary, and Surendra Nath Sastri. 'The Prabodhacandrikā of Baijaladeva along with the Incomplete Commentary, Subodhinī.' *Annals of the Bhandarkar Oriental Research Institute* 44, No. 1/4, 1963.

Govindaprabhu. 'Sri Govindaprabhu-Charitra.'

Gupta, Satya Prakash. 'Jhain of the Delhi Sultanate: Summary.' *Proceedings of the Indian History Congress* 34, 1973.

Haig, Wolesley. *The Cambridge History of India.* Vol. 3. London: Cambridge University *Press, 1928.*

Hardy, Peter. *Historians of Medieval India: Studies in Indo-Muslim Historical Writing.* United Kingdom: Luzac, 1960.

Hari Ram Gupta (ed). *Life and Letters of Sir Jadunath Sarkar.* Hoshiarpur: Punjab University, 1957.

Hasan, Mohibbul (ed). *Historians of Medieval India.* India: Meenakshi Prakashan, 1982.

Hodivala, S.H. *Studies in Indo-Muslim History.* (Original publisher name unavailable), 1939.

Hughes, Thomas Patrick. *A Dictionary of Islam: Being a Cyclopaedia of the Doctrines, Rites, Ceremonies and Customs, together with the Technical and Theological Terms, of the Muhammadan Religion. Italy:* W.H. Allen & Company, 1885.

Hunter, W.W. *A Statistical Account of Bengal.* London, Trubner & Co, 1876.

Hutchinson's Story of the Nations. London: Hutchinson & Co. (Publishers), Ltd., 1915.

Ibn Battuta. *The Travels of Ibn Battuta.* United Kingdom: Murray, 1829.

Isami, Abdul, *Futuhu's Salatin*, Vol. 2. Translated by Husain, Agha Mahdi. New York: Asia Publishing House, 1969.

Jackson, Peter. *The Delhi Sultanate: A Political and Military History.* Cambridge: Cambridge University Press, 2003.

Jain, Kailash Chand. 'History of Mandor.' *Proceedings of the Indian History Congress* 22, 1959.

John Andrew Boyle. 'The Death of the Last Abbasid Caliph: A Contemporary Muslim Account.' *Journal of Semitic Studies*, Vol. 6, Issue 2, Autumn 1961.

Joshi, R.M. 'Ala-Ud-Din Khalji's First Campaign Against Devagiri.' *Dr. Ghulam Yazdani Commemoration Volume*, Hyderabad: Maulana Abul Kalam Azad Oriental Research Institute, 1966.

Journal of the Asiatic Society of Bombay, Vol. 31, Bombay, 1862.

Kalidasa. *Meghaduta.*

Kamran, Tahir, and Amir Khan Shahid. 'Shari'a, Shi'as and Chishtiya Revivalism: Contextualising the Growth of Sectarianism in the Tradition of the Sialvi Saints of the Punjab.' *Journal of the Royal Asiatic Society*, Third Series, 24, No. 3, 2014.

Kane, Pandurang Vaman. *History of the Dharmasastra, Vol. III.* Pune: Bhandarkar Oriental Research Institute, 1973.

Kate, P. V. *Marathwada under the Nizams, 1724-1948.* Delhi: Mittal Publications, 1987.

Kautilya. *Arthasastra.* Translated by R. Shamasastry. Books 2.10, 6-7, 10.

Lal, K.S. *History of the Khaljis.* Allahabad, The Indian Press, Ltd, 1950.

Lal, K.S. *The Legacy of Muslim Rule in India.* Voice of India, 1992.

Lal, Kishori Sharan. *Studies in Medieval Indian History.* Delhi: Ranjit Printers and Publishers, 1966.

Law, B.C. 'Vidisa in Ancient India.' *Journal of the Ganganatha Jha Research Institute*, Vol. 9, 1951.

Layard, F.P. *The Journal of the Asiatic Society of Bengal*, No. 22, 1853.

M. Venkataramayya. 'Maser Inscription of a Sulki Chief.' *Epigraphia Indica*, Vol. 29, 1951.

Majumdar, R.C. *Corporate Life in Ancient India.*

Majumdar, R.C. *The Struggle for Empire.* Bharatiya Vidya Bhavan, 1957.

Majumdar, R.C. 'Hindu Reaction to Muslim Invasions.' Professor D.V. Potdar Commemoration Volume, 1950.

Majumdar, Ramesh Chandra. *Ancient India.* Motilal Banarsidass, 1977.

Minhaj-i-Siraj. *Tabakat-i-Nasiri*. Translated by H.G. Raverty, London. Asiatic Society of Bengal, 1873.

Minorsky, V. 'The Turkish Dialect of the Khalaj (Excerpts).' *Bulletin of the School of Oriental Studies* 10, No. 2 (29 August 2005).

Mintage World. 'Coins of Bengal Sultanate Part 1': https://www. mintageworld.com/blog/coins-bengal-sultanate-part-1/.

Mirashi, V. V. 'Purushottamapuri Plates of Ramachandra.' *Epigraphia Indica*, Vol. 25, 1939.

Misra, Ram Gopal. *Indian Resistance to Early Muslim Invaders Up to 1206 AD*. India: Anu Books, 2018.

Mohammad Habib, K.A. Nizami, et al. *A Comprehensive History of India: The Delhi Sultanat*, Vol. 5. Delhi: People's Publishing House, 1970.

Nilakanta Sastri, K.A. (edited by). *Age of the Nandas and Mauryas*. Motilal Banarsidass, 1988.

Nilakanta Sastri, Kallidaikurichi Aiyah. *A History of South India: From Prehistoric Times to the Fall of Vijayanagar*. Delhi: Oxford India Paperbacks, 2005.

Niyogi, Roma. 'A Note on Turuska-Danda.' *The Indian Historical Quarterly*, Vol. XXV, no. No. I, Mar. 1949.

Nizamuddin Ahmad. *Tabaqat-i-Akbari*. Translated by B. De. Calcutta: Asiatic Society of Bengal, 1927.

Parasanisa, Dattatraya Balavanta., Kincaid, Charles Augustus. *A History of the Maratha People*. Kiribati: H. Milford, Oxford University Press, 1931.

Patel, Alka. *Architectural Cultures and Empire: The Ghurids in Northern India (ca. 1192–1210)*. Bulletin of the Asia Institute, 2007.

Piggott, Stuart. *Some Ancient Cities of India*. Bombay: Oxford University Press, 1945.

Prasad, Ishwari, *History of Medieval India*. Allahabad: The Indian Press Ltd, 1933.

'Qur'an Wiki.' Accessed 19 August 2022. http://www.quran-wiki.com/

Ramakarna, Pandit. 'Kinsariya Inscription of Dadhichika (Dahiya).' *Epigraphia Indica*, Vol. 12. Archeological Survey of India, 1913–14.

Ramakarna, Pandit. 'Manglana Stone Inscription of Jayatrasimha.' *Indian Antiquary*, Vol. 41. British India Press, 1912.

Rashid, S.A. 'Jalaluddin Firoz Shah Khalji.' *Muslim University Journal*, Vol. 1, No. 1, 1931.

Ray, N.B. 'Career of Jalaluddin Firuz Khalji.' *New Indian Antiquary,* Vol. 2, 1939.

Reu, V.N. *Marwar Ka Itihas,* Vols 1 & 2. Jodhpur: Rajasthani Granthagar, 2019.

Rice, Lewis Benjamin (ed). *Epigraphia Carnatica: Inscriptions in Hassan District,* Vol. 5 Part 1. Bangalore: 1902.

Ritti, Shrinivas. *The Seunas: The Yadavas of Devagiri.* Dharwad: Karnatak University, 1973.

Rizvi, Saiyid Athar Abbas. *Muslim Revivalist Movements in Northern India in the Sixteenth and Seventeenth Centuries.* Munshiram Manoharlal Publishers, 1965.

Sachau, Edward. *Alberuni's India,* Vol. 1. London: Kegan Paul, Trench, Trubner & Co. Ltd, 1910.

Sahai, Ishwar. 'The Crime of the Thagi and Its Suppression under Lord W.C. Bentinck.' *Indian Culture,* Vol. VIII, No. 1–4, July 1936.

Sahni, B. 'Yaudheya Coin Moulds from Sunet, near Ludhiana in the Sutlej Valley.' *Current Science,* 10, No. 2, 1941.

Saklani, Dinesh Prasad. *Ancient Communities of the Himalaya.* Delhi: Indus Publishing Company, 1998.

Saletore B.A. *Karnataka's Trans-Oceanic Contacts.* Dharwad: Karnatak University, 1956.

Sankalia, Hasmukh Dhirajlal. *The Nalanda University.* Madras: B.G. Paul &, 1934.

Saran, Paramatma. *Sultan Nasir-Uddin Mahmud and His Two Ministers: General Survey and Estimate. Proceedings of the Indian History Congress,* Vol. 5, 1941.

Sarda, Har Bilas. *Speeches and Writings.* India: Vedic Yantralaya, 1935.

Sarkar, A.K. 'Coins and Weights of Ancient India.' *The Indian Historical Quarterly VII,* 1931.

Sarkar, Jadunath. *Military History of India.* Calcutta: M.C. Sarkar & Sons, 1957.

Sarkar, Jadunath. *The History of Bengal Volume II: Muslim Period.* Delhi: B.R. Publishing Corporation, 2003.

Sastri, Hiranand. *Nalanda and Its Epigraphic Material.* Sri Satguru Publications, 1986.

Sharma, Arvind. 'Did the Hindus Lack a Sense of History?' *Numen,* 50, No. 2, 2003.

Sharma, Dasharatha. *Early Chauhan Dynasties.* Delhi: S. Chand & Co, 1959.

Shourie, Arun. *Eminent Historians: Their Technology, Their Line, Their Fraud.* HarperCollins, 2014.

Shourie, Arun. *The World of Fatwas.* Revised edition-, Noida: Harper Collins, 2012.

Shourie, Arun. 'How History Was Made up at Nalanda.' *The Indian Express:* https://indianexpress.com/article/opinion/columns/how-history-was-made-up-at-nalanda

Singh, Surinder. 'Political Culture in the Delhi Sultanate: Compulsions of a Transitional Phase.' *Proceedings of the Indian History Congress,* Vol. 63, 2002.

Sinha, C.P.N. (1969). 'Origin of the Karnatas of Mithila—A Fresh Appraisal.' *Proceedings of the Indian History Congress,* 1969.

Sircar, D.C. *Studies in the Religious Life of Ancient and Medieval India.* Delhi: Motilal Banarasidass, 1971.

Sircar, D.C. 'Two Inscriptions from Bhilsa.' *Epigraphia Indica,* Vol. 30, 1953.

Sircar, Dineschandra. *Select Inscriptions Bearing on Indian History and Civilization,* Vol. 1. Calcutta: University of Calcutta, 1942.

Sircar, Dines Chandra. 'Successors of the Satavahanas in the Eastern Deccan.' *Journal of the Department of Letters,* Vol. XXVI 1935.

Sircar, Dines Chandra. 'The Divyas.' *Journal of the Andhra Historical Research Society,* Vol. VII, 1933.

Sirhindi, Yahya bin Ahmad bin Abdullah. *Tarikh-i-Mubarakshahi.* Translated by K.K. Basu, Baroda. Baroda Oriental Institute, 1932.

Smith, Vincent A. *The Oxford History of India.* Oxford: Clarendon Press, 1919, 231.

Srivastava, A.K. *Khalji Sultans in Rajasthan.* Gorakhpur: Purvanchal Prakashan, 1981.

Srivastava, Ashirbadi Lal. *The Sultanate of Delhi.* Agra: The Educational Press, 1950.

Srivastava, Kanhaiya Lal. *The Position of Hindus Under the Delhi Sultanate, 1206-1526.* Delhi: Munshiram Manoharlal, 1980.

Suri, Nayachandra. *Hammira Mahakavya.* Translated by Kirtane, N.J., Bombay Education Society's Press, 1879.

Taranatha. *Taranatha's History of Buddhism in India.* Edited by Chattopadhyaya, Debiprasad, Delhi: Motilal Banarsidass, 1990.

Thakur, Upendra. 'Early Indian Mints.' *Journal of the Economic and Social History of the Orient,* 16, No. 2/3, 1973.

'The Religion of the Arabs.' *The Indian Antiquary,* Vol. XV. Bombay, 1886.

Thomas, Edward. *The Pathan Kings of Dehli.* London: Trubner & Co, 1871.

Tod, James. *Annals and Antiquities of Rajasthan Or the Central and Western Rajput States of India: In Three Volumes.* India: Motilal Banarsidass, 1987.

Uris, Leon. *The Hajj.* United States: RHUS (Reprint), 1985.

Verfasser Hansen, Erik. *The Ghurid Portal of the Friday Mosque of Herat, Afghanistan: Conservation of a Historic Monument.* Aarhus University Press, 2015.

Wink, Andre. *Al-Hind the Making of the Indo-Islamic World: The Slave Kings and the Islamic Conquest: 11th–13th Centuries.* Vol. 2. New York: BRILL, 1997.

Yule, Henry., Crooke, William., Burnell, Arthur Coke. *Hobson-Jobson: A Glossary of Colloquial Anglo-Indian Words and Phrases, and of Kindred Terms, Etymological, Historical, Geographical and Discursive.* United Kingdom: Murray, 1903.

Zilli, I. A. 'Successors of Shaikh Nasiruddin Mahmud and the Disintegration of the Chishti Central Organisation.' *Proceedings of the Indian History Congress,* 44, 1983.

Index